The Internet For Macs® For Dummies® 3rd Edition

Cheat Sheet

Y0-BPT-075

How to Get Started

If you don't have an Internet connection yet, here are some useful phone numbers for you.

America Online

Dial 1-800-827-6364 and ask for a set of Mac software to sign up. AOL is probably the friendliest introduction to Internet services.

Earthlink

I've been pretty happy with these people as a service provider. When you call 1-800-395-8425 and ask for Mac start-up disks, they send you just what you need for an automatic sign-up with no hassles.

ISP Finder

If you're a hardier sort or more experienced, a call to 1-888-ISP-FIND gets you the phone numbers of Internet service providers for your area code.

MacConnect

This is a Mac-only national ISP. When you call 1-800-923-2638 (x14) and tell them you have a two-year-old Performa, no one laughs.

Mindspring

They're one of the few ISPs to show much interest in consumer accounts. Call 1-800-719-4660.

Mac Hotspots

If you want to keep up with the latest Mac news, these sites are your best bet.

The Site	The Story
www.tidbits.com	Adam Engst runs the best Mac gossip hotline of all time
www.macaddict.com	This clever magazine also provides links to the best and most current shareware
www.webintosh.com	A great set of links to every important Mac site
www.macintouch.com	Ric Ford's inside track to what's actually going to happen in Cupertino
www.macworld.com	Macworld, MacUser, and MacWeek rolled up under the same corporate umbrella

The Internet For Macs® For Dummies,® 3rd Edition

Cheat Sheet

Fun Time

The Web was a fairly quiet place as a research facility, but it got ridiculous when its popularity soared. Check out these places when you feel like goofing off.

The Link	What's There
www.mrshowbiz.com	Mostly movies, but links to all sorts of other entertainment stuff.
cool.infi.net	This site reviews other sites for their coolness factor. Does a good job, too.
www.suck.com	And this site reviews for lack of coolness. Very funny comments.
www.rockweb.com	I like these guys. They don't do Bach, but they do range from Alternative to Zydeco.
www.hotwired.com	Most Web trends have the life span of mayflies. If you want to see if these trends are taken seriously, check here.

Browser Clicks

These commands work with Netscape Navigator, Internet Explorer, and the custom version of Internet Explorer used by America Online.

Keystrokes	Action
Cmd-L	Open a Web page by URL
Cmd-O	Open a page from your hard drive
Cmd-[	Go back a page
Cmd-]	Go forward a page
Cmd-S	Save the current page
Cmd-.	Stop loading page
Cmd-R	Reload current page
Cmd-N	Open a new browser window
Cmd-P	Print current window contents
Cmd-D	Add page to bookmark/favorite list

...For Dummies®: Bestselling Book Series for Beginners

TM

BESTSELLING BOOK SERIES

References for the Rest of Us! ®

Are you intimidated and confused by computers? Do you find that traditional manuals are overloaded with technical details you'll never use? Do your friends and family always call you to fix simple problems on their PCs? Then the *...For Dummies*® computer book series from IDG Books Worldwide is for you.

...For Dummies books are written for those frustrated computer users who know they aren't really dumb but find that PC hardware, software, and indeed the unique vocabulary of computing make them feel helpless. *...For Dummies* books use a lighthearted approach, a down-to-earth style, and even cartoons and humorous icons to dispel computer novices' fears and build their confidence. Lighthearted but not lightweight, these books are a perfect survival guide for anyone forced to use a computer.

> *"I like my copy so much I told friends; now they bought copies."*
>
> — Irene C., Orwell, Ohio

> *"Quick, concise, nontechnical, and humorous."*
>
> — Jay A., Elburn, Illinois

> *"Thanks, I needed this book. Now I can sleep at night."*
>
> — Robin F., British Columbia, Canada

Already, millions of satisfied readers agree. They have made *...For Dummies* books the #1 introductory level computer book series and have written asking for more. So, if you're looking for the most fun and easy way to learn about computers, look to *...For Dummies* books to give you a helping hand.

IDG BOOKS WORLDWIDE ®

THE
INTERNET
FOR MACS® FOR
DUMMIES®

3RD EDITION

THE
INTERNET
FOR MACS® FOR
DUMMIES®

3RD EDITION

by Charles Seiter

IDG BOOKS WORLDWIDE

IDG Books Worldwide, Inc.
An International Data Group Company

Foster City, CA ♦ Chicago, IL ♦ Indianapolis, IN ♦ New York, NY

The Internet For Macs® For Dummies®, 3rd Edition

Published by
IDG Books Worldwide, Inc.
An International Data Group Company
919 E. Hillsdale Blvd.
Suite 400
Foster City, CA 94404
www.idgbooks.com (IDG Books Worldwide Web site)
www.dummies.com (Dummies Press Web site)

Library of Congress Catalog Card No.: 98-87107

ISBN: 0-7645-0364-2

Printed in the United States of America

10 9 8 7 6 5

3O/RS/QX/ZZ/IN

Distributed in the United States by IDG Books Worldwide, Inc.

Distributed by CDG Books Canada Inc. for Canada; by Transworld Publishers Limited in the United Kingdom; by IDG Norge Books for Norway; by IDG Sweden Books for Sweden; by IDG Books Australia Publishing Corporation Pty. Ltd. for Australia and New Zealand; by TransQuest Publishers Pte Ltd. for Singapore, Malaysia, Thailand, Indonesia, and Hong Kong; by Gotop Information Inc. for Taiwan; by ICG Muse, Inc. for Japan; by Norma Comunicacions S.A. for Colombia; by Intersoft for South Africa; by Eyrolles for France; by International Thomson Publishing for Germany, Austria and Switzerland; by Distribuidora Cuspide for Argentina; by Livraria Cultura for Brazil; by Ediciones ZETA S.C.R. Ltda. for Peru; by WS Computer Publishing Corporation, Inc., for the Philippines; by Contemporanea de Ediciones for Venezuela; by Express Computer Distributors for the Caribbean and West Indies; by Micronesia Media Distributor, Inc. for Micronesia; by Grupo Editorial Norma S.A. for Guatemala; by Chips Computadoras S.A. de C.V. for Mexico; by Editorial Norma de Panama S.A. for Panama; by American Bookshops for Finland. Authorized Sales Agent: Anthony Rudkin Associates for the Middle East and North Africa.

For general information on IDG Books Worldwide's books in the U.S., please call our Consumer Customer Service department at 800-762-2974. For reseller information, including discounts and premium sales, please call our Reseller Customer Service department at 800-434-3422.

For information on where to purchase IDG Books Worldwide's books outside the U.S., please contact our International Sales department at 317-596-5530 or fax 317-596-5692.

For information on foreign language translations, please contact our Foreign & Subsidiary Rights department at 650-655-3021 or fax 650-655-3281.

For sales inquiries and special prices for bulk quantities, please contact our Sales department at 650-655-3200 or write to the address above.

For information on using IDG Books Worldwide's books in the classroom or for ordering examination copies, please contact our Educational Sales department at 800-434-2086 or fax 317-596-5499.

For press review copies, author interviews, or other publicity information, please contact our Public Relations department at 650-655-3000 or fax 650-655-3299.

For authorization to photocopy items for corporate, personal, or educational use, please contact Copyright Clearance Center, 222 Rosewood Drive, Danvers, MA 01923, or fax 978-750-4470.

About the Author

Charles Seiter got a Ph.D. from Caltech, was a chemistry professor for seven years, and won enough money on *Jeopardy!* to skip out to rural northern California with his family and write about computer topics for Macworld and other publications.

His current IDG Books Worldwide titles include *Macworld Web Essentials*, *Yahoo! Unplugged*, and *Everyday Math For Dummies*. His main interest is modern computation-intensive methods in statistics, but he also (no kidding) writes scripts for a German television cartoon series.

ABOUT IDG BOOKS WORLDWIDE

Welcome to the world of IDG Books Worldwide.

IDG Books Worldwide, Inc., is a subsidiary of International Data Group, the world's largest publisher of computer-related information and the leading global provider of information services on information technology. IDG was founded more than 30 years ago by Patrick J. McGovern and now employs more than 9,000 people worldwide. IDG publishes more than 290 computer publications in over 75 countries. More than 90 million people read one or more IDG publications each month.

Launched in 1990, IDG Books Worldwide is today the #1 publisher of best-selling computer books in the United States. We are proud to have received eight awards from the Computer Press Association in recognition of editorial excellence and three from Computer Currents' First Annual Readers' Choice Awards. Our best-selling ...For Dummies® series has more than 50 million copies in print with translations in 31 languages. IDG Books Worldwide, through a joint venture with IDG's Hi-Tech Beijing, became the first U.S. publisher to publish a computer book in the People's Republic of China. In record time, IDG Books Worldwide has become the first choice for millions of readers around the world who want to learn how to better manage their businesses.

Our mission is simple: Every one of our books is designed to bring extra value and skill-building instructions to the reader. Our books are written by experts who understand and care about our readers. The knowledge base of our editorial staff comes from years of experience in publishing, education, and journalism — experience we use to produce books to carry us into the new millennium. In short, we care about books, so we attract the best people. We devote special attention to details such as audience, interior design, use of icons, and illustrations. And because we use an efficient process of authoring, editing, and desktop publishing our books electronically, we can spend more time ensuring superior content and less time on the technicalities of making books.

You can count on our commitment to deliver high-quality books at competitive prices on topics you want to read about. At IDG Books Worldwide, we continue in the IDG tradition of delivering quality for more than 30 years. You'll find no better book on a subject than one from IDG Books Worldwide.

John Kilcullen
Chairman and CEO
IDG Books Worldwide, Inc.

Steven Berkowitz
President and Publisher
IDG Books Worldwide, Inc.

IDG is the world's leading IT media, research and exposition company. Founded in 1964, IDG had 1997 revenues of $2.05 billion and has more than 9,000 employees worldwide. IDG offers the widest range of media options that reach IT buyers in 75 countries representing 95% of worldwide IT spending. IDG's diverse product and services portfolio spans six key areas including print publishing, online publishing, expositions and conferences, market research, education and training, and global marketing services. More than 90 million people read one or more of IDG's 290 magazines and newspapers, including IDG's leading global brands — Computerworld, PC World, Network World, Macworld and the Channel World family of publications. IDG Books Worldwide is one of the fastest-growing computer book publishers in the world, with more than 700 titles in 36 languages. The "...For Dummies®" series alone has more than 50 million copies in print. IDG offers online users the largest network of technology-specific Web sites around the world through IDG.net (http://www.idg.net), which comprises more than 225 targeted Web sites in 55 countries worldwide. International Data Corporation (IDC) is the world's largest provider of information technology data, analysis and consulting, with research centers in over 41 countries and more than 400 research analysts worldwide. IDG World Expo is a leading producer of more than 168 globally branded conferences and expositions in 35 countries including E3 (Electronic Entertainment Expo), Macworld Expo, ComNet, Windows World Expo, ICE (Internet Commerce Expo), Agenda, DEMO, and Spotlight. IDG's training subsidiary, ExecuTrain, is the world's largest computer training company, with more than 230 locations worldwide and 785 training courses. IDG Marketing Services helps industry-leading IT companies build international brand recognition by developing global integrated marketing programs via IDG's print, online and exposition products worldwide. Further information about the company can be found at www.idg.com.
1/24/99

Author's Acknowledgments

In ascending order in the publishing food-chain, I would like to thank Suki Gear, Mary Bednarek, and John Kilcullen of IDG for convincing me that IDG has many of the finest people in computer publishing.

Jim Heid and Tom Negrino, Macworld colleagues who are the unquestioned authorities on their topics (audio/video for Jim, Microsoft Office for Tom) contributed great guest chapters. For this I also thank the corresponding forbearances of Maryellen Kelly and Dori Smith. Kathleen Calderwood also contributed much perspective on the ways real companies in advertising and market communications make money on the Web.

Loretta Toth, besides offering valuable advice, kept me from actually dying during two years of disastrous medical problems that delayed production of this work, parts of which were typed two-fingered left-handed propped up in bed. Mary Seiter Toth, our daughter and a notorious Web-design hotshot in her own right, also helped make this difficult effort possible.

Finally, I would like to thank the original pioneers of the Internet for finding a path for us all to a destination we can't yet imagine. We can no more predict where the Net will take us than Ben Franklin could have predicted TV.

Publisher's Acknowledgments

We're proud of this book; please register your comments through our IDG Books Worldwide Online Registration Form located at http://my2cents.dummies.com.

Some of the people who helped bring this book to market include the following:

Acquisitions, Editorial, and Media Development

Project Editor: Nate Holdread

Acquisitions Editor: Michael Kelly

Copy Editors: Paula Lowell, Constance Carlisle

Technical Editor: Tim Warner

Editorial Manager: Mary C. Corder

Editorial Assistant: Paul Kuzmic

Production

Project Coordinator: Karen York

Layout and Graphics: Lou Boudreau, J. Tyler Connor, Maridee V. Ennis, Angela F. Hunckler, Jane E. Martin, Drew R. Moore, Brent Savage, Rashell Smith, Michael A. Sullivan

Proofreaders: Vickie Broyles, Michelle Croninger, Rachel Garvey, Brian Massey, Nancy L. Reinhardt, Mildred Rosenzweig

Indexer: Rebecca R. Plunkett

Special Help

Jennifer Ehrlich, Kevin Spencer

General and Administrative

IDG Books Worldwide, Inc.: John Kilcullen, CEO; Steven Berkowitz, President and Publisher

IDG Books Technology Publishing Group: Richard Swadley, Senior Vice President and Publisher; Walter Bruce III, Vice President and Associate Publisher; Steven Sayre, Associate Publisher; Joseph Wikert, Associate Publisher; Mary Bednarek, Branded Product Development Director; Mary Corder, Editorial Director

IDG Books Consumer Publishing Group: Roland Elgey, Senior Vice President and Publisher; Kathleen A. Welton, Vice President and Publisher; Kevin Thornton, Acquisitions Manager; Kristin A. Cocks, Editorial Director

IDG Books Internet Publishing Group: Brenda McLaughlin, Senior Vice President and Group Publisher; Diane Graves Steele, Vice President and Associate Publisher; Sofia Marchant, Online Marketing Manager

IDG Books Production for Dummies Press: Michael R. Britton, Vice President of Production; Debbie Stailey, Associate Director of Production; Cindy L. Phipps, Manager of Project Coordination, Production Proofreading, and Indexing; Shelley Lea, Supervisor of Graphics and Design; Debbie J. Gates, Production Systems Specialist; Robert Springer, Supervisor of Proofreading; Laura Carpenter, Production Control Manager; Tony Augsburger, Supervisor of Reprints and Bluelines

Dummies Packaging and Book Design: Patty Page, Manager, Promotions Marketing

♦

The publisher would like to give special thanks to Patrick J. McGovern, without whom this book would not have been possible.

♦

Contents at a Glance

Cartoons at a Glance

By Rich Tennant

page 5

page 35

page 63

page 279

page 119

page 305

Fax: 978-546-7747 • E-mail: the5wave@tiac.net

Table of Contents

· ·

Introduction

*W*elcome to the third edition of *The Internet For Macs For Dummies!*

The Internet is a gold mine of serious stuff, silly stuff, and simply amazing opportunities. The key feature of this book is that it shows you how to get the access you want while blissfully ignoring both Windows and UNIX. The Mac is responsible for about half of all Web sites (if you watch IBM's TV ads closely, you can see that people are using slightly disguised Macs!), so it won't be difficult.

This book is full of cutting-edge material — the Web browsers here, for example, were a few weeks old when their chapters were written. In fact, it may be the first non-obsolete Internet book for the Macintosh, demonstrating the new AOL software Version 4.0. I've kept technical stuff about MacTCP and PPP to a minimum in this edition, because software now shields you from gruesome protocol details. The good news in 1998 and beyond is that you won't have to spend much time on cryptic communications details, unless you absolutely insist.

About This Book

I wrote this book to get you onto the Internet and Web and point out their many interesting features. All the material here has been tested on ordinary users. By *users,* I don't mean the people who hang around at user groups comparing shareware; I mean people who call me with questions about using the spell checker in Word 6.

This book should be easier to follow than, say, a *Macworld* article. I explain some key points in this book:

- ✔ What the World Wide Web is (and isn't)
- ✔ How you get connected
- ✔ What you'll find in newsgroups
- ✔ Where to get free software
- ✔ How to make friends on the Net
- ✔ How to search the World Wide Web

Not Just a Job, It's an Adventure

If you just want to get on and get out there, this is the right book for you. This is a reference book, but that doesn't mean that it's a computer-systems manual. It's a guide to launch you onto the Web and the Net, and it's a map to help you navigate the system after you get connected.

Learning about the Internet is not just another computer chore, such as learning Adobe PageMaker shortcuts. When you sign on to the Internet, you participate in one of the most exciting intellectual adventures in history. Out there on the World Wide Web is a big chunk of all the information accumulated by the human race since the dawn of time, from satellite photos to Shakespeare. Many of the coolest people on the planet are out there, too. It's now also a great place to look for jobs and a great place to go shopping.

Nobody knows where the Web's headed, how big it's going to get, or how it will evolve next. For example, although businesses have flocked to set up Web sites, at the moment, it's an open question how they'll actually make money. All I know is that hundreds of millions of intelligent people can now communicate and do business all over the planet (or *off* the planet, according to some Internet UFO discussion groups). Because you're reading this book, you're going to be able to help determine the future.

How This Book Is Organized

This book is divided into six parts; each has a different function.

Part I: Internet and Web Basics

In this part, I explain the world of the Internet — what's in it, how it came to be, and who's there. You can read this part to learn some Internet background so that you can impress your friends and associates, or you can use the new knowledge to plan real adventures.

Part II: Getting on the Internet

Good news! Getting on the Internet is easy, or at least it's easier than it was two years ago. I'll tell you how to pick a modem to buy, how to use your Mac's built-in modem (especially a snap for new iMac owners), how to pick an Internet service provider, and how to get connected. The Mac has its own special Control Panels and Extensions for online work, and these are explained from a get-connected-fast perspective.

Part III: Working the Web

There are now two main browsers and one national online service after five years of brutal market shake-out. Netscape Navigator, Internet Explorer, and America Online are going to be your windows on the Web, at least for now.

Part IV: Your Mac in the Web World

If you want to play in the big leagues, I tell you what you need in this part. Probably the most useful single Internet fuction is e-mail, so that topic has its own chapter. Then there are Web sites — sometimes it makes sense to be your own Web site and sometimes it doesn't, so I cover the options. In the brave new world of the Apple-Microsoft peace treaty, Office 98 has emerged as a great overall program and a pretty good Web tool, so you'll see a special guest chapter by Tom Negrino, author of the Mac version of *Office 98 For Dummies* (IDG Books Worldwide, Inc.). Also, in another guest section, the Mac specialties audio and video get their own chapter by multimedia guru Jim Heid.

Part V: The Part of Tens

Some of these top-ten lists are serious, and some are just for fun.

Part VI: Appendixes

In the appendixes, I reveal some extra hints and tips. I also offer you some useful lists that are too long to put in the middle of the book.

Icons Used in This Book

Hey, look here, everyone: Pictures in a computer book. These icons highlight special information.

Believe me, the Internet has plenty of technical aspects. You can skip these sections if you like, but read them if you're curious.

A Tip is a recommended way to accomplish an Internet task with your Mac. Often, a Tip is a shortcut.

This icon flags background information that you should keep in mind. "Eat your dinner first and then eat the salad" would be a Remember icon for traveling in Italy.

 "Drive on the left" would be a Warning for traveling in Britain.

 This icon alerts you that I'm going to tell you how to get to some cool places on the Internet. Hey, on the highway, do it my way.

Where to Go from Here

It's time to take the plunge.

But first, I'd like to offer a few words of encouragement: Some parts of the Internet world are fairly confusing. If you find them confusing, it's not just you. Some aspects are hard — the way English-language spelling is hard — because the Internet evolved through a series of historic accidents.

I was the contributing editor in charge of stuff-that's-too-hard-for-English-majors at *Macworld* for twelve years. And I've found some fancier aspects of Internet use to be as hard as, say, advanced topics in Microsoft Excel. So if you are puzzled by the Internet from time to time, remember that it's not your fault.

IDG Books is paying me to make this easy for you. I think that this addition to the good ole *...For Dummies* series will make Internet access almost as easy as word processing — and considerably more fun.

Tell Us What You Think

Please send me your comments; you can reach me at

IDG Books Worldwide
7260 Shadeland Station Suite 100
Indianapolis, IN 46256

I'd give you my Internet e-mail address, but it's already so jammed with stuff that I'm more likely to find your comments on paper! Here's a hint, though — if you look at some of the screens in this book, you can figure out my name on America Online. I'm stuck belonging to a bunch of service providers to produce works like this.

Part I
Internet and Web Basics

The 5th Wave — By Rich Tennant

In this part . . .

The Internet is the wild and woolly frontier of electronic communication. A huge part of all the information ever accumulated is out there somewhere on the Internet. It's just a matter of finding a way to navigate this digital ocean with your Macintosh.

This book assumes that you want to use the Internet the same way you use a Macintosh, with icons, menus, and lots of the little details smoothed over.

In this part, you'll travel the Internet, seeing what it has to offer and how you get it for yourself. I hope you enjoy the journey!

Chapter 1

Welcome to the Net

*A*t one time, way back in the early '90s, people thought that the Internet was the natural habitat of rocket scientists. Then suddenly, everyone from the President to *Time* magazine started telling us that the Internet is for everyone — most newspapers now have weekly Internet columns, and half the ads you see on TV say "www.something.com" in a line at the bottom of the screen (see Figure 1-1). People talk about *surfing the Net* or *surfing the Web,* a peculiar sport played by people who rarely get wet. And commercials about the so-called Information Superhighway promise that you'll soon have data coming out of your ears and that a portable fax machine strapped to your wrist will be proper fashion for a beach vacation.

Whew.

Well, when you get into the Internet, you find out two things:

✔ It really is pretty amazing.

✔ You really don't have to be a computer hotshot to use it. And it won't follow you on vacation, unless you insist.

Caught in the Net

Most computers in business offices or universities can talk to each other over *networks,* which are just sets of wiring and software that let computers communicate with each other.

Figure 1-1:
GM
endorses
the Web.

The Internet is a way for these computer networks to connect to other computer networks. In fact, you can contact people all over the world from your computer through the Internet.

You see, the Internet lets you send files from one computer to another over a big, high-speed system of computer network connections, which the U.S. government paid for, installed, and then turned over to a private group of companies in 1995. Because all computers all over the planet can transfer files or look at information anywhere, anyone (even you) can access any information that someone wants to place in the *public domain,* meaning that it's available to everyone with no restrictions.

That's right — people develop programs, movies, music, books, and other valuable stuff, and then give them away, or use the free stuff as an entice-ment to buy (see Figure 1-2). They also develop a lot of amusing nonsense and give that away, too. With the rise of the World Wide Web as the major Internet feature, everyone from Apple to little Timmy Wilson of Fried Trout, Idaho, can be an Internet citizen. The problem used to be mastering the technical details of file transfer; now it's just coping with the explosion of both useful and non-useful stuff out there. And besides files and World Wide Web pages, now just about everyone has an e-mail address.

Combining all this information with electronic mail (always called *e-mail*) means the following:

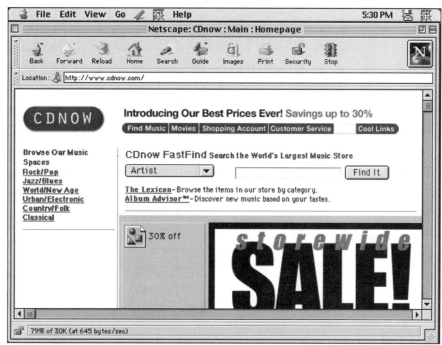

Figure 1-2:
Listen to the
new stuff,
online.

✔ You can send messages to anyone across the Internet, and they get the messages in a few minutes, usually.

✔ You can find tons of useful information and lots of free programs and games.

✔ You can *chat* online with people anywhere (computer chatting is something like talking via CB radio, and it's insanely popular).

✔ You can get instant, up-to-date news, typically twelve hours ahead of your local newspaper (see Figure 1-3).

Macintosh: The easy network machine

Even if you're just sitting at your own Mac and aren't wired to anyone else, you have network capability anyway. The Mac's survival originally hinged on its success in the graphics/printing market, so Apple had to provide a way for several Macs to hook up to one (expensive) laser printer, usually on a network. So it was a relatively easy matter for Apple to make software components to put Macs on the Internet. At this point, anything you need to know about Internet connection will take only a few minutes of reading in this beginner's-level book.

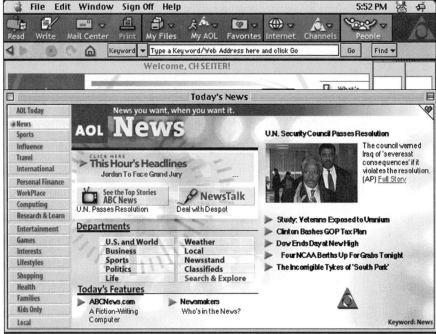

Figure 1-3:
Online
news is
faster than
print. Way
faster.

If you're having trouble visualizing the Internet as a network of networks, think about this: You, at your own Macintosh, use a modem to dial into a central computer that many users can connect to. The central computer has a direct connection to the Internet, so it can dial up any other Internet-connected computer across the country. And that computer can look for anything, say a page on the World Wide Web, on any other computer that's been assigned a type of Internet address. To summarize: After you make an Internet connection, you can reach tons of files or information on any Internet-linked computer. This process is not *hacking,* which means gaining illegal access to files; it's legitimately accessing material that people on other networks *want* you to see.

Mail: Snail versus electronic

Snail mail is computerese for letters delivered by the U.S. Postal Service. *E-mail* is computer messages (which can now include sound and pictures) that are sent over a network. When you send a piece of e-mail, it reaches the recipient almost immediately. (The only catch is that the person receiving the mail has to connect to the network to receive it.) As a result, the Internet has evolved into an international instant post office because it can pick up e-mail on one network and deliver it to another.

Internet Archaeology

How did all this Internet stuff happen? Like many bits of modern technology, the Internet started as a military project. In the 1970s, the Department of Defense decided that research efforts would speed up if investigators with funding from the Advanced Research Projects Agency (ARPA) could communicate from one network to another. Usually, these networks were at big national labs like Los Alamos or universities like MIT.

ARPANET, as the new networking setup was called, originally linked about 30 sites, most of which used computers that are now ancient (Burroughs, Honeywell, and early DEC hardware). Some of the first ARPANET designers were hired for another project that would let ARPANET connect to radio- and satellite-based computer communications. This effort defined the communications hardware and software that make an Internet connection (that's why some of it is so weird, in modern computing practice).

In the 1980s, the old ARPA sites converted to the new Internet connections. Then the National Science Foundation (NSF) put together a high-speed network for Internet sites. Companies selling gateway hardware and software (a *gateway* is the actual connection from one network to another) for connecting to the NSFNET began to appear. Commercial Internet service networks were born. By 1995, the whole shooting match was so big that the Feds bowed out and turned maintenance of the Internet backbone over to a consortium of private companies (see Figure 1-4). Those companies are now struggling bravely to keep up with demand.

Letting all existing networks connect to the single, big Internet produced the well-documented explosion of Internet connections; now almost every business card has both an @ address for e-mail and an http:// address for a World Wide Web page. A big part of the system is the nationwide, high-speed NSFNET, which has been funded through the year 2003 as a sort of government experiment in communications infrastructure.

The number of people connected to the Internet has simply exploded in the last four years. As a simple example, when I started working on the book *Yahoo! Unplugged* for IDG Books Worldwide, the Yahoo! service indexed about 200,000 Web pages. When I finished the book *six months later,* the index had 30,000,000 pages! Nothing like this has ever existed. Ever.

Some authorities estimate that the system can handle about a billion users eventually, with some reworking of connection strategies. After that, the Internet may need to handle e-mail addresses differently — just as phone companies have had to adjust over the years to the increase in telephone use, mainly by making up new area codes.

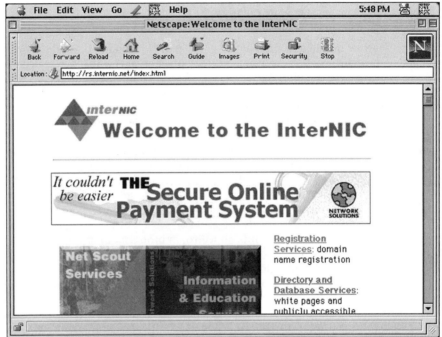

Figure 1-4:
One of the
"ruling
companies."

This amazing growth is one of the reasons that it took a while for Internet access to show a decent interface for Mac users. In January 1993, the typical Internet user had a research job and was used to dealing with a clunky command-line interface worked out for computers using the UNIX operating system. Very few people involved in designing the Internet, way back when, foresaw that you and I would be pounding on the gate(way)s some day, demanding a user-friendly Mac interface to Internet services. But twenty million Mac users beating down the doors at America Online and Internet service providers radically changed the game.

E-Mail, the Internet, and the Web

If you glance at a business card these days, most likely you can find a line on the card that lists an e-mail address (look for the @ symbol). Think about it: Ten years ago most cards didn't even list a fax number! For example, an Apple employee named Kermit T. Frog could have the following e-mail address:

```
kermitf@apple.com
```

The @ symbol is the tip-off that this code is actually an Internet-valid e-mail address; the notation `.com` (the Internet *zone designation*) means that the address is a business. When you read this address, you say, "kermit-eff at apple dot com" (the @ is pronounced "at" and the `.` [period] is pronounced "dot").

Here's why addresses are important: If you have an e-mail address, you can communicate with anyone else on the planet with an e-mail address — that includes everyone who's anyone in the computer business and many of the powerful people at most organizations. To be taken seriously as a computer user or business person, you need your own e-mail address.

For example, today you can send a message to

`vicepresident@whitehouse.gov`

and help educate Al Gore on environmental issues. ("Sir, I'd like to volunteer several distant states as nuclear waste dumps.")

By the way, the zone designation .gov means that the e-mail address is at a government site. Professors at universities usually have addresses that end in .edu (for education). Sometimes, an address is a location instead of a job category. For example, an address that ends in .uk means the institution is part of Her Majesty's domain, and .ca is the Great White North (Canada). See Table 1-1 for a few more examples.

When you get your own e-mail address, I promise that you'll feel very official. I know I did.

Table 1-1	Ten Internet E-Mail Address Types
Address	*Interpretation*
user@coombs.anu.edu.au	Australian National University
user@netcom.com	A commercial Internet service provider
user@aol.com	America Online, another commercial Internet service provider
user@nic.ddn.mil	A military site
user@whales.org	A (mythical) nonprofit organization
user@nsf.net	The National Science Foundation network
user@unicef.int	An international organization
user@informatik.uni-hamburg.de	A computer science department in Germany (.de means Deutschland)
user@leprechaun.ie	A fantastic address in Ireland

In 1995, the Internet saw an explosion in World Wide Web addresses for businesses and organizations as well (see Table 1-2). A Web address, called a *Uniform Resource Locator,* or URL, lets you connect, using a piece of software called a Web browser, to *Web pages* with graphics, sound, and occasional bits of video. Web pages are typically full of *hyperlinks,* underlined words that lead you to yet another page with its own URL address. In this way, you can jump from one page to another for hours, in a determined research effort or in a random day's goof. You'll see lots more on the Web elsewhere in this book, and even more in IDG's *Yahoo! Unplugged* (by myself and some friends), a book on the Web Index site called Yahoo!. Also check out *Macworld Web Essentials,* another fine IDG Books product by myself and Tom Negrino. URL addresses mostly follow the same conventions as e-mail addresses (.gov means government, .com means business, and so forth).

Table 1-2	Some World Wide Web Addresses
Address	*Interpretation*
http://www.yahoo.com/	The Yahoo! index site, now a giant business (it used to be an .edu inside Stanford)
http://www.wustl.edu/	Washington University
http://www.netscape.com/	Netscape, developers of the popular Navigator Web browser
http://www.amazon.com/	A store with a million books online (including fifteen of mine)!

Electronic Libraries on the Net

As an Internet user, you can exchange messages with other Internet users from Brazil to Baltimore and look at Web pages. By itself, that capability makes the Internet extremely useful. But, wonder of wonders, you also can use the Internet to access incredible amounts of information stored all over the world.

The Library of Congress, for example, contains copies of all the books (and nearly all the magazines and newspapers) published in the United States. (Of course, only 40,000 or so of the most useful books have been prepared for you to access through the Internet, but several library groups are working to get the whole collection ready for the Internet.) The U.S. Patent Office has files on all the patents it has ever issued. Medical info sites contain first-rate information about nearly any disorder you can have. And university libraries across the country (Harvard, Yale, and Illinois are the largest) house all sorts of foreign research material not found in the Library of Congress. You can find comic books, today's Dilbert cartoon, campaign fliers, recipes, jokes, and back issues of *TV Guide* on the Internet. You have instant access to everything, including tons of idiotic opinions, pornography, and just plain junk (see Figure 1-5).

All this stuff is being merrily scanned into a Web format that your Macintosh can read with a browser, such as Netscape Navigator. Text, pictures, movies, and sound are all yours.

Now, on-screen reading isn't great for novels; you don't want to try scrolling through an 800-page paperback at the beach on your laptop. On-screen reading is ideal, though, if you're looking for specific pieces of information because you can search Web pages for key words.

Light reading?

Here's an example: The library in the small town where I live has its own Internet connection. (Your library probably also has a connection, because Internet access is *the* hot topic at librarians' meetings in the late '90s. Come to think of it, it's about time the poor old librarians had a hot topic.) Last week, from my house, I checked the local university library for holdings on a particular topic. I didn't find what I wanted, so I clicked into libraries at the University of California at Berkeley and at the University of Illinois, Champaign-Urbana.

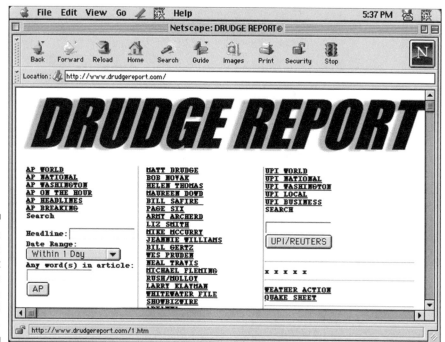

Figure 1-5:
The Web site that brought us Clinton's 1998 scandals.

Greek to me

Just about everything ever written in Latin or ancient Greek is available online as part of a huge project involving Classics departments all over the world (see the following figure). You can, for example, consult the author Lucian, who provides these three rules for getting through the day:

1. When things aren't working, stop for a minute and smile.

2. Remember not to take it too seriously.

3. See whether you can make the situation better by trying harder, or see whether you should try something else.

In the immortal words of Dr. Kent Wilson (UC San Diego), "You know, those old guys weren't so dumb." This advice comes in handy when, every now and then, the software keeps crashing and you're getting busy signals from your modem and you get "connection refused" messages. The classical stuff is especially nice because you can read *finished* documents — I don't think that these authors will be writing new editions any time soon. These ain't betas, they're the shipping release.

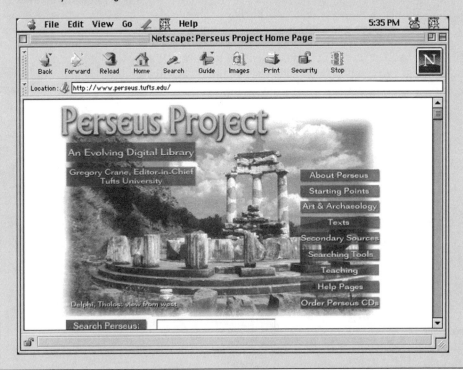

I could have tapped into libraries at Oxford, for that matter. Finally, I came back to my own library and made an interlibrary loan request for a book at Berkeley. Not bad for ten minutes' work at my own Mac! In the next few years, with faster modems and more books online, even this interlibrary loan stuff will disappear, and a huge assortment of reference books will just be routinely downloaded.

In other words, even if you're sitting in front of your Macintosh, you can browse the stacks of most of the world's libraries. Although you may not always be able to get individual books transferred to a library near you, the information in these books is, as I write, steadily being converted to online files that you can download.

Looking for love?

The Internet has a service called *Internet Relay Chat* (IRC), a sort of global conference call. It used to be a separate Internet function, but now it's usually part of a Web site. But the chat lines on specialty bulletin boards and AOL are actually better for this stuff than the Web.

A connected world

The Internet isn't all serious. Sure, it has resources on programming languages and mathematical physics, but the Internet also is the planet's chief pipeline to news and plain old, silly gossip.

For example, I regularly check comments made by fans of the great TV program *Mystery Science Theater 3000*. This program still has thousands of avid fans who chatter away online every day in a huge, open, online bulletin board, called a *newsgroup*. Because *MST3K* specializes in obscure, funny references, any given line from the show is capable of generating an endless stream of linked messages from fans explaining various perspectives on the wisecrack.

Inevitably, the Internet reflects what's on people's minds. Just as Egyptians filled their tombs with pornographic graffiti (no kidding), and just as the first artsy pictures of naked ladies appeared within a single year of the invention of photography, many private computer bulletin boards specialize in adult material. And many of those boards are connected to the Net. In fact, it's a matter of historic record that two of the newsgroups most frequently accessed are `alt.sex` and `rec.arts.erotica`, and Web porno sites are big business.

All Aboard!

On a drizzly, spring morning in San Francisco in 1994, I decided to see for myself what sorts of people were willing to take a beginning Internet class at the dawn of Net history. The crowd, amazingly enough, consisted of equal parts

✔ Generation X-ers, complete with the occasional nose ring and I'm-an-artist-don't-bother-me-OK? fashion

✔ Retired high-school teachers

✔ Mysterious business guys in suits on a Sunday

This pattern has held through several years of classes. I've been asked to give Internet talks to every community group north of the Golden Gate Bridge, and my guess is that the sociological profile of Internet users now looks just like the general population, and that newcomers correctly see the Web and the Internet as the same thing in practice.

You and Your Mac

Mac users buy a Mac for the easiest access to serious computer power. Naturally, you and I both want Internet access that uses a self-explanatory Mac interface. Fun fact: Macs are responsible for about half the sites on the Web.) Apple's new iMac ships with a 56K modem and Web access software as standard equipment, because Apple realizes that's going to be a big part of its use. (What do you think the "i" stands for?) If you have free Internet access (for example, you're a university student or your employer has given you an account), someone has already explained some basics to you. The aim of most of this book, however, is to explain Internet access to people who don't have large organizations with systems administrators supporting them.

In the first edition of this book, back in the age of stone modems and chipped-flint wiring, I had to admit that no way existed to get full Internet access easily in a single software or service package. That's all changed now. If you have a Mac, a modem, and a credit card number, you'll have no more trouble getting on the Internet and the Web than you have running Microsoft Word.

Think about it. If you have a research topic that you've always wanted to pursue, you can command the resources of most of the world's universities with your fingers. If you're an expatriate Australian frustrated by America's utter lack of interest in cricket (or in Australian-rules rugby, or really in anything but Foster's), you can get yesterday's scores by making a local call. If you just want to find a large group of people who share your obsessions, you no longer have to leave your home. And if you just want to buy stuff, you'd better believe the Web wants to meet *you!*

Check these topics

To motivate you and to give you some idea of what's out there, I list here some of the kinds of information on the Internet. You also can take it for granted that there are gigabytes of hard-core techie stuff, too.

✔ **Urban legends:** Folklorist Jan Harold Brunvand, author of *The Choking Dober-man* and *The Mexican Pet*, maintains files on urban myths in a newsgroup called `alt.folklore.urban`. You can check here to convince yourself that all known poodle-in-a-microwave stories are fiction. I personally think the ghostly hitchhiker stuff is true, however.

✔ **QuarkXPress at Indiana University:** Authors of books on Quark have downloaded files to this huge archive of tips and information on using QuarkXPress. Now you can look at this week's tips instead of last year's. By the way, sometime you should notice the huge concentration of computer publishers in Indiana.

✔ **GUTENBERG:** Project Gutenberg is the name of an initiative to put almost everything important that was ever printed into online form. Time for a bigger hard drive, eh?

✔ **Is funny, nyet?:** An Internet service exists that reports jokes from the former Soviet Union. These days they need all the humor they can get.

✔ **Agriculture:** On a huge range of university-maintained databases, every bit of agricultural research ever assembled is indexed and available. If you're a farmer, there's no need any more to wait for the agent from the ag school to get around to your county.

✔ **Sumo:** The Yahoo! index started out as two graduate students' after-hours Web-page project to provide some basic information on the Japanese sport of Sumo. Then they added more stuff, and then more stuff, then dropped out of school to run Yahoo! as a business that indexes the whole Web and has a stock market valuation bigger than Apple's.

✔ **Business:** Pick the name of any business, for example, IBM. Now go to `http://www.ibm.com`. Amazing, isn't it? Now try Apple, Ford, or Microsoft instead. Yup — they're all there. Check out `http://www.camelliainn.com` to see what little individual businesses are doing. The Web has seen the fastest high-tech Gold Rush in history.

Chapter 2
The Online World

● ●

In This Chapter

▶ A network of networks

▶ Newsgroups, the first Internet fun

▶ And now, the Web!

▶ Is this educational?

▶ Greetings from the government

● ●

*T*he basic history is that the U.S. Defense Department set up the protoypes of the Internet as a sort of nuclear-attack-proof communications system for the military. What got devised in the 1960s, and then became the Internet, was actually just a messaging system that allowed computers to forward messages over a network. Some part of the network could be missing, but the software would find a way to get a message from the originating computer to the destination computer. So what really came out of these efforts was a universal e-mail scheme.

But at the same time that the government agencies were working on a communications protocol for connecting research networks, computer use by ordinary people exploded. In the early 1980s, as the earlier military-based Advanced Research Projects Agency system gave way to the Internet, Apple II sales soared into the millions, and the IBM PC essentially became a new industry. Meanwhile, cheap, fast modems appeared, making computer bulletin boards and assorted online services practical for the first time.

Connections Galore

When you start exploring the Internet, most likely by heading for the World Wide Web, you'll find all sorts of information, opinions, hucksterism, and outright bafflement. Not only are there nearly 240 million Internet users, but comparable numbers of people are connected to other nets that pass information to the Internet. Some of these other nets are just tiny, private networks (now glamorously called intranets) that service five people per day. Some of them are government networks that span the whole globe and connect thousands of solid, hardworking citizens in white shirts and ties.

Although thousands of nets can exchange messages and data with the Internet, only a few are really important. Four big sources — Usenet, university special-interest groups, government organizations (see Figure 2-1), and businesses exploding on the World Wide Web — contribute most of the stuff that you find on the Net, and in this chapter I'm going to give you a quick rundown on each of them.

Figure 2-1:
Recognize
these guys?

What's a Newsgroup, Anyway?

Although the Internet was designed as a sort of e-mail equivalent of the worldwide telephone system, it didn't take people long to find a way to use e-mail to set up interactive conferences on particular topics of interest. It was quite simple, really — all it takes is a program that will forward collections of e-mail messages from one computer to another so that everyone who is "signed up" with an interest group gets automatically updated on all the group's messages.

When people think of the Internet, they often think of Web pages with sound and movies. Actually, a lot of interesting action still takes place on what's technically another network, called Usenet. But plenty of Internet sites also are Usenet sites, so the information tends to slosh across the two systems. When you check into a big Web search service such as AltaVista, you also have the option of searching Usenet (see Figure 2-2).

On the Internet, you can talk to Usenet people, and they can talk to you. Usenet was really the first "fun" use of the Internet, and it is still sufficiently interesting that good World Wide Web software also gives you access to Usenet.

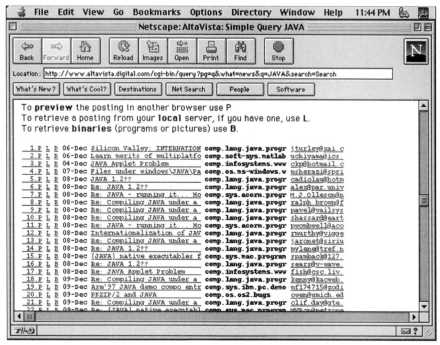

Figure 2-2:
Looking up
Java.

Usenet newsgroups are the source of the most entertaining text-based material on the Internet. For example, the newsgroup `rec.humor.funny` is the most-accessed topic on the Internet; `rec.humor.funny` includes jokes selected diligently from the material found in the larger selection `rec.humor`. That's right — someone screens out the unfunny jokes for you! Is this a great service or what?

Newsgroups are also an interesting discussion forum for topics that don't get a lot of mainstream daily coverage. Check the topics I've gathered in Figure 2-3 for your curiosity.

Usenet also is the source of serious stuff. If you want to study mathematical chaos, for example, you can join a newsgroup called `sci.nonlinear`.

Joining conferences

Table 2-1 lists a tiny sample of the conferences on Usenet that you can join from an Internet site. In Chapters 5 and 6 on current Web browsers, I tell you how to get a current list — many changes occur every few months.

Usenet sites, as a rule, still use the UNIX operating system. One of my goals in writing this book is to insulate you from UNIX; I don't want you to have to learn a lot of UNIX commands just to get Internet access.

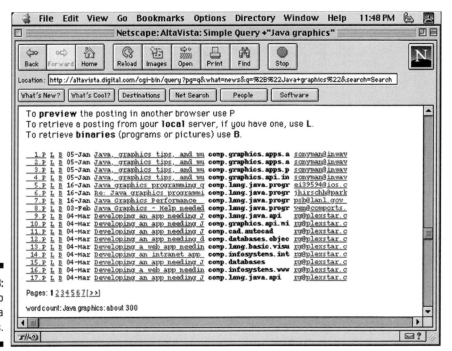

Figure 2-3: Looking up Java graphics.

The reason UNIX appears all over the Internet is that UNIX is a real industrial-strength, bulletproof, network operating system, better at network management than the Mac OS or the much-hyped Windows NT. It's also very efficient with computer resources, and both computer memory and computer time used to be more expensive. It's nerd heaven, too. If you feel the urge to learn more, just check out *UNIX For Dummies,* 3rd Edition or the UNIX command sections in *The Internet For Dummies,* 5th Edition, both by IDG Books.

Table 2-1	Welcome, Stranger!
Newsgroup	*Topic*
comp.ai	Artificial intelligence
sci.med.aids	Current AIDS information
alt.hotrod	Souped-up vehicles, natch
alt.rush-limbaugh	Please note the hyphen
alt.sports.baseball. chicago-cubs	Seminar on congenital optimism
talk.abortion	Abortion controversies of all kinds
rec.arts.poems	Write a poem, put it here
misc.answers	About Usenet itself
comp.sys.mac.wanted	Macs for sale

Drinking from a fire hose

The relatively specialized newsgroup for magnetic resonance lists about a hundred messages a day. But face it, even though magnetic resonance has elbowed its way into hospitals, it remains a pretty obscure subject. My point: Newsgroups for popular topics (in other words, where practically anyone may have an opinion) really run some high volume. Figure it out: If magnetic resonance is worth a hundred postings on a good day, how much traffic do you think shows up during a World Series in alt.fan.baseball?

If you join lots of newsgroups indiscriminately, I promise that you won't be able to find the time to read most of the stuff.

The World Wide Web Takes Over

You can have loads of fun with Usenet newsgroups, but they consist mostly of text messages and typing. (Okay, heaps of dirty pictures are in newsgroups too, but they're encoded, so technically they're text files, too.)

So it was inevitable that in a TV culture people would want pictures, and they finally got them when the World Wide Web moved to center stage on the Internet by early 1995. The Web spent a few years waiting in the wings, but when it arrived it was certainly ready for prime time. If you look at the typical Web screen shown in Figure 2-4, you will see at once why a nation of channel-surfers voted with their modems as soon as Web access became available.

Web history is worth a brief mention. Around 1989, a fellow named Dr. Tim Berners-Lee wrote a modest computer program for his own use in research. It was basically a sort of notepad program, with the interesting wrinkle that individual pages of notes were linked by keywords. You could call up a page about a scientific conference, for example, and click the title of a particular lecture, and the program would then call up an abstract of the lecture. The abstract itself might contain other links to articles or reference tables. His supervisors at CERN in Geneva (a big physics lab) thought it would be interesting to develop this idea to become a general-purpose way of exchanging information among the other far-flung, big-time physics labs around the globe. If you could dial up a central computer, and if you had one starting-point page with an index, it would be possible to access all the latest and greatest in physics research from anywhere, assuming that someone had set up the information and established the links. A group at CERN did just that, and in 1991, the first World Wide Web site was set up at CERN as a service to the world's physicists.

Figure 2-4:
A Web site.

Dr. Berners-Lee (see Figure 2-5) made a formatting language that would support hypertext links as well as plain text formatting (bold, italic, size, fonts, and so forth) and called it *Hypertext Markup Language,* the now famous HTML. HTML, with a few extensions over its original version, is still the basis of the World Wide Web.

The first version of the Web was essentially text-only, with hypertext links scattered throughout long passages of scientific literature. But at the National Center for Supercomputing Applications in Illinois, a graduate student named Marc Andreessen decided to do something amazing — he produced the text-plus-graphics NCSA Mosaic, the first really cool Web browser software, and then *gave it away*!

This development put the Web at the center of Internet computing. Mosaic had an interface that was fun to use, and it encouraged the use of pictures and sound clips. The offspring of Mosaic (Andreessen's own Netscape Navigator, and its rival, Microsoft Internet Explorer) have focused on speeding up graphics and supporting the Web programming language Java, but they are still recognizably the same software. Mr. Andreessen is now one of the principals of Netscape, which was the biggest stock-market news in 1995 when the company went public. Now he's rich, from giving a program away. There is some justice in this world — it's just rare.

Figure 2-5:
This guy made the Web.

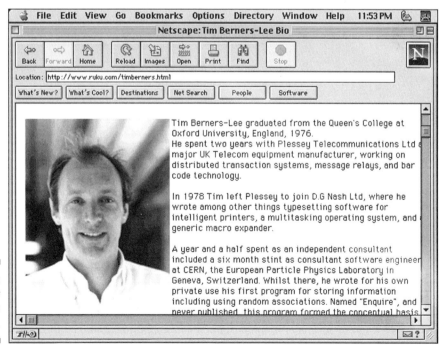

Anyway, you see more on the Web in the next few chapters because it's where the big action is on the Internet these days. When the first edition of this book went to press, only 120 commercial Web sites existed; in other words, there were many more .edu sites. When I wrote the second edition of this book in 1995, there were 90,000, and the number in early 1998 was close to 100,000,000. The Gold Rush was a lazy Sunday afternoon by comparison.

Too Cool for School?

Hundreds of regional Internet service providers offer full Internet access to one and all. The big national Internet services, for example, Earthlink (`http://www.earthlink.net`), have complete Internet access with really simple setup software, too.

You can find all sorts of shareware to download. You can find special-interest groups with an unlimited (and, I dare say, unhealthy) interest in the details of old Partridge Family shows. You can track the entire universe of day-to-day data (stock quotes, sports scores, weather). One really unique feature of the Internet, aside from its unmatchable vast connectivity, is the contribution made by university networks: If you want to look up biographical details on Marilyn Monroe, you can probably do so in a library. But if you want to keep up with developments in molecular biology, you need the Internet. Internet access means access to most of the important areas of modern scholarship.

In fact, special initiatives now exist on the Web for a sort of virtual reality international conference for biologists, in which scientists compare data and analyses — including journal figures and photos — online. In a more pedestrian Internet mode, Web pages are increasingly the standard warehouses for fast-moving information — newspapers, magazines, movie reviews, and sports results (see Figure 2-6).

The Internet may someday help level the research-competitive playing fields between richer and poorer institutions. Already, Internet access — and particularly the World Wide Web — have enabled people in some fields, most notably mathematics, to enjoy a level of contact that's a vast improvement on the traditional once-a-year-let's-all-meet-in-Chicago style of interaction.

Taking classes at Electronic U

Universities are using the Web not just to exchange research results but to offer courses (see Figure 2-7). Think for a moment about the quality of student/teacher interaction in a freshman physics course: It's not uncommon at large universities to stuff 400 students in a lecture hall (and those sitting at the back have to watch the lecture on TV monitors). Doesn't your own private online tutor sound better?

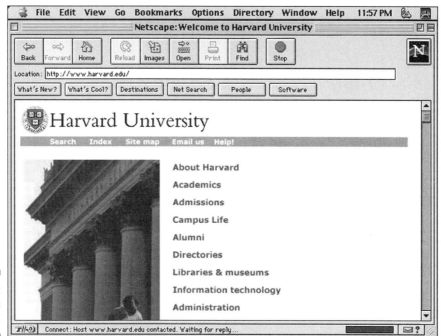

One big argument in favor of online courses is the appallingly short shelf life of course material. For example, there's not much you could have learned in a digital-design course in electrical engineering ten years ago that would look very compelling in your personnel file today. In most engineering professions, it's taken for granted that the whole stock of information needs to be overhauled every five years. The need for fluid information flow keeps many schools interested in online education despite the hassles involved in designing a new instructional format.

Personally, I really hope that Web-based classes develop into a major part of the degree process and adult education market. I'm old enough to remember *television* being touted as a fabulous new educational medium, so I'm not 100 percent convinced that this will work out, but it would solve a tremendous number of financial and other access problems.

Getting the latest info online

Many of the academic journals on the shelves of a university library now have a *one-year* lead time — articles make it into print about a year after they're submitted. That time lapse may be okay for medieval historians — the last time I looked, Charlemagne was still dead — but it's not fast enough for biotechnology or AIDS research or dozens of other hot topics. On the Internet, you can encounter not just newsgroups discussing current research but also Web databases that are updated almost daily by diligent university types. If you have any medical questions, you owe it to yourself to do some research on the Web (see Figure 2-8).

Jumping on the bandwagon

The whole business world signed on the Internet in 1996. It took about six months. Every major business on earth, and plenty of smaller shops, are busy refining their Web sites. The question is simple: Will a system originally designed for a few thousand researchers to trade notes finally collapse under catalog orders, online banking, and porno image downloads? You get to see the answer yourself, sometime between now and 2001.

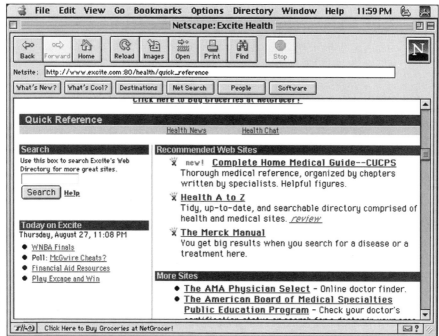

Netscape: Excite Health

Back   Forward   Home   Reload   Images   Open   Print   Find   Stop

Netsite: http://www.excite.com:80/health/quick_reference

What's New?   What's Cool?   Destinations   Net Search   People   Software

CLICK Here to Buy Groceries at NetGrocer!

Quick Reference

Health News   Health Chat

Search
Use this box to search Excite's Web Directory for more great sites.

Search   Help

Today on Excite
Thursday, August 27, 11:08 PM
● WNBA Finals
● Poll: McGwire Cheats?
● Financial Aid Resources
● Play Excape and Win

Recommended Web Sites
new! **Complete Home Medical Guide--CUCPS**
Thorough medical reference, organized by chapters written by specialists. Helpful figures.

Health A to Z
Tidy, up-to-date, and searchable directory comprised of health and medical sites. *review*

The Merck Manual
You get big results when you search for a disease or a treatment here.

More Sites
● **The AMA Physician Select** – Online doctor finder.
● **The American Board of Medical Specialties Public Education Program** – Check your doctor's

Click Here to Buy Groceries at NetGrocer!

Figure 2-8:
Do a little research.

Your Tax Dollars

Universities around the world contribute a great deal to the information base of the Internet, but the U.S. government started it all and maintains a big presence. The U.S. used to pay for the Internet hardware backbone, too, until April 1995, when it turned maintenance of the Net over to a group of private companies.

It's pretty clear that almost no one in the government had any idea (what else is new?) what was being created when the funding for the high-speed NSFNET and another Net called NASA Science Internet was approved. Actually, I'm talking about a trivial amount of money by Defense Department standards — remember, we live in a world where new fighter-plane designs cost tens of billions of dollars. It would have taken Nostradamus to realize that the world could be stood on its ear by a few hundred million doled out over a few decades to scientists.

Good guys and bad guys?

Although many Internet old-timers are convinced that the U.S. government in total is too dumb to impose any sort of regulation on the Net, lots of advanced thinkers working for the government have become quite agitated about the prospect of a high-speed, nearly anonymous, nonwiretappable, international communications network.

As a result, topics of Net access and security are controversial. Most traditional Internet people favor unrestricted use, but a minority favor some way of guaranteeing law-enforcement access to suspicious activities. It's probably naive to disregard the possibility that some Internet users will find a way to use the Net to foster criminal activities (send opinions to psuarez@medellin.cartel.com?), and that plenty of gray areas, such as offshore gambling, exist, but it's also naive to suppose that an unobtrusive way exists to check a significant fraction of messages. Expect plenty of debate in these areas in the years to come.

If you have access to the America Online version of *Time* magazine, you can watch government concern express itself by doing a search on the keyword "Internet". Almost every title you find is a horror story, from credit scams to what-if-the-North-Koreans-are-watching to a notorious, entirely fabricated cover story on child access to porn. *Time* is a pretty accurate reflection of the concerns of the Washington establishment, and it's clear that unlimited instant access to all types of facts and rumors gives many government people a case of the whim-whams.

Dear Congressman (from a concerned citizen who can afford a computer)

You can find lots of old-time government data on the Internet. Some of it is the kind of info the government's printing office still ships from Boulder, Colorado, with a hundred fun recipes for powdered milk, or pamphlets on *The Soybean, Our Versatile Friend,* or travel tips on avoiding exotic diseases.

Another way to use the Internet is to make yourself heard in the corridors of power. Because newspapers have many staffers in the forefront of the online revolution, you're likely to find Internet e-mail addresses for everyone with the slightest pretensions to authority, including state legislators, congressional representatives, governors, senators, and cabinet members. Usually these e-mail addresses are listed on the editorial page of the paper (sometimes printed as a shameless way to fill space).

The handful of people I know who have worked this contact channel (some old hands at PeaceNet and EcoNet, both pioneering public-interest network groups) claim to have obtained better results electronically than with traditional paper and pen. You can throw letters right in the trash, but you have to clear e-mail or it clogs up your electronic in-box.

Despite the millions of Net residents now online, the whole scheme is still new enough to politicians that an Internet message still has some impact. And if you send an Internet message to a politician, you're more likely to be taken seriously. The U.S. Senate, by the way, now has a Web site full of current Senate information (see Figure 2-9).

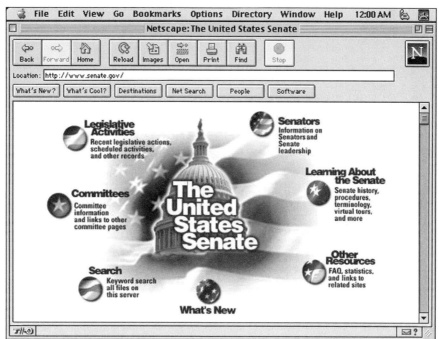

Figure 2-9:
Visit the Senate online.

Part II
Getting on the Internet

The 5th Wave   By Rich Tennant

"IT'S JUST UNTIL WE GET BACK UP ON THE INTERNET."

In this part . . .

Getting set up to navigate the Internet has never been easier. In this part, I tell you what you need to know about modems and how to set yours up. I also tell you what software you need and about some you may find helpful.

I also explain how to use mail programs and how to configure them and other settings on your computer for optimal performance. I also explain what all those strange acronyms stand for, like PPP and TCP/IP.

Chapter 3

Modems and Beyond

● ●

In This Chapter

▶ Understanding what modems do

▶ Selecting the right modem for Internet connection

▶ Finding out why faster is better, up to a point

▶ Choosing software for signing on

● ●

*A*ll the wonderful stuff on the Internet is out there on other computers. And your Macintosh is sitting on your desk. If you want to join the Internet, a cable has to connect your Mac to the rest of the world.

That cable plugs into the little port with a picture of a telephone on the back of your Mac. The other end of the cable goes to a modem, which plugs into your phone line. That's all there is to it. Actually, if you bought a Mac with a built-in (internal) modem, you don't even need to know *that* much.

You may, of course, decide to get really fancy and go for a high-speed ISDN connection (more on that later), or you may live in an area where super-speed cable modems are already a reality. But for most people in most places, a good modem is the answer to connection questions.

Now, this assumes that you're an individual Mac user. If someone has handed you a network-connected Mac at a university or business, you're a separate case. You can skip this chapter, unless you also want to get online at home.

A modem is one of the more mysterious computer accessories. In the Mac world, for example, a printer is fairly self-explanatory. That's because the Macintosh was *designed* to be the first computer that worked easily with printers.

A modem, in contrast, is distinctly *not* self-explanatory. The bulk of the modem business is still in the hands of electrical engineers who don't have much interface-design expertise. Nearly all modems respond to a mysterious command code developed back in the 1970s, and Apple itself is powerless to save you from some of the confusion this situation produces. I am going to try to get you through modem installation as painlessly as possible. Consult the "Warning signs for modem users" sidebar later in this chapter in case I succeed too well — and you become a modem junkie.

Buying the Right Modem

 Modem-buying calls for just a little background. For historical reasons, modem speeds are based on funny multiples of 300 bits per second, and several different data compression formats have been developed. Manuals for modems tend to feature cable-connect pinouts, timing diagrams, arcane CCITT standards jargon, and tables of the time-honored Hayes AT commands. The Hayes Company declared bankruptcy and reorganized in 1995, but the AT commands will apparently live on unchanged until eternity.

In the Mac world, external modems have been more common than internal modems. An external modem comes in its own case. An internal modem is a card that you stick into a slot inside the Mac. They don't differ much operationally, except that internal modems tend to be cheaper. External modems have the advantage that you can see the little flashing lights, so at least you can tell if they're working. PowerBooks are a special case, as the "Power to the people" sidebar explains.

Warning signs for modem users

You can get into this modem stuff too deeply. Review these warning signs to make sure that you aren't turning into a wirehead:

✔ You hum dial tones in the shower.

✔ You can make modem sign-on noises with your nose.

✔ You remember which colors mean what on the phone jack's teensy wires.

✔ You absentmindedly reset the clock on a friend's VCR.

✔ The blinking lights on the front of your modem send secretly coded messages that only you can understand.

If any of these things happen, go to some live concerts to restore your equilibrium.

Power to the people

PowerBook owners should note that everything I say in this chapter applies to PowerBooks as well, with the provision that the same modem speed costs $100 more for PowerBook internal modems than for desktop Macs, a sort of surcharge for miniaturization engineering. Very small portable external modems are also available, with the advantage that you can unplug them and use them with your desktop Mac. Little pocket modems typically run off their own nine-volt batteries. This feature helps when you're on the road, because PowerBook internal modems tend to run down the PowerBook's own battery at a frightening rate, and you can at least always get nine volts at a convenience store.

Understanding Modems

Despite all the hardware jargon, a modem's job is really fairly simple: It takes output from your files or your keyboard and converts the computer pattern of zeroes and ones into an equivalent pattern of tones. The telephone line can handle the tones reliably, so the message gets sent.

The other common communications accessory is the fax machine, so these days, modem makers tend to build fax capability into the modem. A fax/modem's job isn't much harder — it converts the document into a set of lines containing dark bits and white spaces (blocks of zeroes and ones) and performs the same tone conversion on this data. One of the major Mac communications mysteries is why fax software is often so troublesome. Fax software, however, is getting better.

The circuit boards inside these products reflect this simplicity. They usually contain just a few chips (and only a few popular chip vendors for data communications circuits exist) and other components. In portable modems, the holder for the nine-volt battery is often the biggest physical component. Because not much material is really in them, prices for modems fall steadily every year as the chips get cheaper. Yesterday's $600 modem is today's $99 bargain, and yesterday's mainstream modem is sitting on a closet shelf.

Can I use an older modem on the Internet?

The short answer to this question is No.

Millions of old 14,400 bps (bits per second) modems are still floating around, and if you plan to contact an online service only occasionally and then only use it for text e-mail, you can get along with one of them. Slower modems (9600 bps or earlier) aren't worth having any more, because they're not practical for Web access. Frankly, you shouldn't *buy* a 14,400 bps modem anyway — try to cajole someone into giving you one instead. The typical Mac users group includes dozens of people who have upgraded their communications and may be willing to donate their old 14K or 28K modem to you. But you won't be happy downloading files from the World Wide Web at 14,400 bps, except in emergencies.

I'm only discussing these modem speeds at all because millions of otherwise-useful Performas have these older modems inside. For current Web access you're going to want to do one of the following:

- ✔ Take your Mac to a dealer and change your internal modem to a faster model.
- ✔ Get a fast external modem to plug into the back of your Mac. The instructions will tell you how to override the old internal one.

What does "good enough" mean?

The reality is that you want to plunge into the expanding universe of the World Wide Web. Most modems made a few years ago didn't anticipate this situation. When you download lots of pictures, you simply need an order of magnitude faster access than you did with plain text. About 85 percent of Web access happens at 28.8 Kbps or faster.

What should I buy?

To be happy with a modem connecting to the Internet, you should plan on buying at least a 33.6 Kbps modem.

Most sites on the Web are so jammed with visitors that they can't spit the data out fast enough to take full advantage of your 56 Kbps modem — 56 usually isn't actually twice in practice as fast as 28.8. This situation will slowly improve, but by then even faster stuff than plain modems will be available. So keep saving your "modem money" for the big bangs of cable and faster phone lines (see the next section).

Honest, they gave me this thing!

Apple sold at least a million Performa models with built-in modems and communications software, and clone makers did the same. The catch in this arrangement is that the modems tended to be cheaper units that were discontinued because faster modems were on the way. The built-in modem was okay when the computer was new. Now the computer is probably okay, but the modem isn't. On the World Wide Web, the old built-in modem is an obstacle, not a help.

With a built-in fax, a 33.6 Kbps modem cost a bit less than $60 in January 1998, and 56 Kbps modems were about $120, but the price was dropping quickly. If you are the kind of person who wants a $3,000 trail bike and who bought a Power Mac the first day it appeared, you should know that faster options are also available (see Table 3-1).

Table 3-1	Modem Standards
The Standard	*What It Means*
V.32bis	14,400 bps
V.Fast	28,000 bps
V.34	33,600 bps
K56, X2, and V.90	56,000 bps
ISDN*	128,000 bps
ADSL	64,000 bps upload and 1,200,000 bps download
Cable	1,500,000 bps minimum, both ways

ISDN requires a modem-like card and arrangement with the phone company and service provider.

Early buyers of the 56,000 bps modems had to pick between one of two incompatible standards: K56flex and X2. If you picked the wrong modem standard, that is, if you bought a modem with a standard that your ISP didn't understand, your modem speed was limited to that of a 33,600 bps modem. The confusion put a bit of a damper on the excitement for faster speeds as many ISPs were reluctant to choose between one modem standard or another. (I would, too, if I had to go change the modems at hundreds of dial-up sites around the country!)

By early 1998, an international standards group chose a standard called V.90, which promptly put the kibosh on the 56 Kbps standards war. Fortunately, most of the 56 Kbps modems could be adjusted with some *firmware* (geek-speak for modem reprogramming software) to make it work with the new V.90 standard.

Before you get all gooshy at the idea of reprogramming your modem, I recommend that you visit a Web site: `http://www.56k.com`. This site can help you find out if your modem is upgradable to 56K, if your Internet service can support 56K, and if your Internet service supports 56K in the modem standard flavor you can use.

Don't upgrade your modem until you know that your Internet service provider can support your modem's new standard and speed, or your modem might become slower, or worse, nonfunctional.

Telephone systems themselves are being upgraded to carry more data — even at 28,000 bps, the noise in ordinary voice lines becomes a problem. That's why many national online services took their time about providing faster access. In the first edition of this book, I predicted that it could take a few years to get faster access. But phenomenal demand for Web services forced everybody to upgrade to 33.6 Kbps within a matter of months! Most national Internet providers now support 56 Kbps local numbers and have special hardware/software ISDN packages for their members. Again, however, before you upgrade, check with your Internet provider on what speeds and modem standards they support.

ISDN? Cable? Faster Phone Lines?

The Web, you will see, is more like a TV show than it is like old-time computer bulletin boards. For that reason, the standard modems of the late '90s are likely to disappear as an Internet hook-up in a few years.

This is not a technology issue: It's part of the usual great American debate about who gets the money. The phone companies want your Internet business, of course. So do the cable TV companies, and they're fighting over your future with high-priced lobbying teams in Washington, D.C., and your state capital. Software companies like Microsoft are trying to form alliances with communications hardware vendors to garner some sort of official monopoly on access technology.

This isn't how decisions are made everywhere. In Canada, the Province of Ontario simply decided to get wired, and put in cable modems for everyone. So you get stuck with your crummy modem in California while PacBell figures out how to extract Internet charges, and everyone in Toronto connects at 50 times your speed. Hmmm. No comment.

ISDN

This faster type of digital connection (Integrated Services Digital Network) over phone company lines has, in my opinion, three deadly problems:

✔ It's not *that* much faster than 56 Kbps.

✔ It's usually expensive.

✔ Your ISDN investment will be obsolete in just a few years.

If you are still interested, check out the details in *Macworld Web Essentials* (IDG Books Worldwide). You can read some nice things about ISDN in magazines, but in fact the only happy ISDN campers I know are computer journalists who got their home setup for free. Don't say I didn't warn you.

Cable

At this point in Web evolution, the connection through standard TV-cable wiring really makes the most sense, although the phone companies don't want to hear this. You buy or lease a cable modem for your end, the cable company buys some switching gear for its office, and away you go, faster than any other setup. A modem is walking, ISDN is a bicycle, and cable is a Ferrari. I can't give you prices here (in some small college towns that have insisted on it, the rates have ranged as low as $10/month) because the situation is changing faster than I can type, but you'll probably get the word from your own cable company, included in a monthly statement sometime soon.

ADSL

This abbreviation stands for Asymmetric Digital Subscriber Line, and there is a family of variants under the name "xDSL." They refer, basically, to fancy chipsets that allow fairly fast uploads but cable-speed downloads. They can work over the phone lines you have now, so when your regional Bell company finally gets the picture that ISDN won't be in every home, some sort of xDSL modem will probably be the marketing darling of your phone company's reach of cable. The bottom line here is that Web connection fast enough (with the right streaming software) for movies and everything else on Web pages will be common and cheap, one way or another, in 1998 and beyond.

The Software Connection

The modem, of course, does nothing but sit there until a piece of software tells it what to do. (Also, make sure that the modem is turned on — believe it or not, I've been called out on plenty of consulting calls where pressing the On button was the issue.)

Two kinds of software are important for your Internet journey. First is the software provided directly by an online service, which pretty much means America Online, the Last Man Standing of the Net. If you're going to connect to America Online for Internet service, AOL sends you its own software disks. (Actually, you can walk into any supermarket in the U.S. and still find AOL disks bagged into computer magazines.)

The second kind of software is offered by Internet service providers and includes special communications utilities, direct Internet connection, and whichever Web browser (from either Netscape or Microsoft) the ISP decided to include.

How AOL does it

Sometime in 1998, AOL will introduce a new version of its Mac connection software, AOL 4.0. All you have to do to sign on to this new service, which includes a Web browser based on Microsoft Internet Explorer, is get the disc (usually a CD) and keep clicking Continue (see Figure 3-1).

Figure 3-1:
AOL. At least it's easy to install.

Welcome to America Online!

We will now take you through a quick and easy set-up and registration process. Before you begin, make sure your modem is turned on and that it is connected to your Macintosh and your phone line.

[Cancel ⌘.]   [Upgrade ⌘U]   [[Continue ⌘C]]

The reason you're seeing this in a chapter on modems is an odd touch in the installation process. If AOL says it thinks you have a particular modem, you may as well believe it, even if the identification seems wrong, because the software has determined it knows the codes to make your modem work (see Figure 3-2). The software then dials an 800 number to find your local connection, and away you go. See Chapter 7 for more about AOL.

How EarthLink does it

One example of a successful independent Internet service provider is EarthLink, which I mention for two reasons. First, they faithfully show up at Macworld Expo and hand out lots of installation disks. They also have very satisfactory Mac support in general. All you need to get started on the Net is the usual piece of plastic. The software identifies your modem, gets you a local number, and plunks you on the InfoBahn.

We've chosen a modem for you. If you wish to choose a different one, please select it from the list below.

> Global Village TP Silver
> GUC 14.4 PCMCIA
> GUC 14.4 v.32bis
> GUC 288 Fax Modem
> Hayes Accura 144
> Hayes Accura 28.8
> Hayes Accura 96
> **Hayes Auto Reliable**

Cancel ⌘.   OK

Figure 3-2:
Take their
word for it.

Second, EarthLink has put together a nice home page with great instructions for putting up a modest Web site of your own (see Figure 3-3). If you get a chance, check out `http://home.earthlink.net/~chseiter/` for a sample easy setup.

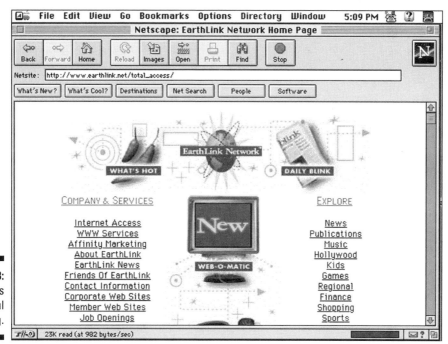

Figure 3-3:
EarthLink's
cheerful
greeting.

More Info for the Hyper-Curious

In this book, I want to tell you only enough modem stuff so that you don't buy something that's disastrously wrong. As you can see, the Internet itself is a big enough subject to occupy your attention. The definitive work on modems is Tina Rathbone's *Modems For Dummies,* 3rd Edition, another fine IDG Books Worldwide product (also check out *More Modems for Dummies,* too). With these preliminaries out of the way, I show you how to communicate with everyone on earth in the following chapters.

Chapter 4

Connecting Your Mac to the Internet

*T*he story of the Mac's Internet connection has an amazing conclusion: After years of different approaches by Apple, the basic software for Internet connection turns out to be *freeware* (software that's free for you to download and use all you want) developed by clever people in Michigan and Australia. Epic Apple projects, which resulted in gigantic early bug-ridden releases of "gee-whiz" software that was high on functionality but low on practicality, produced essentially nothing that you actually use these days for Web or e-mail access.

Nothing really compares anywhere else in computing — Apple's dedicated fans have been more important in Mac Internet history than Apple. Here's a company that makes both the hardware and the system software, whose graphics-oriented systems are ideal for Web development, and who is in a perfect position to have pioneered one-click Web access as early as 1995. Instead, the heavy lifting has been left to a scattered band of volunteers. Too bad Apple couldn't fire its CEOs twice.

Apple Computer of 1998 appears to have learned its lesson. In July 1998, a new version of the software that makes your Mac operate, Mac OS 8, arrived. It came complete with many useful tools to get you quickly connected to the Internet. The latest update of the software, Mac OS 8.5, has many more improvements that can get you online in mere minutes. Mac OS 8.5 comes complete with the Microsoft Internet Explorer 4.01 Web browser, assistant programs to help you type in your Internet settings, and more software to make your trip down the InfoBahn easier than ever.

Your Basic Hookup

Every Internet service provider (ISP) that wants your business these days knows that you want connection to be automatic. In the old "Edition 1" days of the Internet, ISPs figured they were dealing with people who were happy writing their own modem scripts and could probably interpret cryptic error commands in UNIX when things went wrong.

Today, ISPs make the safe assumption that when you sign up for Internet service, that it's the ISP's job to give you setup software that requires only that you have a name and a credit card number. Like America Online, ISPs leave installation disks at computer stores and also send them to you in droves in home and business mail. Mac OS 8 assumes that you want all the goods as well. When you buy a Mac today, it also comes with the basic software you need to connect, preinstalled on your computer.

Setting up an account using an ISP's installation disk isn't much trouble. You double-click an Install icon on a CD (or Disk 1 of a large set), and after five minutes of hard drive grinding and thrashing, the setup software has installed the necessary software you need — typically a Web browser and e-mail program.

You usually see a dialog box asking you for the vital billing information for the new Internet account. Then the program dials up for a first connection, has you pick a local access number, and you're on your way in cyberspace.

If you check your hard drive, you'll find that the ISP's installation disk has installed the following:

- ✔ A Web browser, either Netscape Navigator or Microsoft Internet Explorer

- ✔ An e-mail program, if it's not built into the browser

- ✔ The Internet Config program (more about this item in the next section, "Configuration Made Simple")

- ✔ Sometimes PPP software, usually the FreePPP utility

Macs don't like mixed messages. If you happen to install an ISP's software and not use the built-in Internet software that comes with Mac OS 8, it's a very good idea to turn off all other PPP software that you're not using. Sometimes, having several kinds of software that do the same thing may cause your Mac to connect unpredictably. For more details on how to turn off extensions and control panels that make up PPP software, pick up a copy of *Mac OS 8 For Dummies,* another outstanding IDG Books publication written by Bob LeVitus.

PPP? Should I be going to the restroom?

Before your eyes glaze over from all the technobabble, it's time for a quick explanation. For your Mac to join the Internet, it needs some kind of software that helps it connect to it using your modem — that's the little box you connected to your Mac and attached a phone cord in. That software, called PPP (point-to-point protocol) does the connecting job. Mac OS 8.5 comes with Apple Remote Access 3.1, which contains the PPP software you need. If you've installed an ISP's software, you may have received another version of PPP software such as FreePPP, a program that's, well, free to use. Open Transport/PPP also comes with Mac OS 8 and earlier (just to get you confused). A good tip is to use whatever software the Mac or the software you've installed has configured for you.

Mac OS 8.5 provides you the same types of software in the form of Microsoft Internet Explorer 4.01, an older version of Netscape Navigator, Outlook Express, and a great first-time setup utility called the Internet Setup Assistant (see Figure 4-1).

When you turn on a Mac with Mac OS 8.5 installed for the very first time (or for the first time after you've installed the software yourself), you'll be greeted by the Mac OS Setup Assistant, a program that gathers from you the basic Mac settings such as your name, date, time — those sorts of things. After you complete the Mac OS Setup Assistant, you can start up the Internet Setup Assistant, which helps you create a new Internet account or modify settings you may already have on your computer.

Figure 4-1:
The Internet Setup Assistant of Mac OS 8.5.

Once you've used Mac OS 8.5's Internet Setup Assistant or the ISP's installation disk, you'll probably never come into contact with the TCP/IP control panel, where your most important ISP settings are stored. The control panel is managed by FreePPP, Mac OS 8.5's Apple Remote Access, or whatever PPP software you have.

Most likely your installation will work perfectly, and every time you double-click your browser icon, your PPP software will dial for you, make the connection to the Internet, all will be well, and you'll be surfing happily and downloading your e-mail. You don't need to know any details. Later, though, in the event of a crash, file damage, or even simple changes — the local phone number that your modem calls may change, for example — it will help you to know a little bit about the humble software parts that actually run things behind the browser.

Configuration Made Simple

After you're on the Internet, you'll probably experiment by downloading and installing additional software for using the Internet. What you may not know is that much of the software requires the same Internet settings you give your Mac when you set up your Internet account. You could open up one of the programs already installed to copy the settings, but why bother? That's where software such as Internet Config and the Internet control panel in Mac OS 8.5 helps. Both of these programs remember all of your Internet settings and provide the settings to any program you use that looks for Internet Config on your computer.

Internet Config, the ingenious work of Peter N. Lewis, the Australian fellow who also developed the essential FTP search utility Anarchie at the dawn of Macs on the Internet, some guy nicknamed "Quinn the Eskimo" (I'm not kidding!) and many others, ships with most Internet software because it provides a single convenient container for a whole raft of unrelated settings. Internet Config is also included with Mac OS 8.0 and 8.1, where you'll find it hiding inside the Internet Utilities folder, inside the Internet folder on your hard drive. Those of you who installed software from an ISP's installation disk may need to use the Mac OS Find command from the File menu to locate it. After you find Internet Config, open it, and gaze on the magnificence of its scope (see Figure 4-2). If you're using Mac OS 8.5, the Internet control panel is probably the repository for most of your settings. As you see in Figure 4-3, it's not quite as pretty as Internet Config but is just as functional.

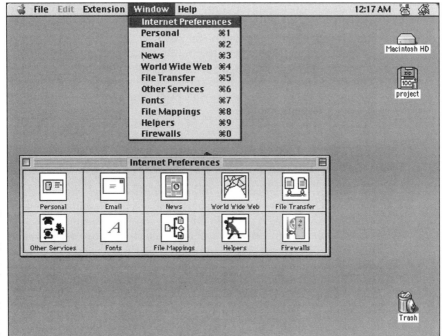

Figure 4-2:
Internet
Config: A
central
switchboard
for Internet
wires.

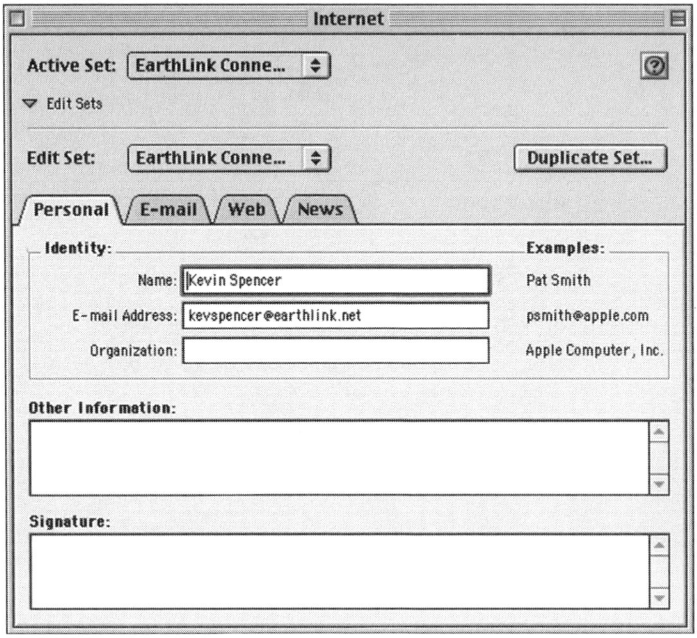

Figure 4-3:
The Internet
control
panel of
Mac OS 8.5.

Each one of these panels controls a different aspect of an Internet program when the program starts. Some of these are obscure programs that have their roots in UNIX and will be mainly of interest to users on university Internet connections where the administrators cling to the good old days where terms like *ping, finger,* and *whois* were the staff of connected life. Nowadays, not much need exists for these terms, unless you like to walk around speaking these words out loud. Who knows? Somebody may mistake you for a pinball machine.

Home page, sweet home page

Both Internet Config and the Internet control panel offer much of the same features. Other panels control settings for more familiar everyday activities. The World Wide Web panel in Internet Config, for example, is the easiest place to reset your browser's home page (see Figure 4-4). That's helpful, because both Netscape and Microsoft set their own home pages as the default home page — that's because the price they can charge for links and advertising is based on the number of times the pages are visited (or *hits*).

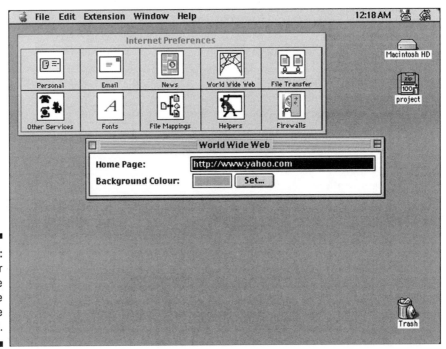

Figure 4-4:
Setting your home page using the World Wide Web panel.

Making the page the default for all free browsers really drives up the number of hits. This panel also lets you set the browser page background color easily. I only wish this book could be printed in color so that you could see the lovely mid-1960s elementary-school-wall green I use for a background.

For Mac OS 8.5, clicking the Web tab of the Internet control panel gives you the same opportunities to change your browser's home page and background colors. (See Figure 4-5.)

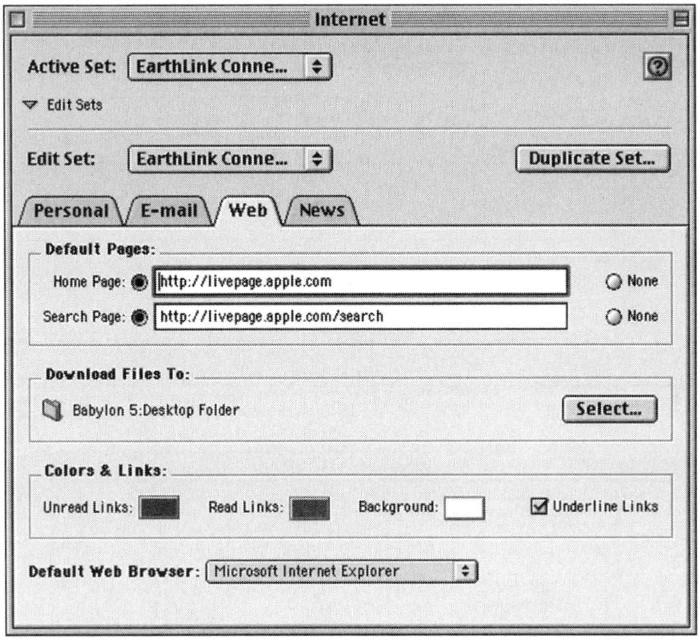

Figure 4-5:
Setting your
home page
from the
Web tab.

Mail call

Another panel you need to open is the E-mail panel in Internet Config, or the E-mail tab in the Mac OS 8.5 Internet control panel. Check out the resulting screen (see Figures 4-6 and 4-7) and write down the information on the inside cover of this book. Having this information lets you copy the settings intact if a disaster occurs. Trust me, if you do a lot of Internet cruising and upgrade every time a new browser is released, at some point your e-mail settings will get screwed up, but you can restore them in less than a minute. After you come to rely on e-mail, you get panicky when you're cut off and don't know why.

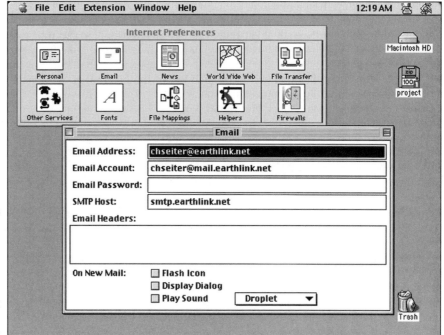

Figure 4-6:
Take down
this
information
if you use
Internet
Config!

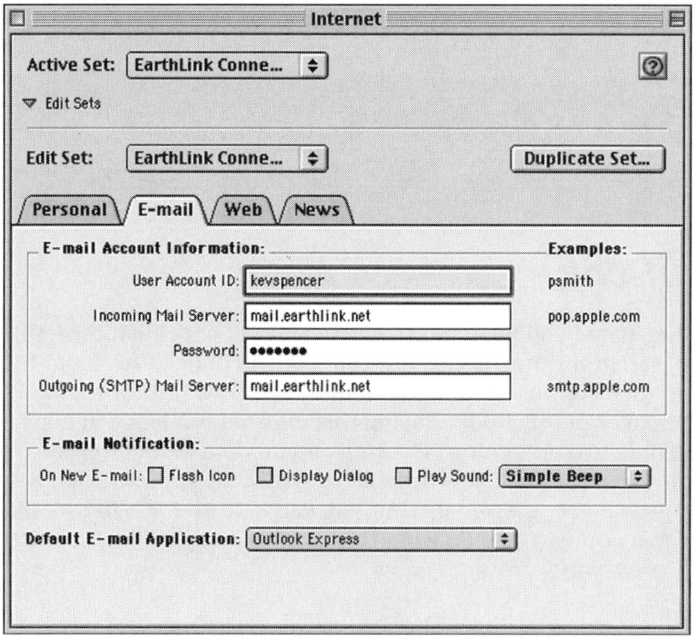

Figure 4-7:
Take down
this
information
if you use
the Internet
control
panel!

If you ever have to retype this information into your Mac (or another computer) to get connected and download your mail, here's a quick guide on what each setting means:

yourname@yourisp.com	Your Internet e-mail *address*.
yourname@mail.yourisp.com	Your e-mail *account* name that the ISP looks for.
mail.yourisp.com	Your ISP's e-mail *server* (geek-speak for big computer).
your password	Well, it's your password, probably the same one you use to log on to the Internet.

Using Helper Applications

Alas, your Web browser is not like Michael Jordan. Sometimes, like a basket-ball player, your Web browser needs other programs to assist you with your Internet viewing. A common name for these programs is *helpers*.

Internet Config lets you tell your other Internet programs what programs you want to use to assist your Web browser. By clicking the Internet Config Helpers menu (see Figure 4-8), you have access to the way your Internet connection interprets the file types that are available through a Web page (such as, http files, ftp files, and files in different e-mail formats). For example, if your ISP has provided you with Internet Explorer as a browser, you'll almost certainly find that it has also set up your system to use Outlook Express as the built-in setting (or *default*).

You may want to use another e-mail system instead of Outlook Express. Claris EMailer or Eudora are prominent alternative choices. Here's how:

1. **Click one of the file types in the list.**

2. **Click the Change button.**

   The Add Helper dialog box appears and gives you a way to select replacements for the default helper programs (see Figure 4-9).

In case you were wondering, the Mac OS 8.5 Internet control panel doesn't hold your helper application settings except for your preferred Web browser and e-mail program, both of which can be changed via the Web and E-mail tabs, respectively. To change your helper settings, open the preferences for your Web browser.

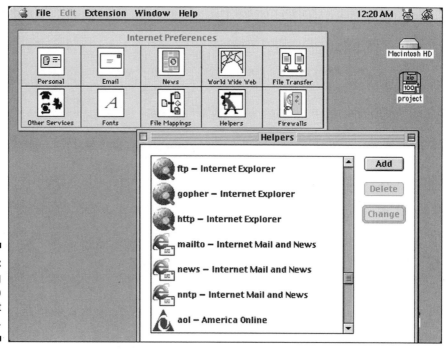

Customizing is a surprisingly unrisky business and lets you construct a very efficient setup. For day-to-day work, you can combine an older browser (usually smaller and faster) with newer e-mail services (that support multimedia). For downloading files using a process called *ftp* (geek-speak *and* an acronym for file transfer protocol), you can use the fast and robust program Fetch (from Dartmouth University's Web site at www.dartmouth.edu) to do your downloading — for big downloads on a modem, it really helps.

Add Helper	
Helper For:	http
Helper:	Internet Explorer
	Choose Helper...
	Cancel OK

Using FreePPP and Apple Remote Access 3.1

For some of you who've received and installed software provided by an ISP, you're likely to see a little telephone-shaped menu on the right side of the menu bar (it appears in most of the screen shots in this book). In general, you can just ignore it — any time you open your Web browser or another Internet program, your computer already knows to fire up FreePPP automatically to make a connection using point-to-point protocol (PPP).

If you're using Mac OS 8.5 and have set up your Internet connection with its built-in software, accessing your PPP settings is as easy as opening the Remote Access control panel from the Apple menu.

I just know that some of you aren't crazed to run out to get the latest and greatest versions of the Mac OS, so it's more likely that you have an earlier version of the Mac's PPP software, called Open Transport/PPP. All that Apple did in Mac OS 8.5 was to combine the features of what were two separate programs: Apple Remote Access and OT/PPP. I'd say that 98 percent of what I speak of here still applies to your version of PPP, and may likely be found in the same places of the control panels. Just open the PPP control panel from the Apple menu to get started.

As is the case with Internet Config, though, you can save yourself some trouble if you take a look at the insides of FreePPP. Because it controls the actual details of a dial-up or direct Internet connection, it's the place to look when something goes wrong.

Isn't there a Motown song by Aretha called "T.C.P.I.PPP"?

The heart of your Internet settings are stored in two places. FreePPP (or Apple Remote Access) stores what phone number you dial out to and how your modem and your ISP's modem should talk to each other. A second control panel called *TCP/IP* stores some otherwise-meaningless numbers that tell your computer what server to connect to on the Internet to make your Internet connection.

If you must know, TCP/IP stands for *Transmission Control Protocol/Internet Protocol*. It's just the way that all Internet-based computers connect and transfer information. Okay? Okay.

If you click FreePPP's little Telephone menu or open the Remote Access 3.1 control panel, you get choices for opening and closing a connection and for setting up your connection. The FreePPP Setup option, shown in Figure 4-10, brings you to a single convenient place to modify your communications settings. Likewise, Figure 4-11 shows some of the guts of the Remote Access control panel settings. But you don't *want* to modify them if everything's okay. What you do want is some specific information.

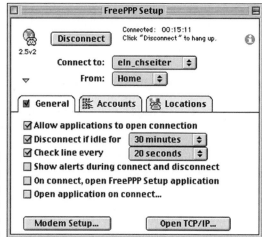

Figure 4-10:
All settings
in one place
for FreePPP.

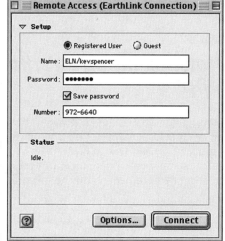

Figure 4-11:
The Remote
Access
control
panel.

1. **Click the TCP/IP button in FreePPP or choose TCP/IP from the Remote Access control panel. The TCP/IP control panel opens.**

   The top two pop-up menus should always say Connect via PPP and Configure Using PPP Server. The next three items: IP address, subnet mask, and router address don't matter a whit. Skip 'em.

2. **Copy down the numbers in the Name server address box, then close the TCP/IP control panel, so that you're back at whatever PPP program you're using.**

3. **Back in your PPP software, write down *exactly* how your username is spelled, then dig up that password from your memory and write that down, too.**

   For example, if I didn't type in "ELN/" before my username, I don't connect. Period. Computers are funny about these things.

4. **Click any of the settings/options tabs or buttons you may find.**

   The most important ones to find are Connect Automatically When TCP Programs Are Opened, Use TCP Header Compression, and Use Error Correction. If any of these items are checked, write down the name of the item and indicate that they were checked.

5. **Last, but not least, open your Modem control panel from the Apple menu and make a note of the name of the *modem script* you're using to prepare your modem before PPP dials to the Internet.**

   Modem scripts just send more of those cryptic codes to your modem, but different ones exist for different modems. Make sure that you jot down your script's name.

I dwell on getting your settings copied down because a great variety of ways exist in which these settings can get wrecked. You can sign up for AOL and accidentally make these numbers change. Sometimes merely upgrading your browser or switching to a different browser can make the numbers disappear. So, if you find that your modem is dialing but somehow not making a connection, go back to the version of PPP that you use and the TCP/IP control panel and see what turns up. You can enter the numbers here directly if they're missing, and then you're back in business. Compared to waiting 45 minutes on hold on your ISP's help line, this method is significantly more convenient.

Note also the Connection Via button on the TCP/IP settings page. You may be surprised to see all the possible connection modes that have somehow found their way into your System file. The implication of all this for America Online is discussed in the sidebar at the end of this chapter.

A setting saved is a setting earned

FreePPP setup and Remote Access 3.1 are the route to most other sorts of settings changes. If your ISP changes your local access number, for example, the Account tab in FreePPP or your PPP software needs to know the new number (see Figure 4-12). In fact, you should routinely check the PPP software you use every time you change providers or when you change browsers because

✔ Occasionally, an installation makes assumptions on its own, and changes your settings.

✔ The installation may flash a bunch of questions to which you just press Return as an answer, but sometimes Return isn't the right answer (that is, you were supposed to check something other than the default).

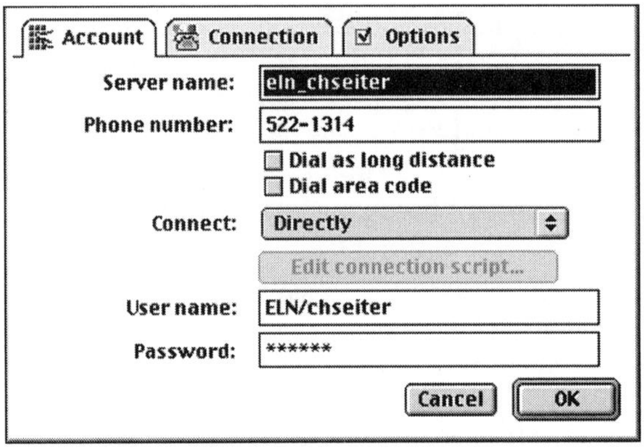

Figure 4-12:
Change
your
number.

| 🔳 Account | 📇 Connection | ☑ Options |

Server name: `eln_chseiter`

Phone number: `522-1314`

☐ Dial as long distance
☐ Dial area code

Connect: `Directly` ⬍

`Edit connection script...`

User name: `ELN/chseiter`

Password: `******`

`Cancel`   `OK`

If you keep a record (on paper, in a safe place) of your PPP settings, you can always restore your previous settings to your Mac.

Why does my computer dial up the Internet by itself?

The not-so-funny thing about FreePPP and Mac OS 8.5's Remote Access is how they help out a bit too much sometimes.

Some of you may discover that your Mac starts to dial up the Internet automatically when you open up your Web browser or other Internet program. This behavior isn't particularly bad — except when you don't need to really connect. For example, many Internet programs you may come across online or at a store have manuals or setup instructions that are actually Web page documents. That's a novel idea, because most people who need Internet software probably have a Web browser that can read these files. Or, if you're designing your own Web pages, you may want to open up your Web browser to see how things are formatted.

But the rub is that PPP software such as Remote Access may assume that you need to connect to the Internet because you're opening up an Internet program. This practice becomes very annoying after a point, particularly if your spouse or roommate is talking on the phone at the time. Nothing gets a person's goat like getting an earful of a modem's screeching sound that's vaguely reminiscent of a terrified, sick pig.

To keep your Mac from automatically connecting to the Internet, you need to find the setting in your PPP software that says something like Allow Programs to Open a TCP Connection. In the Remote Access control panel, click the Options button, then click the Settings tab and uncheck the Connect Automatically When Starting TCP/IP Connections box.

For every silver lining, there's a cloud, however. When you do want to connect to the Internet later, you need to open your PPP software and click the Connect button yourself to start a connection, *before* you open your Internet programs. Because you're manually controlling when your Mac connects, you won't be able to take advantage of Web hyperlinks in word processing documents or e-mail messages until you turn on your Internet connection yourself.

Oh, sure, the browser may open, but because the Mac won't create an Internet connection, you'll soon see dreaded messages such as `There Is No DNS Entry` or `The Connection Has Failed` because the browser has no connection to search through. Just remembering *why* things work sometimes can make your life flow nicely, don't you think?

Speaking of work, the usual circumstance is that if you pick the Edit option on the Accounts tab, it indicates Direct as the Connect option. You can see what this means by selecting the Connection Script option and then clicking the Edit Script button. What you see is the set of commands that FreePPP actually sends out, first to the modem and then to the service where the modem connects. (See Figure 4-13.)

What's interesting is not the script itself, but the fact that you don't have to know what any of it means. The first edition of this book had to explain to users the details of modem code commands, just so they could log on to a bulletin board and check out some text-oriented services. For speed, it's as if the color television were invented the year after the first radio.

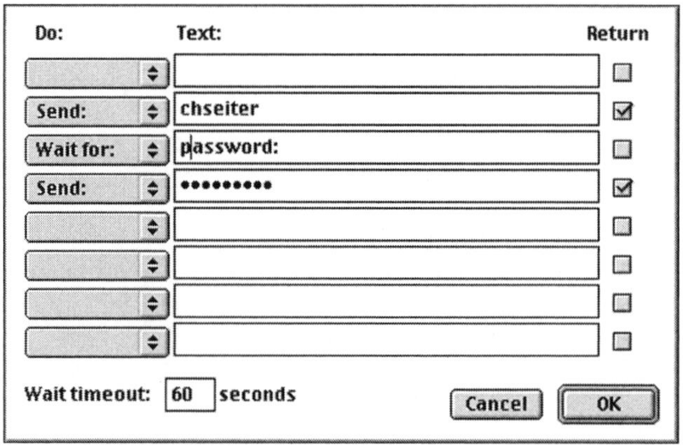

Do:		Text:	Return
	◆		☐
Send:	◆	chseiter	☑
Wait for:	◆	password:	☐
Send:	◆	••••••••	☑
	◆		☐
	◆		☐
	◆		☐
	◆		☐

Wait timeout: `60` seconds   [Cancel] [**OK**]

Figure 4-13:
A universe
you can
now ignore.

TECHNICAL STUFF

The special case of AOL

For reasons probably lost in the depths of time, America Online chose a distinctive approach when it added outside-ISP access to its service, in addition to the more familiar AOLNET dial-up network connection. I'm putting these notes here because they're a techie sort of detail. They have more to do with the details of Mac's TCP/IP implementation than most AOL users need to know.

You'll find that on your opening connection screen, in the pop-up list for locations, you have Home as a choice, and also a choice for TCP/IP through an ISP (you get these choices if you told AOL that you had another Net connection when you installed AOL). The catch is that for a dial-up connection you can't just pick Home or TCP, because AOL sets up the dial-up connection internally.

If you want to switch from one type of connection to the other, start AOL and find the Preferences command under My AOL. Scroll down the list at the left, through the eighteen zillion settings options (hard to believe there were about six items here a few years ago) and find AOL Link. When you click this option, you are given the option of setting AOL for a TCP connection or for standard AOLNET. Pick the type you want and then restart your Mac.

As an alternative, you can just pick a connection type, and follow the dialog boxes that result when AOL decides your setup is wrong. In principle this works, too, but it takes longer and can wreak havoc on your settings if restart isn't the very next thing you do.

Part III
Working the Web

The 5th Wave   By Rich Tennant

TOM'S COMPANY OCCASIONALLY CONDUCTED SPOT CHECKS TO MAKE SURE THE EMPLOYEES WEREN'T SNEAKING THEIR MACINTOSHES INTO THE OFFICE.

In this part . . .

Now for the fun part — surfing the Web. However, you need the right software to do so. In this part, I discuss the three big browsers — Netscape Navigator, Microsoft Internet Explorer, and America Online. With these browsers, the World Wide Web is your oyster.

Chapter 5

Netscape Navigator 4.0

· ·

In This Chapter
▶ Browser basics
▶ Bookmarking details
▶ Get what you prefer
▶ Communicator: Navigator plus
▶ Quick tips
▶ A look backward

· ·

*N*etscape Navigator is the basic piece of software on the Web. It was developed from the original graphical browser, Mosaic, by many of the same Web pioneers who developed Mosaic in the first place. Netscape Navigator 2.0 and the rise of the Web are roughly synonymous.

Navigator 4.0 is a bit different from its predecessors. Like Internet Explorer, Navigator 4.0 has been gleaned to just its Web browser component. You can't send e-mail or create Web pages in Navigator 4.0. Turns out that the Netscape Corporation, as part of a change in marketing, changed what we knew as Navigator Gold 3.0, changed some features and added new ones, and called it Netscape Communicator 4.0.

Netscape Navigator 4.0 was quickly created by Netscape Corporation *after* Communicator arrived. Netscape had no intention of creating a stand-alone Web browser without the perks. But, apparently, many users of the new Communicator complained about the program's slow speed and its desire to hog most of their computer's memory for itself. These folks liked the Navigator browser but didn't need the other gee-whiz parts.

Whether you use Navigator 4.0 as part of Communicator or as the stand-alone version, this chapter is for you. Given the changes of Navigator 4.0, however, users of earlier versions of Navigator won't find a lot of help here because many of the menus and settings have been rearranged. Besides, it's really a good idea to use the latest versions because they have been improved quite a bit in style and substance. In other words, Navigator and Communicator 4 are easier to use and may crash your Mac less often because Navigator 4.0 is designed to handle the latest Web tricks and technology, such as Java and Dynamic HTML, that might choke an earlier version of Navigator.

Battle of the browsers

Because Microsoft wasn't paying much attention to the Mac for most of the late 1990s, Netscape Navigator was the browser for more than 80 percent of Mac users in mid-1998. And if you mastered Netscape Navigator 4.0 in detail and then looked at Microsoft's browser, you'd find most features, down to the level of keyboard shortcuts, have been faithfully copied into Internet Explorer as well. The future of this odd arrangement is unclear: Netscape released source code for Navigator Version 5.0 into the public domain, and then it got bought as a company by America Online. None of this browser upgrading matters much to the average Web fan — it will take Web sites years to catch up with the currently supported Web page features anyway.

Although Netscape Navigator now "competes" (gee, who will make the most money giving away browsers?) with Microsoft Internet Explorer for market share, it's fair to say that Microsoft has put more effort and money lately into Mac software, and there's not a tremendous argument in favor of one over the other browser. In the short term anyway, things have settled down a bit, and the Mac (and iMac) are sitting pretty.

Setting Preferences

Before getting too deep into exploring the Internet, you can make a couple of customizations to Netscape Navigator 4.0 to tailor it better for your own operations. Call up Preferences under the Edit menu. Under Navigator in the list at the left, one of the simplest tricks is to pick out the home page that's most useful to you (see Figure 5-1). Netscape's Netcenter has lots of useful links, but it takes a while to load with a plain old modem connection. For a general starting point, a faster load is Yahoo! at www.yahoo.com, but you almost certainly have a higher priority in life than general searching. For absolute fastest startup, this Preferences page lets you pick Blank Page as a startup alternative.

Another set of choices is the extensive list of helper applications. The choices in this list tell Netscape Navigator how to process different file types it encounters. Although when you first install a current version most of these items (see Figure 5-2) are the right choices, as the months roll on, you'll find you will likely want to update these. Particularly, the multimedia options on the Web are changing quite rapidly (see Chapter 8 for more perspective on sound and movies in a Web page). You can also use this list to direct Netscape Navigator to use a favorite mail program to handle mail files and a program like Dartmouth University's Fetch to handle file transfers. Although the program Internet Config or Mac OS 8.5's Internet control panel (see Chapter 4) will probably be the main way to do these customizations fairly soon, Netscape Navigator was still having occasional glitches at Version 4.05 in its dealings with Internet Config.

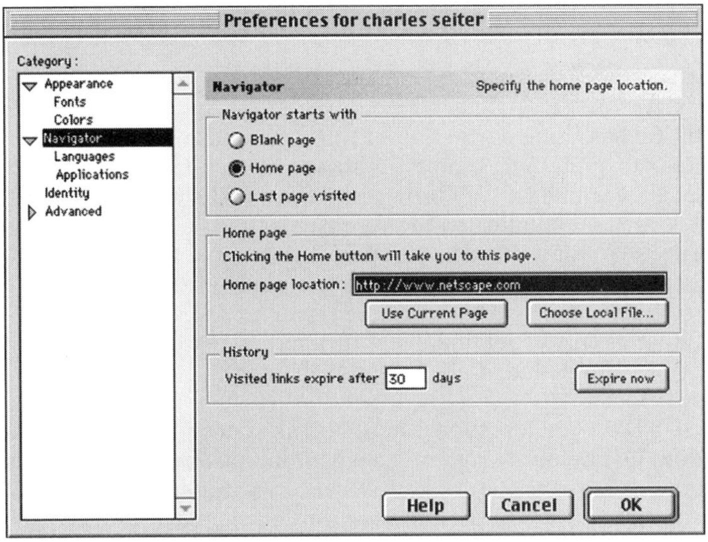

Figure 5-1:
Which way
home?

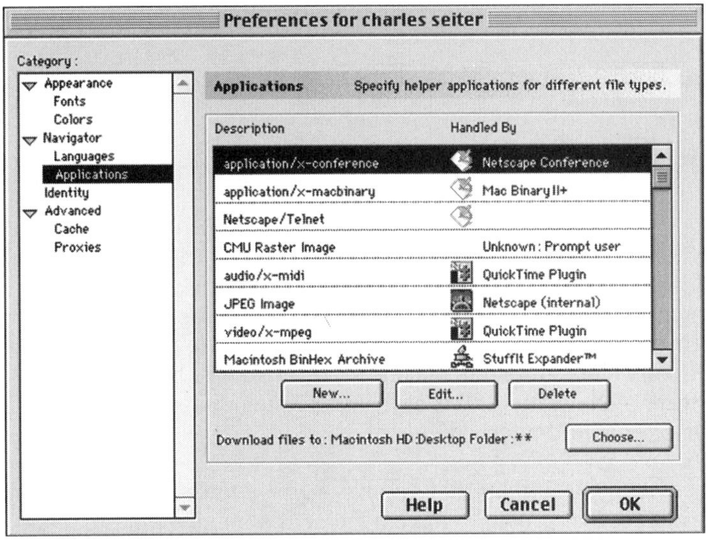

Figure 5-2:
Navigator's
file of file
handlers.

URL, She's RL, We're All RL!

Netscape Navigator and other Web browsers work by searching for Web sites by their particular names. Okay, what you type in aren't really names — they're more like addresses. A Web site's address is formally called a *URL*, which stands for *uniform resource locator*. Wow. Sounds like three words that mean "address" to me.

The parts of a URL are rather simple. Take, for instance, this example:

```
http://www.yahoo.com
```

Each URL has three parts. The `http://` part tells a program, "Hey, I'm trying to speak to something that understands **h**ypertext **t**ransfer **p**rotocol." Basically, you need a Web browser to open URLs with `http` as its first part. Next, `www.yahoo` indicates the Web site to find — in this case, Yahoo!, an Internet searching site. The last part, I guess, is a subpart. See the .com part? That tells you that the page is a commercially created page; that is, a page owned by a company that might be trying to sell you something. Other parts include .`org` (for educational institutions), .`net` (for Internet services), and .`gov` (for federal- and state-created Web sites).

To use a URL, you just type it in the blank space provided near the top of window, just below Navigator's navigation buttons, and then press your keyboard's Enter or Return key. When Navigator searches, the "N" button at the top-right corner of the browser window displays a mystic animation of stars and planets (heck, it beats the Mac's "watch" and "beach ball" wait symbols!). The browser begins to transfer and arrange the pictures and text to form the Web page. When the page is completely done, the "N" animation stops.

Browser Basics

Unless you're using the software you received from an Internet service provider to install a copy of Netscape Navigator 4.0, you'll probably need to download the new version. Mac OS 8 comes with an older version of Navigator, but most of the features that I describe to you in this chapter may confuse you, because the menus and settings are different. If you can find a copy from a Macintosh magazine's CD, that's the best way to obtain the software — Navigator 4.0 is still several megabytes in size and will take a while over a modem to download.

Let's start by assuming that you have given your credit card number to an Internet service provider, have been sent some installation disks or a CD, and have patiently let the software install itself.

Moving around the Web

After starting your computer, start Netscape Navigator. The program will dial the connection itself (during installation you were probably prompted to select a local number from a list) and you will see either your ISP's home page, the Apple/Excite home page, or, more likely, the glorious display of

Figure 5-3, cooked up as Netscape's one-stop attraction Netcenter, the Netscape Corporation's combination welcome, search-for-something, and buy-something home page.

On the Web, you move around simply by clicking *hyperlinks* (or *links,* for short) — highlighted words (colored or underlined) in a page. Each click takes you to another page of information. Well, actually, it takes you to another page of words and pictures — you get to decide whether it's "information." On the toolbar, you have Back and Forward toolbar buttons to take you back (or forward) through the set of pages you've seen in this connection session. Holding down either button brings up a list of Web pages you have visited to which you can immediately jump forward and back. The mechanisms here are pretty simple. Every highlighted word in a site, or "link," has the address of another Web page, and the browser simply keeps track of these addresses.

Watch the screen as you move your cursor over highlighted items, and you see the links for those items appear in the little flat zone near the bottom of the screen. Also, when you click a highlighted item, you're likely to see the progress bar, also at the bottom of the screen, which tells you how the loading process for the linked screen is going. If you're lucky enough to have a fast connection, such as cable modem, you may never have to watch this, but if you use a standard phone modem, you'll gaze at the progress bar and realize why it's called the World Wide Wait.

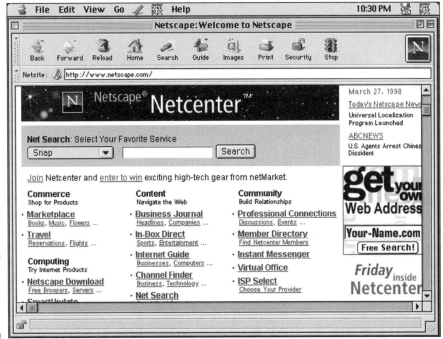

Figure 5-3: Square one of the Web board.

Browsing the Web more efficiently

You could easily spend a month just clicking aimlessly through the high-lighted links on the Netcenter page, but Netscape has put a new toolbar button, called Guide, on Version 4.0 of Netscape Navigator to help make your browsing pay off quicker (see Figure 5-4). The Guide home page has lots of links to serious areas, but the Guide button itself shows a pull-down menu with a built-in goof-off choice for slackers called What's Cool.

For my money, What's Cool is the best search button on this page. What's Cool is located next to a pop-up window that gives you a choice of six popular *search engines* (places to search for Internet-based material). You can find more on searching in Chapter 12, but for now, you can conclude that the Netscape Navigator Netcenter page really isn't a bad place to use for a home page. To try a first search from any page on the Web (not just Netcenter) using Netscape Navigator, click the Search button on the toolbar. This button displays a page of links to Internet search engines and other search services. Typically, you then type in some search words, click a button, then wait for the engine to find your search words in a database of Web pages. The results are usually presented as a list of links to pages containing your search words.

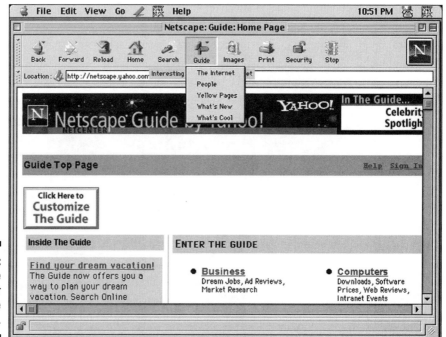

Figure 5-4:
Netscape
Navigator
wants to be
your guide.

You should also know that one more search command is useful — the Find command stashed under the Edit menu. Very often, search results will be big enough text piles that finding your search words "by eyeball" may take longer than you'd like. Call up this within-page word search with ⌘+F, and look for the word again with ⌘+G.

Windows as usual . . .

Web pages, like typical Macintosh windows, have scroll bars that you can use to see any content too large for your monitor's current size. (If scrolling is new to you, it might be a good idea to brush up on your Mac basic skills by getting a copy of *Macs For Dummies,* 5th Edition by David Pogue, also published by IDG Books.) You can probably also guess that the File menu for Netscape Navigator, like every other Mac application, has a Save As item for saving page contents. You have a choice between saving as text, usually the best option for later editing in a word processor, or saving as HTML source, which gives you a page with the same layout as you see on the Web, as long as you open it in a browser.

That's almost true. If the page has lots of pictures, you have to click each picture and hold the mouse button down until a tiny menu appears over the item you are clicking. From that menu, choose the Save Image As option and accept the name that the browser finds for the image. (You don't want to change the name because the Web page you have copied contains programming that looks for the original name of the image.) This process can be tiresome if the page has dozens of tiny images, but if you're trying to make up your own Web site by partially cloning someone else's, it's less work than producing your own visuals.

. . . and frames

One simple variation on the standard page, which first appeared in Netscape Navigator a few versions ago, is called *frames* (see Figure 5-5). Using frames, Navigator can display pages within a page (like the picture-in-picture feature of television sets). Frames divide a page into rectangular areas, and each frame area can display its own mini-page. A link in a frame works the same as a link in a standard page, and you can resize a frame or move it around just by treating it as a Mac desrĀop window. Because frames make for complicated pages, and frequently produce annoyingly chopped-up results when a page with frames is saved as text, you may want to use a different text-selection method. You can select text by clicking once at one end of a selection, then holding down the Shift key and clicking a second time at the other end of the selection. Unlike a word processor, Navigator won't show you a blinking insertion bar.

Figure 5-5:
Framed up.

Saving Pages with Bookmarks

The practical problem in Web navigation is that in a few days of leisurely clicking around (having spent my high school and college years on the great beaches of San Diego, I just can't bring myself to call Web activity "surfing"), you will have visited hundreds of Web sites and a dozen pages per site. Some will be very interesting to you, but most won't. You want to keep the good ones and forget the rest. So now it's time to look into the topics of Bookmarks and History, the Netscape Navigator facilities that make up your personal roadmap to the Web.

Bookmark basics

Bookmarks are a list of Web site addresses you've saved to a file on your hard disk. (Technically, these locations are called Uniform Resource Locators, or URLs, but these days you can live a happy Web life without really knowing what URL or other abbreviations mean.) When you add a bookmark to your list, the item stays until you remove it or change lists (see Figure 5-6). That's what makes them valuable for personalizing your Internet access. History, instead, offers a way to redisplay all pages you've previously viewed. Unlike bookmark lists, which store page locations only when you tell the browser to make a bookmark, history items (see Figure 5-7) are saved automatically whenever you display a page.

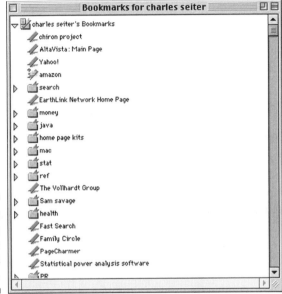

Figure 5-6:
Checking
the
Bookmark
list.

Netscape Navigator offers lots of ways to create and update a bookmark list. When looking at a page you like, you can create a bookmark for the page by

✔ Opening the Bookmarks menu and choosing Add Bookmark.

✔ Pressing ⌘+D. This shortcut adds the current page as an item in the Bookmarks menu.

You can edit and organize your bookmarks by choosing Bookmarks from the Navigator menu (the menu symbol that looks like a sailing ship's steering wheel).

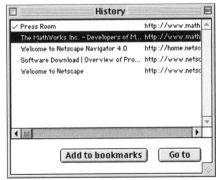

Figure 5-7:
Short-term
history.

More advanced options in the Bookmarks window let you create hierarchical menus and multiple bookmark files. The Bookmarks window not only lists your bookmarks but also offers menu items for list organizing. Each item in a Netscape Navigator list contains the title of the Web page, the associated URL, and date information. You double-click a bookmark icon to access the corresponding page.

To edit Bookmarks, follow these steps:

1. **Click the Navigator icon on the menu bar.**

   In case you're looking for the word "Navigator" on the menu bar, the Navigator menu is actually the sailboat steering wheel icon, to the right of the green bookmark icon that is the Bookmarks menu.

2. **Click and hold the Bookmarks item to get the Bookmarks option.**

3. **Choose Edit Bookmarks.**

You can drag and drop bookmark icons or use the window's menu items to arrange the display of your bookmarks and bookmark folders. You can create new folders by picking New Folder from the File menu and giving the new folder a name. To eliminate old, stale bookmarks, you can also select a particular bookmark icon and press the Delete key.

Bookmarks and history

One resource for editing and updating bookmarks is the History list, which is a list of all the Web sites you have visited in the past. To see the History list, click the Navigator icon and choose History. You don't have to do much about History, because it tracks the pages you've visited automatically. But when you open the list, you're given the option of clicking one of the entries and adding it to the Bookmark list. This gives you a quick way to make replacements when a favorite page changes its address — the History list shows both the old address you tried to visit and the new one the page wants you to use.

In your up-to-date Bookmark list, you can double-click bookmarks to access pages, drag and drop icons to arrange your bookmarks, and use the Bookmark window's menu bar to create new bookmark items and manipulate bookmark lists. It's rare for bookmarks to be useful for more than a few years. Netscape Navigator has a fairly good set of built-in bookmarks, and because a new version of the browser comes out every six months or so, the bookmarks are usually correct.

Multiple bookmark lists can also be useful. You can have more than one bookmark list, each with its own set of titles linked to favorite pages, although only one bookmark list can be active at a time. To create multiple bookmark lists, follow these steps:

1. **Open the Bookmarks window from the Navigator (steering wheel) menu and choose Save As to save the current list in the Bookmarks window.**

   The list is saved as an HTML-formatted page file.

2. **Give the list a filename and click OK to create the bookmark file.**

Now with the Bookmarks window open, click the File menu and choose Open to pick the list you want to display in the Bookmarks menu. You can also import Bookmark files — people often like to exchange them with friends. When you open the File menu in the Bookmarks window, you see an Import choice, which shows you an easy-to-follow Import Bookmarks File dialog box. Just select the bookmarks.html file that you wish to append to your current bookmarks set.

Looking at the Rest of the Package

Go to the Netscape download page at www.netscape.com and see what Netscape has to offer. This page is shown in Figure 5-8. Specifically, Netscape Navigator 4.0 was being offered for no charge in mid-1998, and now the whole Netscape Communicator package also will be downloadable soon for no charge. That would be good news for you, because then you get some other interesting programs. With Communicator, when you click the main Netscape icon on the toolbar, you get a longer list of goodies (see Figure 5-9).

Composer

In the Communicator package, Netscape assumes that you don't just want to do passive browsing, but that you may want to try your hand at Web page composition. So it's bundled a separate application called Composer into the full Communicator package.

Web pages used to be simple enough to compose directly in HTML (the programming language used to make Web pages) without too much trouble. That's because in the early days of the Web, pages tended to be text, hyperlinks, and a few simple bits of graphics. Now even a page that's quite simple by today's standards (see Figure 5-10) is a dauntingly large file of text when viewed directly (see Figure 5-11) as HTML (one of the options in the Netscape Navigator View menu).

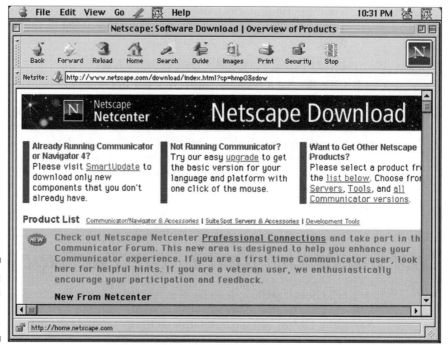

Figure 5-8: Netscape's latest and greatest.

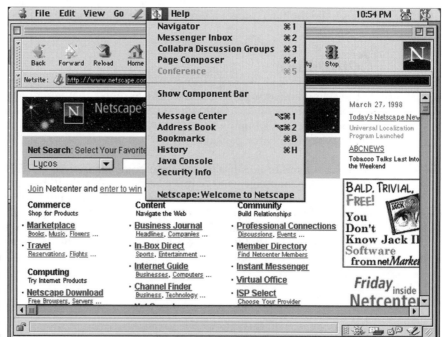

Figure 5-9: Communicator's long list.

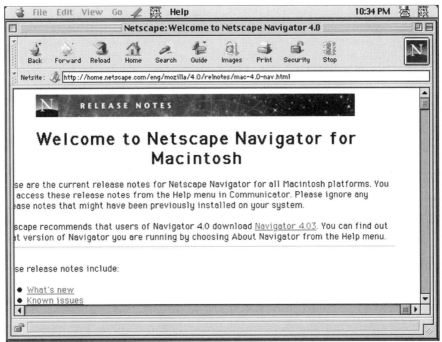

Figure 5-10:
A plain but
useful page.

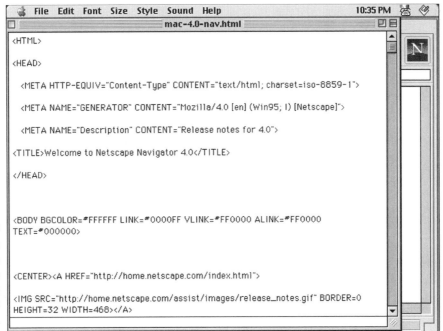

Figure 5-11:
Viewing the
source
code for a
simple Web
page.

You can make your own pages by downloading pages from the Web as HTML and tinkering with them, replacing images and text as you go. Actually, most of the professional Web site developers I know maintain files just like this of pages they tweak to meet client requests. The Composer program lets you make up a page directly (see Figure 5-12) using nifty tools like those in other dedicated Web-page kits. Composer is especially valuable in that if you make up a page in Composer, it looks exactly right when someone views it in Netscape Navigator. Almost any other Web tool for easy page-building calls for some post-composition reworking. This isn't so with Composer because you're viewing the page you create in Netscape Navigator itself as you work.

Messenger

The earlier versions of Netscape Navigator had a simple mail program built into the package. As Netscape tries to position Communicator as serious business software, it needs an industrial-strength mail client program. So Messenger (see Figure 5-13) not only provides a decent online address book and a way to generate sets of folders for mail filing, but is also set to manage mailings to lists (for example, mailing a message to everyone in the account-ing department). Messenger is better than Netscape Navigator's old mail system at handling enclosures and guaranteeing message security, and it automatically highlights message parts (see Figure 5-14) that can be inter-preted as Web hyperlinks.

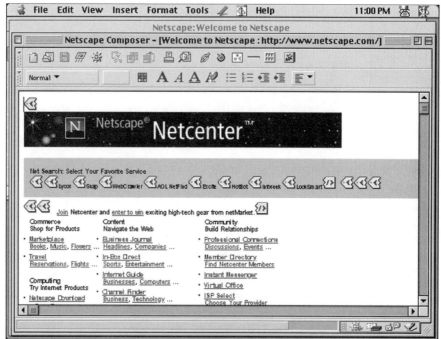

Figure 5-12:
Look at
Composer's
intuitive
toolbar.

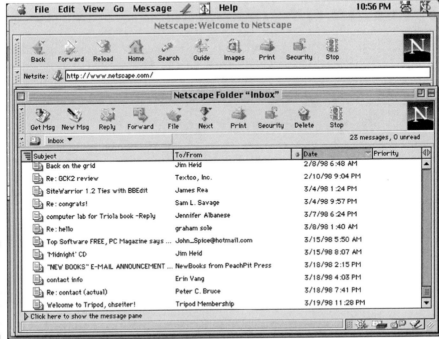

Figure 5-13:
Netscape
Messenger,
showing the
Inbox.

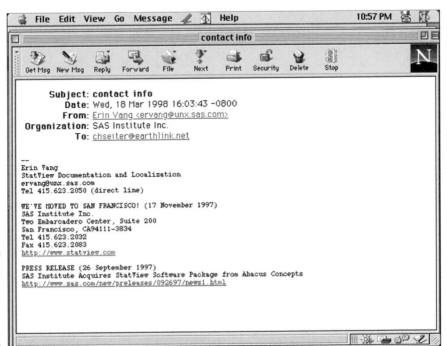

Figure 5-14:
An e-mail
message
with
hyperlinks.

Speeding Up Things

Because nothing's ever fast enough, and certainly nothing to do with the Web is fast enough, here's a selection of speed tips to make Netscape Navigator more pleasant to use.

Increasing your speed

If you're willing to use keyboard shortcuts (see Table 5-1) rather than do everything in mouse/menu style, you gain two benefits:

- ✔ Results pop up quicker, gratifying in itself.
- ✔ If you're just browsing Web sites, the keyboard shortcuts replace a lot of index-finger work on the mouse with a greater variety of movement involving both hands.

Trust me, anything you can do to avoid repetitive movements is worth trying. Your poor old appendages weren't designed for eight-hour shifts consisting of endlessly repeated, identical, small, wrist movements.

Table 5-1	Quicker Clickers
On the Keyboard	*What It Does*
⌘+L	Opens a Web page by URL
⌘+O	Opens a page from your hard drive
⌘+[	Goes back a page
⌘+]	Goes forward a page
⌘+S	Saves the current page
⌘+.	Stops loading page
⌘+R	Reloads current page
⌘+N	Opens a new browser window
⌘+P	Prints current window contents
⌘+D	Adds page to bookmark/favorite list

Increasing Navigator's speed

With your fingers making their own nimble contribution to speed, it's time to make Navigator hustle a bit. The speed tips are all really directed toward the same goal: getting Navigator to avoid downloading material you don't need.

First, click the Edit menu and choose Preferences. In the Preferences window, click the Advanced section of Preferences (see Figure 5-15) — remember, Preferences is an item in the Edit menu. Several little check boxes are here that dramatically affect both startup and downloads, so I consider them in detail. The Advanced options also include check boxes for the mysterious and seldom-explained topic of Web *cookies*. For the story on cookies, please consult the nearby sidebar "Cookie time."

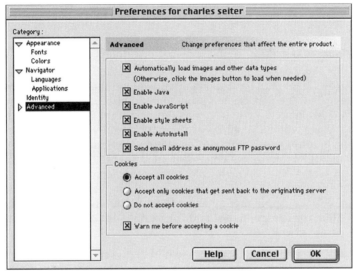

Figure 5-15:
Setting for
speed.

Don't let the pictures load automatically

First, click the Automatically Load Images item to remove its "x." When this check box is unselected, the images in pages are replaced by small icons, a process that's very fast compared to loading every corporate-vanity image on a commercial site. These small replacement icons are sometimes accompanied by little bits of text, shown as a substitution when an image isn't loaded. For most pages, this will be a great help for speed as the text surrounding the graphics (the page's content) gives you enough context to use the Web page. On the downside, some sites use graphics themselves as a link, so if you don't load in the graphic, you can't click anywhere.

If you decide the page is worth checking out in detail, or if there don't seem to be any links to click, then just click the Images icon on the toolbar, or pick Show Images from the View menu. As a simple way to judge for yourself the speed difference between having images always present or not, you may want to go to www.amazon.com and try viewing the site the standard way versus the text-only option. When I'm trying to buy a book and I already know the author or title, I find that using their text-only forms saves me about ten minutes on the transaction.

Java

Java applets (programs written in the Web-oriented language Java) have the potential to do great things. They're just not doing them yet. Instead, they currently waste your time running idiotic scrolling banners and such. When you go to a page that contains a Java applet, you can count on a minute or more of downtime while your browser starts up Java and plays the applet, which is almost always a piece of advertising junk. In Netscape Navigator, you can uncheck the Enable Java box in our old friend the Advanced Preferences screen. You may want to turn it back on someday, but worthwhile Java applets are taking a while to develop generally.

A cache speed-up

There's a place on your Mac where copies of Web page content are stored so the browser doesn't have to always download the same graphic or text. This place, called the disk *cache* (pronounced "cash"), can hold a lot of previously downloaded content. But as the size of the cache increases, Navigator slows down while trying to get information from it for previously viewed pages. In other words, though Navigator's disk cache is supposed to save time, a large cache slows you down. Here's what to do for real speed if you have a system with enough RAM, or system memory (24MB or more is best):

1. **Click the Apple menu, select Control Panels, and then open your Memory control panel and turn RAM Disk on by clicking the appropriate check box.**

   Set the RAM disk's size somewhere between 1024 to 4096K (that's 1MB to 4MB).

2. **Restart your Macintosh by clicking the Special menu and choosing Restart. You have to do this to actually create the RAM disk for the first time.**

3. **After your Mac has restarted, open Navigator, click the Edit menu, and chose Preferences. Then click the Cache item in the Advanced options of Preferences.**

4. **Click the Choose button and select the RAM disk as the new location of the cache from the dialog box that appears.**

Now the disk cache is actually the same RAM you use to run programs, and Navigator runs much faster because it can search a RAM disk faster than trying to access your hard disk. If you're using Netscape Navigator 4.0, you get an impressive browsing speed up even if you just set a RAM cache of 1024 kilobytes, a mere 1MB.

Cookie time

On the page for setting Advanced Preferences, you may have noticed a bunch of check boxes that referred to *cookies*. You ought to understand a bit about these, because they're involved in the background of plans to make money from the Internet. Cookies are small text files that a browser may store on your hard drive. The file may be your zip code, your username, or data you put in an online form. Web sites then look for these cookies when you link to a site, and use the cookie to identify you as a previous visitor.

One main use of cookies is to "personalize" the ad banners you see when you visit sites. If you go to a shopping site and order books, the next time you visit the site, you'll likely see flower ads. Other sites will want to remember that you're a Mac user and avoid showering you with Windows banners. Webmasters like cookies because cookies can tell them how many unique visits their sites have had, how often users return, and where they go.

It's up to you to make a choice here. Your browser is set to send them out by default, but you can, using Preferences, either always decline to accept them, or have the browser tell you when a site makes a cookie request. You may be delighted that many Web sites will be semi-personalized to reflect your interests. You may be annoyed that you're supplying marketing information about yourself. If you firmly believe that this kind of information will never ever be abused, nor ever collected by one Web site and resold to others, please send me a copy of your last year's 1040A courtesy of IDG Books, and I'll recommend some fabulous investment opportunities for you. Seriously, you may want to check the box for the browser notifying you when a site requests a cookie, just so you can track what's happening.

Old Software Never Dies . . . Sort Of

Here's one last speed tip, and it's simple. Keep your copy of Netscape Navigator 3.01 instead of using Navigator 4.0. In graphical interface software, the size of the software is a major determinant of speed, and 3.01 is much smaller than any of the 4.0*x* versions. The figures for this book were almost all done using Netscape Navigator 4.05 over a period of several months. I must admit, I was really impressed with 3.01 when I clicked it by mistake during that time. First, the menu items are set up to give you what you most want with a single click — I like having Bookmarks on the main menu rather than filed somewhere else, and I like the Open icon on the Navigator toolbar (see Figure 5-16). The only caution to observe in this is security, as security is always better in the newer versions of Netscape Navigator. If you're just browsing, security isn't a problem, but for placing credit card orders, you're a bit safer with Version 4.0.

You may have problems keeping a running copy of Navigator 3.01 and Navigator or Communicator 4.0 on your Mac at the same time because the newer versions of Navigator add components that Navigator 3.01 might not be able to understand. As a result, both versions of Navigator may act strangely. If you have problems, I suggest that you drag the folder containing the copy of Navigator 3.01 to the Trash. Depending on the problem, however, you might also want to reinstall Navigator 4.0.

The other nice touch in the older browser is that it has windows for newsgroups, and more importantly, mail (see Figure 5-17). In the new world of Netscape Communicator, mail, as I explain earlier in this chapter, has been packaged away into a bigger and more complete separate application. But if you're pressed for RAM space (a common situation with laptops), it's convenient to have a single compact application that can view Web sites and collect e-mail, whether or not the e-mail system offers every known bell and whistle. Magazines, partly because of the influence of advertisers, always like to assume you're ready to buy upgrades or new computers at the drop of a hat. This, however, is a book, and it doesn't have ads, and I can tell you that a lot of mail from its first two editions asked how to keep up with the Web without spending more money. The simplest quick answer is to use last year's software if you're using last year's machine.

Figure 5-16:
The Open icon on the Navigator toolbar.

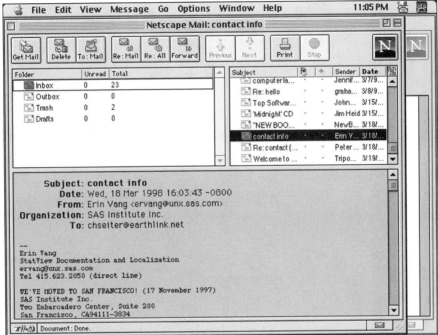

Figure 5-17:
Navigator
offers mail,
too.

Chapter 6

Internet Explorer 4.5

· ·

· ·

*I*nternet Explorer (IE) is Microsoft's means of cashing in on the popularity of browsing the World Wide Web.

The first versions of Internet Explorer for Windows were useful, but the first Macintosh versions were, to put it mildly, unstable and lacking in anything that made it worthwhile to try. Today, however, IE 4.5 for Macs is compact, stable, and nicely packed with convenience features. Given that Navigator's development future is a bit uncertain following Netscape's acquisition by AOL, you might want to get familiar with IE 4.5.

The Plus Side

Internet Explorer is now a pretty handy program. The only part missing, compared to its Windows equivalent, is support for the new Web markup language XML, emerging in 1999 as the next big thing, succeeding the plain old HTML that was the foundation of the Web. So I don't want to make a commercial for Microsoft, but Internet Explorer 4.5 *is* great for Macs if you

✔ Don't have a lot of RAM installed

✔ Don't have a lot of hard disk space

✔ Want a faster browser

✔ Like to browse Web pages while not connected to the Internet

✔ Want to use pages loaded with Java programming

Getting It

Internet Explorer 4.5 comes as part of the new update to the popular system software update, Mac OS 8.5. (See Bob LeVitus's book, *Mac OS 8.5 For Dummies,* for more about it.) Or, you can find it on CD-ROMs included with such magazines as *Macworld* or *MacAddict,* or download the program from Microsoft's Web page at www.microsoft.com/ie.

There were some bugs in Internet Explorer 4.0, which were fixed in 4.01. But 4.5 is also a serious features improvement on 4.0, so get yourself the latest version of Internet Explorer, not just for the bug fixes, but for changes in security and convenience features.

The entire IE software package is a reasonable download with a fast modem. But Microsoft, realizing that you want to download only the parts you need, lets you download the browser separately from Outlook Express (the accompanying e-mail program). Just visit www.microsoft.com/ie and click the link that encourages you to download IE 4.5 by itself. You get a browser that needs only 4MB for the Power Mac version, quite an accomplishment for the organization that virtually invented bloatware. Microsoft's Web site also currently offers to sell you the browser on a CD for $6.95, but warns that the delivery might take up to six weeks. That makes downloading it, even overnight with the slowest modem, look fairly attractive.

Cool Features

Internet Explorer looks much like Netscape Navigator, with the exception of several additions and a name change or two (see Figure 6-1). Aside from the standard Macintosh menu bar at the top of the screen and the browser area where pages are viewed, IE's window breaks down to the Button bar, the Address bar, the Favorites bar, and the unique Explorer bar. Hey, it wouldn't be Microsoft if we didn't get more new names and terminology, right?

Figure 6-1:
Internet
Explorer.
The unusual
Explorer bar
consists of
the four
tabs on the
left side of
the window.

About the Button, Address, and Favorites bars

The Button bar works just like the Navigator bar, with buttons to take you forward and back through previously viewed Web pages, stop loading a page, and so on. The Address bar is where you'd type in a Web site address, such as `http://www.dummies.com`, as you would with Navigator. Below it, the Favorites bar is a place where you can drag your most-used links to Web pages. *Favorites* is the name that IE gives to what Navigator calls *bookmarks* (which are a library of Web page addresses that you save with your browser, in case you were wondering). If you see me switch between using "favorites" and "bookmarks," just remember that they are one and the same thing in function.

The Button, Address, and Favorites bars have a great feature that's useful if you want to create more room in the Internet Explorer window where a Web page loads. See the crinkled barbershop-pole-like bar thingie on the leftmost side of each bar? That's a handle of sorts for moving a bar. When you click and hold down your mouse button on one of these bars, you can move the bar so it appears to the left, right, or above the other bars.

A popular way to gain more browser space is to place the Button and Address bars alongside each other, as shown in Figure 6-2. Now, depending on your monitor's screen size, you might lose the ability to use the last few buttons on the Button bar, but you gain more vertical space to see a Web page.

Though I don't recommend it, you can also hide any of the bars if you don't need to see them. Follow these steps:

1. **Choose Edit⇨Preferences.**

2. **Click Browser Display under the Web Browser section on the left side of the screen.**

3. **Uncheck the box that says Show Button Bar, Show Address Bar, or Show Favorites Bar.**

I suggest that you always keep the Button and Address bars visible because they're the most convenient way to navigate through any page. You can do some Button bar commands by using the keyboard (such as ⌘-[and ⌘-] for Back and Forward, respectively). You can probably get by with not showing the Favorites bar — you gain more space to view a Web page with this bar closed. And, of course, all the commands you need are available from the standard Mac application bar anyway.

Figure 6-2:
I've moved
my Address
bar to the
right of my
Button bar.

The Explorer bar: Some parts are useful

The Explorer bar is Microsoft's compromise in adding the features of the Windows 95 and Windows 98 versions of Internet Explorer to the Macintosh version. In IE 4.0 for Windows 95/98, a feature called the Active Desktop allows you to access special Web sites named *channels* by clicking a special toolbar on the Windows desktop. Because Microsoft couldn't change the Mac OS to add this browser/operating system hybrid, Microsoft puts the Explorer bar in IE 4.5 for Macs to allow you to get some of the same features of the Windows IE. (See Figure 6-3.)

The Explorer bar shows you essentially the same things that you can view using the menus at the top of the screen, such as the History tab (that's a place where IE records in order all the sites you have visited since you started the program), and the Favorites tab (your catalog of Web page links). The Explorer bar also adds a nice touch called PageHolder. PageHolder keeps a "live" copy of a page you want to visit frequently, so that you can return to that page instantly during a browsing session. Like everything else on the Explorer bar, it just presents something the older browsers could do, in a slightly more immediate format at the expense of screen space. PageHolder, hardcore Web addicts may note, replaces the Channels tab in 4.01 — even Microsoft has had a hard time making many Webmasters sign up for its channels program.

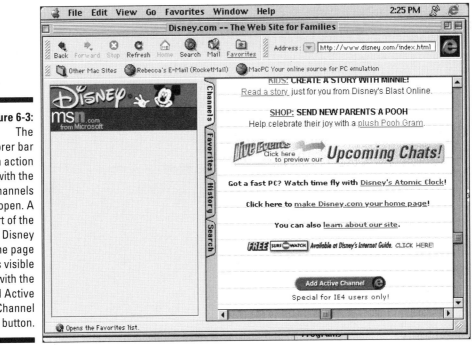

Figure 6-3: The Explorer bar in action with the Channels tab open. A part of the Disney home page is visible with the Add Active Channel button.

The Search tab on the Explorer bar really is helpful because it keeps all popular search sites in one place. When you click the Search tab, you're greeted by a scaled-down version of one of the popular *search engines* (that's a Web site that you can use to search for information in or other kinds of Web sites). You can select a specific search page by choosing the page from the pop-up menu at the top of the Search tab window.

The cool thing about searching for sites and content with the Search tab is that you don't have to create a new browser window or have IE take away valuable time loading in yet another page in the main browser window, which in turn shoves out the page you were last viewing. This saves space on the screen, and it's faster and much more efficient.

Printing superiority

It may seem like a small detail, but in practice it's a great help. The File menu in IE 4.5 has a Print Preview selection, and, astonishingly, it works. All Web browsers, including every version of Netscape Navigator and all previous versions of Internet Explorer, have been laughably bad at producing printed versions of Web pages. IE 4.5 actually produces usable printed output. At last!

A Better Way to Download

Internet Explorer also offers a great feature not available in Netscape's browsers: a window that monitors the status and keeps records of any programs or items you download. Behold the Download Manager, shown in Figure 6-4.

Figure 6-4:
The Download Manager not only watches your downloads, but records their progress and whether the download was successful.

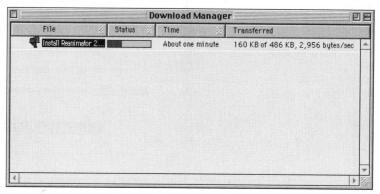

Microsoft and Apple: Peace treaty in force

Microsoft's antitrust trial in 1999 has showed many that Microsoft really isn't picking on the Mac in particular, it just wants to crush all other companies in general. It probably would rather squash Sun Microsystems than Apple, at least as a first choice.

Thanks in part to Steve Jobs' influence, Microsoft has realized lately the importance of (and profit to be made by) making Mac users happy. Because Mac users want *functioning*, useful software, Microsoft finally showed it can listen to Mac users by totally rewriting Microsoft Word and other parts of the Microsoft Office software suite to create the fast and powerful (though not very affordable) Office 98, Macintosh Edition. Naming the program suite "Office 98" was also a bow of respect to the Mac world, as the Windows version of Office 98 would not show up until months later.

Internet Explorer 4.5 for Macintosh follows Microsoft's renewed improvements to the Mac way of life. The whole point in using your computer is to *use* it, not to follow some philosophy that spurns Microsoft or other companies just because they're huge and compete against Apple and others. IE 4.5 is pretty impressive free software, so it's worth your time to try it.

The Download Manager performs three functions and does them very well. When you click a link for a downloadable item, such as a program, the Download Manager window appears and shows the item you are downloading in a Finder-like list view. In that view, you see the name of the item, the amount that has been downloaded to your Mac in the form of a progress bar, a human-like estimate of the time needed to download the remainder of the file (like, "About one minute"), and the size of the download and the speed at which your modem is downloading the file.

The Download Manager also remembers if a download was not fully completed. Incomplete downloads happen when your Internet connection is cut off either by you or accidentally. When that happens, the Download Manager saves the incomplete part of the download file. If you were to click the same download link again, the Download Manager would resume downloading where it left off, saving you the time of downloading the whole file again.

Sometimes a busy Web site will not transmit files to you quickly and so your download appears to move slowly or to even stall (no data is being transmitted from the download site). Your Internet connection probably is fine, but there's something wrong at the download site that prevents the download from continuing. In Netscape Navigator, a tiny window appears that tries and fails to show the speed of a download. But in the Download Manager, you'll know a file is stalled if you see the words "Waiting for data" in the line of information about the download you're receiving.

The Download Manager can also give you special information about any file listed in the Manager's window. Figure 6-5 shows the Get Info window for a file I downloaded. To get more information about a file that's in the Download Manager window, click once on the item's name and choose Get Info from the File menu in Internet Explorer (or just double-click the item's name).

Figure 6-5: The Download Manager Get Info window. Nice to have if you've forgotten where you found a file.

This useful window shows you where you downloaded this file (in case you've forgotten), the status of the download (whether or not it was completed), and the Reveal in Finder button, which enables you to immediately open a window in the Finder that contains the item you downloaded. That's a great feature because it keeps you from having to switch to the Finder and double-click a bunch of folders to get to an item. You can also reload a file by clicking the Reload button in the Get Info window.

You can open the Download Manager window at any time by choosing the Download Manager command from the File menu.

Importing Netscape Navigator Bookmarks

Say that you're using Netscape Navigator or Communicator but want to transfer a copy of Navigator's bookmarks to IE, where bookmarks are known as Favorites. No problem — just follow these steps:

1. **Click the Favorites menu and choose Open Favorites.**

   A window containing a list of Favorites appears.

2. **Click File⇨Import.**

   A dialog box appears.

3. **Open the System Folder on your hard drive and find the Preferences folder. Inside, depending on your version of Netscape Navigator, you'll find a folder named Netscape or Netscape Users.**

4. **Find the bookmarks.html file, select the name in the dialog box by clicking it once, and then click the Open button.**

   The bookmarks from Netscape are placed in your Favorites window. From here you can reorganize them by dragging links or folders up or down in the window.

5. **When you're done, click the Close box at the upper left of the Favorites window.**

You can now view your imported Favorites with the Favorites tab on the Explorer bar or from the Favorites menu.

Tweaking Internet Explorer's Settings

You can change many things in the Preferences window of Internet Explorer to make your Web browsing easier or more pleasing to the eye. In a previous section in this chapter, I talk about using the Preferences window to rearrange or hide the bars at the top of the screen to gain some extra room and see more of a Web page. I also go over some of the other options that it's worth your while to change. To open the Preferences window, choose Edit⇨Preferences. You'll see the window shown in Figure 6-6.

Figure 6-6:
In the Preferences window, you can make IE into a lean, mean browsing machine.

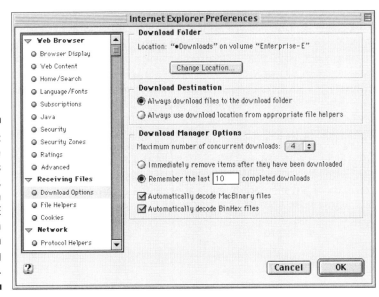

Browser Display and Web Content options

You can hide or change the appearance of the Button bar with the settings under the Browser Display option, located under Web Browser preferences. The Web Content option allows you to make pictures in a Web page display better or faster, and before or during the loading of the page. This option is important because sometimes it takes too long to view a page that's loaded with pictures. Using the Progressive Formatting section's Refresh after each image saves you time on a slow connection, such as a modem. For more speed, you may also want to uncheck the Play Sounds, Show Video, and Show Animated GIFs options to keep your Mac from spending more time than you need in processing sounds, video images (such as QuickTime movies), or animated GIFs that you may find in advertising banners at the top of a commercial Web page.

Language/Fonts options

The traditional fonts for Web browsers, Times and Courier, are automatically selected by Internet Explorer when you first use it. I recommend the optional fonts Trebuchet, Verdana, and Monotype.com, very appealing fonts specifically for Web page viewing that are preinstalled with Internet Explorer 4.5 in Mac OS 8.5. You can also download the fonts from the Microsoft Internet Explorer site.

Java

Java is a computer programming language that (in the case of the World Wide Web) lets Webmasters (people who create Web pages) add programs to their Web pages that any other browser that understands the Java language can use or view. That means, in theory, that a Webmaster using a Windows PC can make and add a Java *applet* (a Java program in a Web page) to her Web site that works when viewed with any Web browser on a Mac that handles Java.

Java's cross-platform promise hasn't been realized yet, in large part because of Microsoft's efforts to foil it and thus make the world safe for Windows. But in Version 4.5, partly in response to legal pressure, Microsoft has retreated a bit. Instead of using Microsoft's own non-standard Java software, IE 4.5 now uses Apple's own "virtual machine" (the software that interprets Java code) that's built into system software.

And hey, it works! It works so well that it's currently your best bet for seeing decent performance on Java-rich sites. I've been using it in connection with development of a very sophisticated mathematics site for a college textbook publisher, and it's been wonderful. It's still possible to turn Java off by using the Preferences panel, but there's not much need to do it.

Download Options

To make it easier to find items you've downloaded, you can tell Internet Explorer to save downloaded items to any folder by clicking the Change Location button in the Download Options section. You can also tell your browser to remember any number of previous downloads (as shown in the Download Manager window) and whether to automatically decode files you receive as BinHex or StuffIt archives. (I recommend that you keep these settings on; it just makes your life easier by not having to fuss with additional programs.)

Selected Goodies with Internet Explorer

Internet Explorer 4.5 by itself is a great Web browser. But if you want to view Internet newsgroups or read your e-mail, Microsoft has other options for you to use.

Chances are, your Mac already has something for you to use to view Usenet groups or your e-mail, so consider these add-ons for Internet Explorer as options and not really important stuff.

Outlook Express

If you aren't using the free Claris E-Mailer Lite program that comes with Mac OS 8 or other e-mail program, and you don't have a newsgroup reader, Outlook Express is a good companion. Outlook Express (a "lite" version of the program available as part of the new Office 98 Macintosh übersoftware) works well with Internet Explorer to send e-mail messages and newsgroup messages without a hitch. Outlook Express is also available as a separate free download from Microsoft's Web site.

Essential and supplementary Web fonts

I mention these earlier, but it bears repeating: Microsoft's Web fonts make it much easier to read a Web page. If you didn't get them by downloading the complete IE installer package, use the Active Installer to download them, or just visit `www.microsoft.com/ie/download/addon.htm` to get more information on how to download them.

When is a drag not a drag?

It won't necessarily save your life, but IE 4.5 now lets you drag links and images directly from a Web page to the Mac desktop. This will be most useful if you have a nice big monitor; but if you hide all the toolbars, you can make yourself a little "drag zone" at the bottom of smaller screens as well. With some experimentation, you'll find you can assemble document components from Web pages in record time.

Chapter 7

America Online

*I*f you have a copy of the second edition of this book, you'll find a long middle section on six national online services. The only one left, three years later, that still resembles the original service, is America Online. That's significant, and it's actually good news for you.

In this chapter, you see how to do everything you could want to do online, using only AOL. It has e-mail, Web connection with a built-in browser (a customized version of Microsoft Internet Explorer), chat rooms, instant messaging, every Apple support file, games, education, and more. Best of all, AOL has gone through the experience of being the first online stop for about ten million people, so you see how easy they've made it (finally).

The AOL Timeline

Because it has a great deal of bearing on whether you as a Mac user should bother with AOL, I want to give you a little survey. I really think AOL is a pretty good deal, especially for *Internet For Dummies* customers, but a bit of background will help you understand the frequent complaints you hear about this service.

Then

For years, during the mid-1990s, AOL was the butt of hundreds of Internet jokes for two reasons. First, it was fairly primitive compared to sophisticated UNIX-based Internet access favored by the pioneers of the Net based in universities. Second, AOL, intent on driving up its registration numbers, gave away AOL sign-up disks everywhere — with newspapers, magazines, new computers, or to anyone who stood still for more than twelve seconds at a computer show. Cynics called AOL the "National Blank Disk Distributor" and ridiculed AOL's marketing strategy.

Trying to drive up membership, AOL switched from per-hour pricing to fixed pricing per month. This drove membership up all right, resulting in constant system crashes, downtime, and busy signals on AOL access numbers. It also allowed AOL to lose a small amount of money per customer, even as the number of customers increased wildly.

In its defense, it might be pointed out that nobody, including mighty Microsoft (and certainly not Apple, host of the long-gone eWorld), has yet figured out how to make a profit, much less a reasonable return on investment, from online services. If AOL had twenty million customers who would volunteer to pay $30 per month and then only dial up once a week, everything would be great financially, but that's unlikely. We'll see.

Now

AOL hands out CDs instead of floppy disks, because the newer versions of AOL include Microsoft's Internet Explorer as a Web browser, making the whole package about a five-floppy set. The service now has about fourteen million customers — fairly close to a theoretical break-even point financially. It's also been successful at making exclusive content deals, so that the inside-AOL versions of many online operations (Morningstar investments, *The New York Times,* interactive games, and so forth) offer more features than the equivalent independent Web sites.

Right now, AOL is promoting its new software, Version 4.0, that makes it simple to move back and forth between AOL's own proprietary services and the rest of the Internet (see Figure 7-1). That's the software used for the figures in this chapter, because

- ✔ Version 4.0 makes sense for newer Macs.
- ✔ Version 4.0 will be upgraded to use Netscape features.
- ✔ Older AOL software is not great on the Web.

It's nice to see also that AOL develops its Mac software on an equal footing with Windows — the beta versions of 4.0 for both systems tracked each other pretty closely.

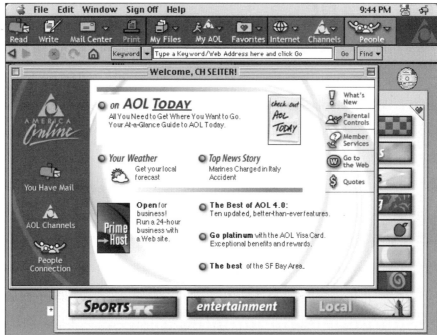

Figure 7-1:
AOL 4.0
lights up the
screen.

Next

By 1998 the problem facing the earlier online services was simple. And impossible. How could they provide more interesting content than the World Wide Web, which offered it all for free? Well, they couldn't.

AOL instead took the approach of making everything easier. Basically, with its new software that offers a choice of browsers, it has morphed into an Internet Service Provider with special content deals and better e-mail. It used to be that AOL was a "set of training wheels for the Internet." Now it's about as good a system as you'll find. Once you get used to it, you'll probably find few compelling reasons to switch services.

Will AOL survive, especially in competition with Microsoft's well-funded Microsoft Network (MSN), now virtually installed as the default online service on new Windows computers? So far, it's doing fine, and MSN just flounders and loses money. As you'll see in the next few sections, AOL offers several really important features you don't get with the usual ISP's browser-and-a-phone-number setup.

Inside AOL

Three big arguments exist in favor of using AOL as a main Internet connection:

- ✔ First, there's control over content. There's stuff on the Internet that a 45-year-old prison guard would find repellently raunchy. America Online has a great parental control system for keeping underage users from browsing, accidentally or otherwise, hard-core sites.

- ✔ Next, America Online has done a creditable job of putting together special content areas and creating an "online community" that's big enough to be viable.

- ✔ Finally, there's e-mail. Everybody has e-mail, but America Online's is superior in nearly every respect. Let's take a closer look at these inside-AOL features.

A fourth reason might be that it's all pretty simple to get started. You'll find an AOL CD-ROM bundled with half the computer magazines at a newsstand. Just insert the CD and follow the directions, which means pressing the Return key about twelve times and entering a credit card number once. The installer itself can figure out your correct modem and system settings, make a connection, check your credit card, put local phone numbers in your preferences file, and set you up with a screen name and password. If your name is Istvan Szekely, you'll probably get your first choice of screen name; if you're Steve Green, you may get SGreen732. That's what happens when a service has 12 million members.

Setting Parental Controls

So I'm visiting some friends a month ago, and their son (a kid in third grade) pipes up and says, "Hey, you're Charlie the Internet guy. Let me show you something cool." We walk over to the computer in Dad's home office and he calls up a Web page detailing the life story, pix and all, of one of the Spice Girls who had an earlier career as a nude model (guess which one).

Actually, that site is pretty mild compared to some. I won't give you details, but pictures of everybody and everything doing many things that look like fun and many that don't, actually, are out there in Web sites and newsgroup posts. There's software to guard access to minors, but most of the minors I know exchange ways to work around it by e-mail.

America Online has taken this problem seriously, and is the safest mode of Internet access for families with kids. After all, there's plenty of time for the little ones to consign their souls to perdition when they get to college; that's why America Online has such a complete system of Parental Controls. You find Parental Controls in the pop-up menu that appears when you click the

My AOL icon in the toolbar. AOL is so proud of this feature that there is also a Parental Control icon on the sign-on screen. As you see on the main screen for this function, AOL even provides an online movie to show you how to set controls.

✔ If you have kids 12 and under, you can assign the KIDS ONLY category to their children's accounts. This restricts young children to the Kids Only channel. A Kids Only account can't send or receive Instant Messages (private real-time communications), and can't enter member-created chat rooms. Also, they can only send and receive text-only e-mail. That means no file attachments or embedded pictures are allowed in e-mail, so nasty little friends can't send your kids stuff they shouldn't see.

✔ Parents of teenagers can pick young teen (ages 13–15) or mature teen (16–17) controls instead. Young Teens can visit some chat rooms, but not member-created rooms or private rooms. That's because even on good old family-oriented AOL, some chat rooms (online forums where people type little messages back and forth) are too raunchy to display in a screen shot here.

✔ Both kinds of teens are also restricted to Web sites for their age categories, selected by the AOL staff for kid-appropriate content. They are also blocked from Internet newsgroups that allow file attachments (the file attachments for most newsgroups are typically, um, artwork). Although newsgroups were originally started as an e-mail information exchange at universities, and many still serve this purpose, this fine old early-Internet, pre-Web function carries lots of triple-X material these days as well. Finally, the category 18+ gives all-bets-off, anything-goes access to all features on AOL and the Internet. Hey, once they can drive, that's the least of your worries.

Because maturity levels vary, Parental Controls let you pick the appropriate level of access for your own kid. Some parents might consider their 15-year-old a "mature teen," while others may wish to maintain the "young teen" setting. You, as the person with the credit card, make the decision. After setting a control level, you can fine-tune the settings by using custom controls. You can adjust specific activities (chat, the Web, e-mail, newsgroups and file downloads) so the kid can get into chat-room political discussions without also getting access to video clips of Tommy Lee and Pamela on the boat. AOL has just done a great job on this control setup.

Exploring with channels and keywords

You have a couple of ways to explore all the areas America Online has developed through a hard-fought decade of dealmaking. The simplest, and a pleasant way to spend an hour or two, is to go directly to the channels screen. See Figure 7-2.

Figure 7-2:
Channel
surfing.

1. **On the Welcome screen, click the Channels button.**

2. **Click a channel that represents an interest you might have.**

3. **Click a likely channel, and you see a new world of icons leading you into the topic.**

There's a lot underneath these channels. The Travel channel, for example, lets you explore destinations, make plans, and shop for cheap reservations and airline tickets — you can get yourself to Cancun without phoning a travel agent. My own favorite, devoted as I am to an entertainment-free existence, is Computing, shown in Figure 7-3. The system already knows you have a Macintosh, so when you click through the Computing page to software, for example, you get your choice of commercial software for the Mac (often at an AOL-negotiated, members-only price) or else selected, reviewed Mac shareware. No poking around to the bottom of a list full of Windows NT offerings. It's nice to feel wanted.

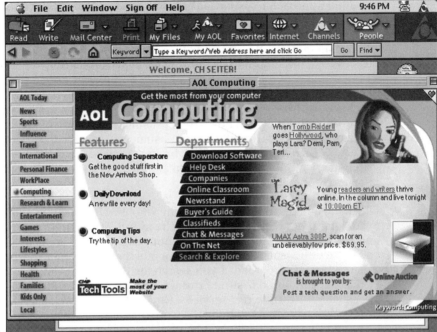

Figure 7-3:
Mac
software
and
hardware,
neatly
arranged.

Lifestyle, anyone?

The only point you may need to investigate here is whether your interests qualify as merely a Lifestyle rather than a separate channel. If you are fascinated by mechanical or electronic gadgets, for example, that's a Lifestyle. It's no trouble to find what you want on AOL (as you'll see later, you can usually do it with a keyword), but the logic of classification is sometimes quite amusing. I'm sorry to say that nearly everything I do is apparently part of a lifestyle, a humiliating bit of stereotype because I live in the Wine Country in California and remember the ratings of every Chardonnay for the last 20 years. They've got my number, I'm afraid.

AOL's special-interest forums are also likened to Lifestyles. The brilliant journalist Mary Eisenhart (editor of MicroTimes), for example,

used to maintain an electronic bulletin board for Deadheads, following them to every concert appearance with a laptop. And she was doing this 12 years ago, when there probably weren't more than a handful of musicians who could identify a modem. Now the AOL Grateful Dead Forum is an amazingly busy spot and a whole universe for fans. And for all the Dead forum users there, I'm really bummed about Jerry, too. I met him a couple of times when he was wandering around the Russian River Jazz Festival, of all places.

Anyway (sorry, I was just flashing back), almost anything you're ever done other than upgrading to System 7.5 qualifies as an AOL lifestyle. You'll find plenty of friends who think you're cool.

Another approach to exploring is to thread your way through America Online's keyword indexing. It's hard to believe now, but the first version of AOL used about twenty keywords. Now, if we printed the mid-1998 keyword list in 9-point Helvetica, it would fill a forty-page appendix and be nearly useless in a few months as keywords get replaced.

Instead, just type anything that pops into your head in the space to the right of "keyword." For this example, I'm using investing as a search topic, partly because America Online hosts the best single collection of investment services for average middle-class consumers anywhere in cyberspace. When a service such as the online stock brokerage service E*Trade sets up an AOL site, America Online helps redesign and simplify the content compared to the corresponding Web site.

If you do an investing search over the whole Web instead of AOL (you could use Netscape Navigator and the Excite search engine to search on the word *investing;* see Chapter 10 for more about Excite and search engines), you get a hundred thousand search results of mostly unusual junk, because the search term is too broad. If you search inside America Online instead, you get about a hundred first-rate results, because AOL has already screened the possibilities down to real services. On a World Wide Web search, you get every Web page that contains the word *investing;* on AOL you get only services that are actually usable. And if you want to do the Web search to see for yourself, you can do that, too.

Sending and receiving letters

America Online always had the nicest online-service e-mail system, even back when e-mail meant plain text messages in a single font and endless hassles dealing with file attachments. Now, along with word-processsor-style fonts and styling (they work inside AOL but don't necessarily transfer correctly through Internet gateways), Version 4.0 sports a whole collection of new "extras."

Extras let you quickly create your own personalized e-mail, add smileys and photos to your e-mail, and use color and styles throughout your messages. See Figure 7-4. To use the extras, just click the Mail Extras button on the Compose Mail window.

AOL Version 4.0 lets you put images directly into the e-mail message, rather than allowing only attachments. To add an image to your message, follow these steps:

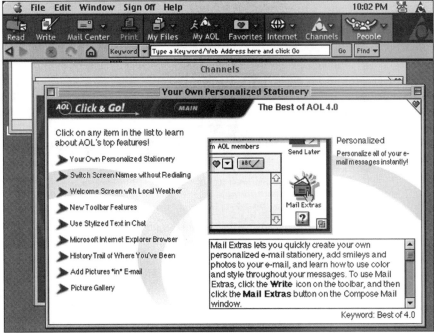

Figure 7-4:
Further
fancy
e-mail
details.

1. **Click the photo icon (on the e-mail toolbar). You'll get a standard Macintosh dialog box for finding your picture.**

   The photo icon looks like a little camera.

2. **Select the picture in this dialog box, and it pops into your e-mail message.**

Although there are obviously tons of personal uses for adding images to e-mail messages, it's also handy for business (for example, including your business card as a PICT file).

Two old standby features of America Online e-mail have not been compromised in the upgrade. AOL still has a more convenient mail-folder structure than the mail systems associated with browsers. See Figure 7-5. That's because America Online e-mail is now in its eighth year of user feedback, and the users are both vociferous and picky. The scheduler feature has actually been made more powerful. See Figure 7-6. You can schedule convenient send and receive times for e-mail and also time-tag individual files for a scheduled download. If you have a modem connection, the right time to download the next 10MB generation of browsers, will, I promise you, be something like 4 a.m. when you're sleeping.

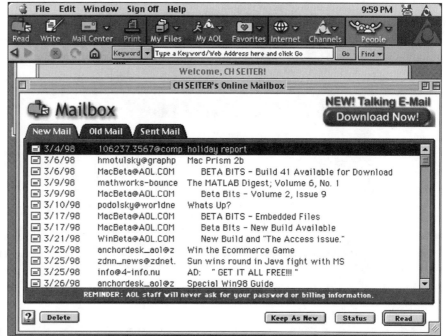

Figure 7-5:
Simple,
reliable
files.

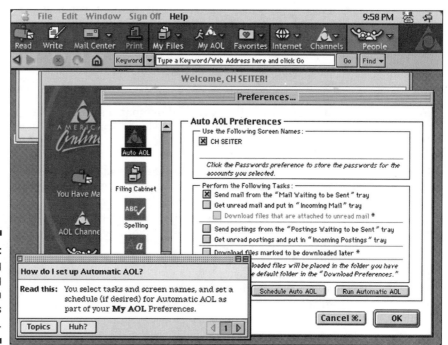

Figure 7-6:
Scheduling
beats sitting
through
downloads
personally.

Chatting with people

If you write computer books, pretty nearly the last thing you want to do for recreation at night is fire up the old Mac and type wisecracks to people thousands of miles away. I mean, they're all wrong about practically *everything* anyway. You may, however, feel like a chat. Click the Personal Connection icon on the Welcome screen, and away you go.

And here's an area where AOL excels. Not only does it have a fabulous range of chat rooms for every topic and interest, it lets you set up your own. America Online has also thought through:

- ✔ The desire of many adults to use chat rooms as a swinging pick-up area, balanced against

- ✔ The nearly universal desire of these same adults not to deal with 13-year-olds posing as hot dating material online

A combination of a great Chat setup and a great Parental Control system is ideal, and America Online's got it. My own advice, having heard hundreds of stories, is that you ought to request an e-mail with a recent photo, and make sure that your correspondent is actually listed in a phone book and has a Member Profile online with AOL.

AOL and the Net

It's a reasonable generalization to say that America Online's main business challenge over the last four years has been to reinvent itself as cyberspace made the transition from online bulletin boards (the early model) to the Web (the current model). A big part of this challenge has been formulating a Web connection that's simple to use and follows traditional AOL navigation, and finding a way to integrate America Online content with Web sites. You can see a first bit of AOL's approach just by clicking the Favorites button. See Figure 7-7. As you'll see, Web sites and locations within AOL itself are just regarded as Favorites page references, in a natural extension of the original concept of "bookmarks" in the first Web browsers. America Online also offers the most user-friendly ways to access some of the older Internet services, such as the file transfer (FTP) and Newsgroup options shown in Figure 7-8, and newer functions, such as Web page composition, so let's work through the list of possibilities.

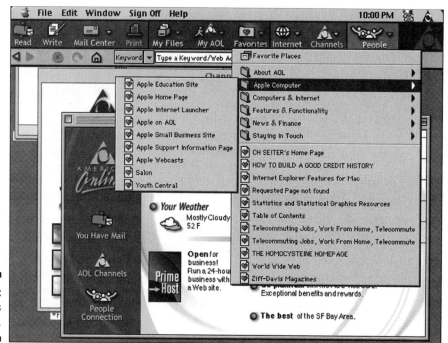

Figure 7-7:
Favorites
everywhere.

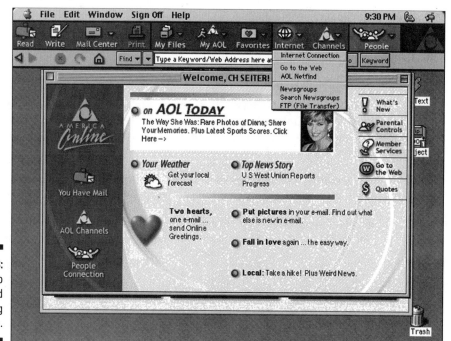

Figure 7-8:
The Web
and
everything
else.

The World Wide Web

You can get to the Web from AOL in any of three easy ways, all of which start up AOL's browser, a custom version of Microsoft Internet Explorer:

✔ Type in a Web address (you'll usually need the full www.blahblah.com instead of just a single word) in the little box on the Web toolbar next to the Keyword button. Then click Go. Up pops the site you wanted. See Figure 7-9.

✔ Click the Internet button on the top toolbar, and pick the Web choice from the pull-down menu.

✔ Choose the Favorites list, and pick either one of AOL's prepackaged Web addresses or one of your own Favorite Web sites.

Any one of these three actions makes a Web page appear in the AOL-customized version of Microsoft Internet Explorer. America Online made a deal with Microsoft that allowed it to use most of the Explorer code while still retaining some corporate identity instead of looking like a mere Explorer clone service (after all, America Online is actually a competitor with Microsoft's own money-losing online service).

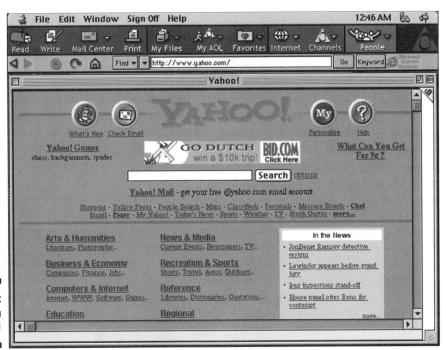

Figure 7-9:
Yahoo! You
found it!

Following its traditional aim of making things easy for beginners, America Online has streamlined a couple of paths for introducing yourself to the Web. It offers its own starting-place site (www.aol.com) that's a sort of simplified version of what you'd see if you went to Excite, except that it also links to America Online's own services as well. The link you'll want to check first is the one at upper left in this screen, the link for AOL Netfind. Once again, you see a page related to Excite. See Figure 7-10. This page, however, has lots of additional nice touches called Time Savers. AOL's market research people did a study (it's easy to do actually — just log the "hits" on sites) to determine which topics people were most eager to find on the Web. Then it made up short lists of the best Web links for these topics, and stashed them here as Time Savers. The links really will save you time, especially compared to poking around the Web with a standard search service.

File transfer protocol

AOL has put its own version of the Net service FTP (file transfer protocol) on the Internet menu, and a jolly good version it is, too. In the bad old days before 1995, one of the main functions of the Internet was simply to ship files from one site to another, and special software and protocols were developed for this function. It was fairly difficult to find files, and even the relatively simple Mac FTP utility called Fetch left something to be desired.

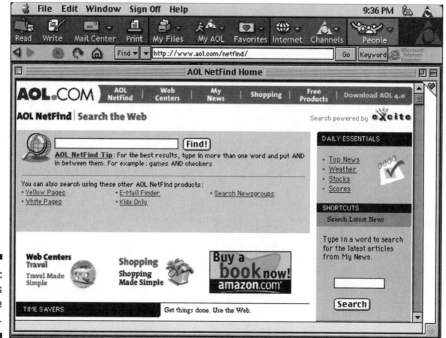

Figure 7-10:
The links
DO save
time.

Now everything is blissfully simple. Even now, in the days of Web dominance, a large percentage of the files you might want for business or for improving your Mac's software capabilities are out there in FTP archives.

In America Online's FTP area (either enter the keyword FTP or click the FTP button in the main Internet screen), you get a screen with some choices for explanation of the service and icons for action. See Figure 7-11. The explanations are important because for many new AOL users, this will be their first glimpse of FTP. And you also see a bit of AOL cleverness: Rather than telling you to learn the earlier Internet search program called Archie and locate file archives on the Net before starting your FTP session, AOL has built in a proprietary search system, and it runs on an index maintained on AOL's own computers. All you have to know is that it's easier than the earlier way. AOL has also collected nearly every file you might want for your Mac, and put it in its own FTP area. You want fonts? You want freeware? You want FAQs? (You can't *handle* the FAQs!! as Jack Nicholson might put it.) They're all here, offering you hours of happy browsing. To try something for yourself, go to AOL's FTP area and try out the giant FTP site that's called sumex-aim. You'll find gigabytes of game files, utilities, font, and programs to try out, all for free.

Newsgroups

Because America Online was building Internet connections before the Web exploded, it has great access to other interesting Net areas, and a big one is newsgroups. If you now click the Newsgroups button on the main Internet screen, you get a personal gateway to the thousands of lively, entertaining, informative, and odd (try alt.conspiracy.diana, for one) newsgroups.

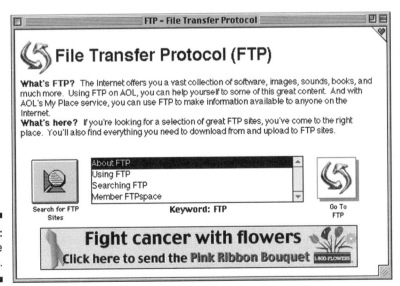

Figure 7-11:
A fast route
to freebies.

To add to this list, you can find newsgroups by searching or by using the Expert Add icon, shown in Figure 7-12. To add a newsgroup with Expert Add, you need the exact name of the newsgroup you're joining. I list some groups in Appendix C, and you can join the group `news.lists` to see the whole list. Actually, using AOL's search procedure is the easiest way.

A key point to watch is the sheer number of messages that crop up in an active group. Newsgroups on what you might think are obscure TV shows can pick up several hundred messages a day. (A lesson from the Internet: The world is big — one percent of millions of people is a lot of people.) You're not going to get around to reading most of the messages unless you feel like spending hours every night online. Fortunately, AOL shows you the subjects of the group's communications, so you can scan them and pick out a few favorites. Then click the Mark As Read icon. Otherwise, you would drown in a week, even with a rigorously austere list.

All these newsgroup correspondences are conducted in plain text. However, you're going to need to know just a bit of Internet code, such as BTW and IMHO, to read and respond to newsgroup messages. A standard set of abbreviations has been developed over the years. Table 7-1 provides a minimal list of these abbreviations so that you know what's going on when you see them. To convey some sort of accent to the text, symbols that look like cartoon faces soon appeared, too. Table 7-2 contains a smattering of these symbols, called *smileys,* and their interpretations.

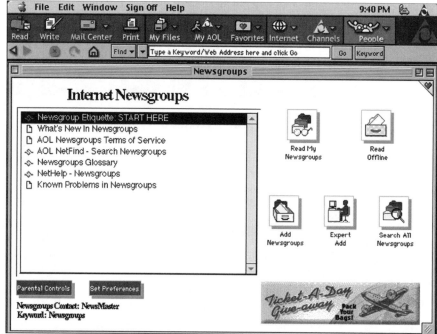

Figure 7-12:
Newsgroups:
information
and
insanity,
too.

Mac newsgroup software may someday let you easily annotate newsgroup messages with sounds and pictures (like America Online e-mail) for impact — a sort of smileys-on-steroids. But for now, these abbreviations and smileys are still standards, and the pictures and sounds are all on the World Wide Web. If you poke around in the AOL communications forums, you can find whole dictionaries of smileys (various jokers have concocted about 500), which may interest you for cultural anthropological reasons.

Table 7-1	Short Takes
Code	*It Stands For*
IMHO	In my humble opinion
BTW	By the way
FYI	For your information
LOL	Laughing out loud
GMTA	Great minds think alike
RTFM	Read the f*&^% manual

Table 7-2	Keep On Smilin'
On the Keyboard	*What It Says*
:)	Smile
;)	Wink
: *	Kiss
: (	Bummer!
: >	Fiendish grin

One last fine feature of America Online newsgroup practice is the ability to block junk messages sent out in batches. These aren't a problem in the professional-oriented newsgroups concerned with geology or statistics, but the more popular newsgroups get hundreds of junk EARN THOUSANDS AT HOME!!!! messages, and worse. So America Online gives you the option of simply screening out all junk. See Figure 7-13. Hey, just do it.

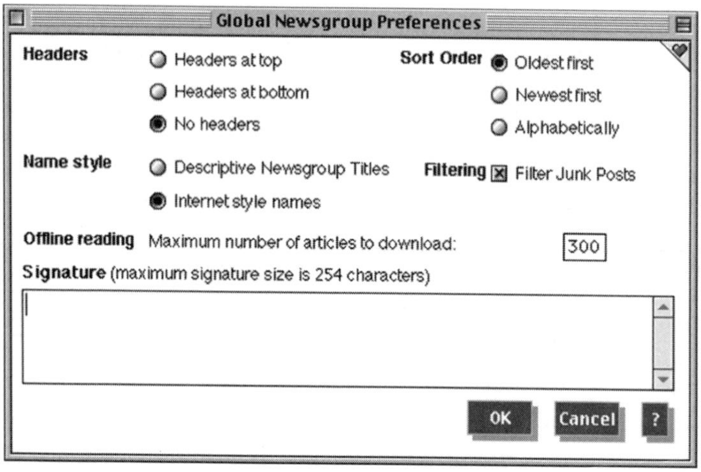

Global Newsgroup Preferences

Headers		Sort Order	
	○ Headers at top		● Oldest first
	○ Headers at bottom		○ Newest first
	● No headers		○ Alphabetically

Name style
○ Descriptive Newsgroup Titles   **Filtering** ☒ Filter Junk Posts
● Internet style names

Offline reading   Maximum number of articles to download: 300

Signature (maximum signature size is 254 characters)

[OK] [Cancel] [?]

Figure 7-13:
Junk
filtering.
Now if they
could do it
for paper . . .

Older Stories: Previous Versions of AOL

Now although the latest version of AOL is indeed bursting with magnificence, the service has done a good enough job of "backward compatibility," which just means that Versions 2.6 and 3.0 are still usable in the new 4.0-based service. Why is this important? For some users it won't be, but for others it's a key point. As each release of AOL software appears, it's about twice as big as its predecessor. If you are trying to run AOL on a laptop with a mere 8MB RAM, you'll find Version 4.0 to be a bulky traveling companion. Versions 2.6 and 3.0 are going to be easier for you to use than 4.0 if you're working with an older Mac or limited RAM.

Version 3.0 had the size advantage that the browser was a separate piece of software, so that AOL itself could run comfortably in a mere 4MB. Not only is that fine for older laptops, but having a separate browser lets you collect e-mail, use AOL services, and perform every function but Web browsing at impressive speed.

The services are the same and are quite comparable in ease of use and features. The main difference between Versions 3 and 4 is really that in 4, the mail system has fancier touches, and the Microsoft Internet Explorer browser has been completely integrated. Again, if you're just using AOL for chat, e-mail, and standard services (America Online's own travel agency and shopping services), you don't necessarily have to rush to upgrade.

To make life even simpler on the road, you can still use the positively tiny AOL 2.6 (less than a megabyte, which is why it shipped on all those floppies). The e-mail in 2.6 is plain text, but it can also handle enclosures, and it's fast, efficient, and small enough to run alongside other applications even on the most limited Mac you're likely to have around the house.

Browser wars, round 5

Under lots of pressure from users, America Online in 1998 came up with a custom version of Netscape Navigator to use with AOL as your Internet service provider. Now that AOL owns Netscape, this feature will likely become standard. That means you can have America Online as your only online connection, and still use Netscape Navigator just like the sophisticates who sign on with a local ISP and think AOL is for kids. Amazingly, speaking of kids, America Online also thought through the process of keeping all the Parental Controls in place when you switch browsers. That's something the local ISPs can't quite do yet.

Part IV
Your Mac in the Web World

The 5th Wave By Rich Tennant

It started as a wrap-around porch, and then Stuart found a section on medieval architecture on the Internet.

In this part . . .

This part is chock-full of information to help you make the most of the Web. I discuss e-mail, effective searching, putting together your own Web page, and making the most of those special audio and visual effects that fill the Web.

I also discuss the Web from a business point of view, using Microsoft Office to run a business, as well as from the consumer's point of view.

Chapter 8

E-Mail: The World on the Wire

In This Chapter

▶ First steps in e-mail

▶ Putting e-mail to work

▶ The Web takes over e-mail

▶ Sound and pictures in the mail

*T*he story on e-mail is that it's the most important business use of the Internet, and also the most important social use. All the buzzing sounds and flashing lights on Web pages are fascinating, but it's e-mail that does the work. It's also the most effective way for most people to keep in frequent touch with each other over long distances.

You can send e-mail to any one of the Internet's 300-or-so million users if

✔ You own a Macintosh and a modem (this is the most typical situation).

✔ Your Mac is on a network, and the network has its own Internet connection.

✔ You have any computer that can connect to the Web, so you can send e-mail by Web-based e-mail services.

✔ Your Mac is directly connected to a network that is an Internet *host* — a computer system with its own Internet numerical address, usually in an office. You don't even need a modem in this case.

The first e-mail services open to the public (businesses have had in-house e-mail since the 1960s) were national organizations like MCI Mail and CompuServe. In the beginning, if you had an MCI account, you could send mail to anyone else with an MCI account, but you couldn't send mail out of the system. Actually, you could have had an MCI message delivered on paper to a regular street address, but for a discouragingly high fee.

By the early 1990s, however, everyone involved in the e-mail business had figured out that universal connection on the Internet was the future of e-mail. If CompuServe, MCI, and Prodigy became Internet hosts, then users could easily send messages from one service to another. It was obviously a good idea.

Surprisingly, given the history of good ideas, they actually followed through. Every business that can afford to advertise in a magazine is now connected to the Internet and has universal e-mail capability. The rise of the Web, with an emphasis on multimedia, has meant a fantastic expansion of e-mail to include sound and video. You can send just about any kind of mail across the Web, except paper.

These connections worked, in the early days, because the messages were primitive. The e-mail messages I'm talking about are plain text; you can create these messages on any type of computer and read them on any other. And because they're just text, they're compact — a one-page color picture file is 500 times bigger than a file containing a page of text. That made a big difference when you used the old slow modems (9600 bps) for Internet connection. Now you can send systemwide sound-plus-picture messages across the Internet, but because the typical 1998 modem (33.6 to 56 Kbps) is only four to five times faster, the real Golden Age of online video e-mail will probably have to wait for widespread adoption of cable modem or some other megabit-speed connection.

Mac Access

Two years ago, I would have felt compelled to offer a few pages full of UNIX mailing commands in a cheat sheet. Now, I can duck the whole, ugly mess. Even UNIX hotshots themselves are converting their systems wholesale to an interface called X Windows, which looks for all the world like a small-print version of a Macintosh screen.

Hosts, mailboxes, and you

Suppose that you sign up with a major Internet service provider, such as AT&T WorldNet. WorldNet gives you a local dial-up phone number. You use the name "Joe Cool," and you choose "joec" as your Net name. Your Internet address, then, is `joec@att.worldnet.com`. WorldNet is the *host,* meaning a computer system with its own Internet numerical address. You, in turn, are a user attached to that host, but you are not a host yourself.

As a service for outgoing e-mail, WorldNet becomes the equivalent of the corner mailbox.

You send a message to your pal Michael Nifty, `miken@aol.com` (America Online). WorldNet routes the message to the receiving Internet host, `aol.com`. The receiving host acts like one of those big office mailbox systems with hundreds of pigeonholes. It finds `miken`, stores the message, and notifies your pal that he has new mail. Usually, he sees this notice the next time he logs into the `aol.com` system, although sometimes mysterious delays occur, for hours and sometimes, although rarely, days.

You can get Internet e-mail access in lots of ways. You can use the plain, guess-your-next-command style that's standard with UNIX, or you can get a really friendly mail interface from America Online. Ironically, Internet e-mail access costs between $10 and $20 a month, whichever type of access you pick. Look, you had enough sense to pick a Mac in the first place — make your own decision.

Using E-Mail

Any time you sign up with an Internet service provider, you are assigned to a mail system, and you pick out an e-mail name. If you are Ted Anzac and you sign up for America Online, you can probably have the address tedanzac@aol.com. If you are Steve Smith, you are probably going to find that name taken, so you have to settle for stevesmith951@aol.com or else do something creative with your middle initial.

Many people, intrigued by the anonymity of the Net, pick colorful e-mail names like bonzo@att.worldnet.com or surfdude@aol.com. My advice: Think about how it's going to look on a business card. Maybe you don't really want to be known as "HotBootie" to your real-estate clients after all.

More advice from an old pro

Every few months (for the last twenty years!), I've gotten a truly anguished phone call from one friend or another. The problem takes several forms:

- Someone finds out weeks later that he was fired because the boss saw an e-mail in which that person called the boss brain-dead.

- Someone finds that a trusted friend has forwarded embarrassing e-mail to a romantic rival.

- A steamy, semi-porn e-mail exchange gets printed out and widely distributed.

I worked at a software company where the marketing vp's online dope deal with the loading dock guy became common knowledge. This was not a career-enhancing move. So my advice, as a Net old-timer who's seen everything go wrong that can possibly go wrong:

DON'T PUT A MESSAGE IN AN E-MAIL THAT YOU WOULDN'T WEAR ON A T-SHIRT.

If you ignore this advice, someday you'll be very unhappy that you did. E-mail is not secure, and it won't be, anytime soon.

Choosing E-Mail Software

Internet service providers now provide you with an automatic dial-up tool, so connecting is a snap (in the Bad Old Days it was quite a chore). All you need is your name and your password, and your Mac's modem dials a local number and connects you to the system's Internet host computer.

In 1998 or later, you'll probably just start your browser and begin surfing because the browser can handle e-mail, too. But consider these reasons for using a dedicated e-mail program instead:

- ✔ One of the best e-mail programs, Eudora Light, can be downloaded free at www.macworld.com or www.eudora.com.

- ✔ An e-mail program is faster than a browser, so if you're traveling and can't get a local number, it's a lot cheaper to use.

- ✔ You may want to use a PowerBook, and not be willing to pay for the expensive memory upgrades for laptops. E-mail programs are always much smaller than browsers — you can collect your mail on an old 4MB PowerBook with Eudora Light, but no popular browser even fits on this system.

With Eudora Light, your mailbox looks like Figure 8-1. It actually looks a lot like the Mail window of a Web browser (and why not, because they all shamelessly copied Eudora), but it actually sports a few more convenience features.

Using e-mail on AOL

On this planet at least, more e-mail accounts are on America Online than anywhere else. And, to be fair, AOL has actually been pretty good to its Mac-using members — AOL 3.0 for us shipped later than the Windows version, but at least it was fast and was pretty well debugged. AOL 4.0 now being the same on both Mac and Windows means that you can buy *America Online For Dummies,* 4th Edition (John Kaufeld, IDG Books Worldwide, Inc., 1998) for more advice. All you have to do is ignore the annoying little Windows underlines on menu items.

The e-mail system is the simplest known to man in terms of connection details: You don't have to know *any* of them. Log on to AOL, and a friendly robot voice (actually, it's the voice of a guy who's a newscaster from Texas) tells you "you've got mail!" Click the mailbox and double-click a mail entry, and you see something like Figure 8-2, complete with its self-explanatory icons (even if this is your first e-mail, you can probably guess what happens when you click Reply).

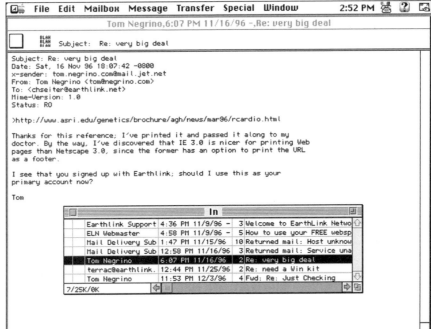

Figure 8-1:
Eudora
Light is
clean,
simple, and
e-mail only.

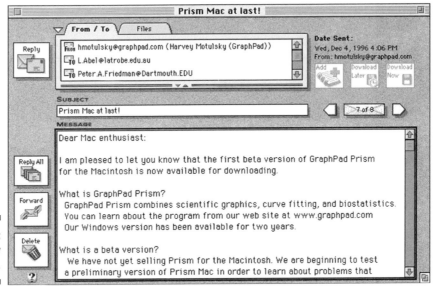

Figure 8-2:
AOL's new
e-mail look.

To write an e-mail on AOL, just select Mail⇨Compose Mail. You get a screen like Figure 8-3, where you have a message space, icons for sending the message or saving it for sending later, a little address space, and a cc space (for addresses of other people who should get copies of the e-mail). Because you're just starting out, why not send a letter to the President? (By the way, president@whitehouse.gov is the real address.)

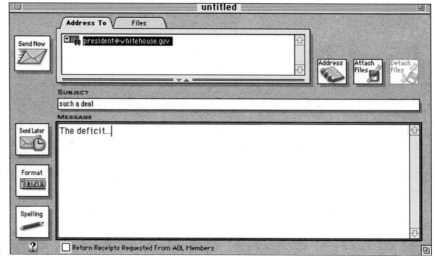

Figure 8-3:
Dear Mr.
President,
on AOL.

The AOL menu contains lots of convenient options, all of which, fortunately, are explained in the Help functions in the Mail Center (see Figure 8-4). You'll want to check out the options for automatically sending and collecting mail, because AOL has gotten a bit crowded and you're likely to be happier with automatically sending your messages at 4:30 a.m. than trying to get through a busy signal at midnight.

Figure 8-4:
A complete
mail menu.

Spel chek your address

If you make a mistake in addressing your e-mail, the message won't get through. Some systems tell you after a brief delay that the address isn't working. Typically, however, the message goes out on the Internet and gets bounced back to you hours later — you'll find it returned the next time you connect to your host system. In other words, it's critical to get Internet addresses exactly right. Unlike the post office, the Internet has no way to work around your typos. I once got a letter addressed to C. Smelter in Hellburg, CA — there is nothing corresponding to this kind of creative interpretation online.

Some useful AOL features deserve a closer look. The main working Mail window has a particularly useful feature — the Ignore button (see Figure 8-5). AOL tries to stop people from sending you electronic junk mail, but quite a bit gets through anyway. Just click the junk item, click Ignore, and it will be gone the next time you check your mail.

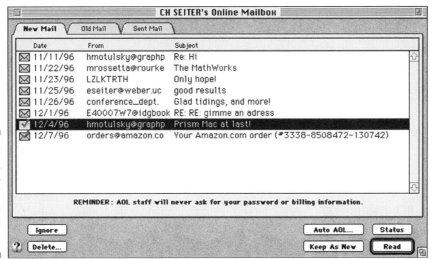

Figure 8-5:
AOL
Ignore —
man's (and
woman's)
best e-mail
friend.

E-mail from Netscape Communicator 4.5

Eudora's great, and AOL is friendly, but Web activity is the big deal on the Internet, so doing your e-mail from within your Web browser is usually the most convenient way to go. Outlook Express, the mail program shipped with

Microsoft Internet Explorer 4.0, is feature-rich, especially because it's heavily "influenced" by features from Netscape and Lotus. The mail system in Netscape Communicator 4.5 is also sufficiently feature-rich for most mail purposes you may have.

Looking at a World Wide Web page in Netscape Communicator, you may well ask, "Where's the mail?" It's there all right, under the Communicator menu at the right (see Figure 8-6).

If you look at a mail sample in Netscape Communicator (see Figure 8-7 — it's actually the same mailbox we looked at with Eudora if you'd like to compare the two styles), you see the first inkling of the expansion of e-mail beyond plain text. The mail message contains a Web address (an `http:\\` reference, and because this mail document has been opened in a browser, the browser knows what to do if you click this address).

But that's only the beginning. It's not much of a programming challenge to make the mail function in a browser do any of the other things a browser can do. That includes, with the appropriate browser plug-ins, sound clips and bits of video; the only caution in this area is that sound and video files are simply gigantic compared to the typical five-line plain-text mail message.

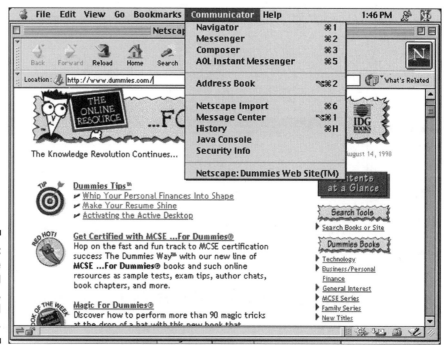

Figure 8-6:
There's the mail program, now called Messenger.

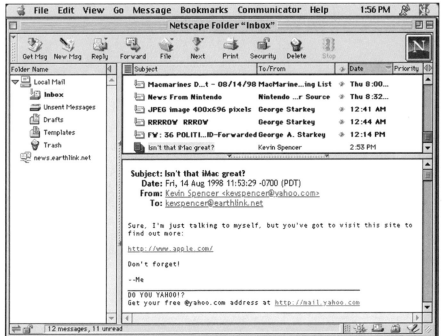

Figure 8-7:
E-mail with
a live URL
link.

The price for all this magnificence is that you may have to know a bit more about setup details than you would with AOL. If you just accept the deal packaged by your ISP, all your mail info will be set up automatically. If you want to change providers, for example, to a local service run in your home town, you'll have to fill in the Mail Preferences screen under Options in the main Navigator menu (see Figure 8-8). Don't worry, though; Navigator is popular enough that most Internet service providers give you guidance on managing your mail settings if you're collecting from multiple services or other such trickery.

I'll have a Web special, hold the mail

You have several options if you need more e-mail addresses (say, one address strictly for e-mail to friends and family, and another for business). In AOL, for example, you can create more screen names that act as additional e-mail addresses. Internet service providers such as EarthLink will provide you with additional addresses for a fee.

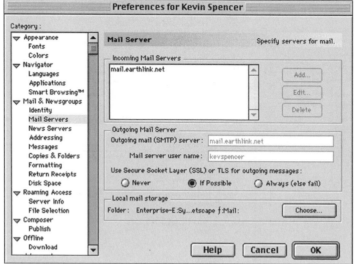

Ten Internet e-mail tips

1. The best way to find someone's address is simply to ask for it over the phone. Sometimes you can even state your message. Ain't technology neat?

2. If tip 1 fails, try looking up the address at http:\\sss.four11.com.

3. Make your Internet name recognizable instead of using squiggy@netcom.com or something like that.

4. DON'T USE ALL CAPITALS IN A MESSAGE. THEY MAKE IT SEEM LIKE YOU'RE SHOUTING.

5. Remember the Golden Rule, and be nice, because everyone else can do unto you automatically. Over and over. Over and over. Over and over.

6. E-mail jokes don't always work. In plain text, it's harder to tell when you're kidding, you lamentable buffoon (just kidding).

7. Try to keep it short. U dnt hv 2 wrt lk ths, but if you have a long message, send it as an enclosure instead of a text message.

8. Make sure that the person receiving the message can tell who you are (put your name and phone number in the text of the message).

9. In unsolicited messages, you should put a ? first in the subject line, as in ?are you the joanm who went to high school in Greenwood, WI?

10. Pay attention to the ongoing discussions of electronic message security in the news. You may want to watch Big Brother instead of letting him watch you.

But the best option is to sign up for a Web-based e-mail account with one of several free Web e-mail services, such as Hotmail (www.hotmail.com) and Yahoo Mail (mail.yahoo.com). These services work just like your e-mail account through AOL or your ISP, except that, in order to access your mail account, you must be able to access anything that can display Web pages off the Internet. That means that you could actually use that *PC* at work to read your e-mail! (And *you* thought that computer wasn't useful!)

Chapter 9

Looking Around in Cyberspace

· ·

In This Chapter

▶ Finding a job

▶ Getting educated

▶ Getting healthy

▶ Discovering the Web's first topic: Science

▶ Climb aboard for fun time!

· ·

*1*t took about two years, but the world has put together an interesting and nearly complete image of itself on the Web. Whatever you may find interesting, you can bet that other people find it interesting also, and you can bet they're out there setting up Web sites, too.

I'm not just talking about looking up pictures of the cast of *Friends* or finding Mac shareware. I'm talking about every topic thought up by mankind since the dawn of civilization. Literally. You can find out how to make flint arrowheads. You can discover how to play *senet*, a five-thousand-year-old game so popular in the Egypt of the pharaohs that people were typically buried with their senet sets. You can look up the full text of all the research available from classical Greece. Zooming toward the present, you can find out everything you need to know about the cultures of the Orient, Apple's plans for your Mac's future, and the complete script of any popular movie (my favorite is the script of *Dumb and Dumber* — the parakeet scene is immortal). What more could you want?!

This chapter lists many Web sites you can browse, including sites to help you find a job, sites that offer online continuing education courses, sites about health and health-related issues, sites about science, and sites for fun. One thing you may want is a much longer section on fun than you'll find in this chapter. Try *Yahoo! Wild Web Rides* by Tarin Towers, Ken Badertscher, Wayne Cunningham, and Laura Buskirk (IDG Books Worldwide, Inc.). In real life, I'm a respected authority on lots of topics, but fun isn't one of them. My wife, looking over my shoulder as I was working on this chapter, had to point out to me that *online scientific calculators* would probably best be filed under science and not fun. It's that bad. I collect antique slide rules, too. Umm, the other people who write computer books tend to be like that too, you know.

Now Hiring

I do know about work, however, and the Web has become the best place to look for some kinds of jobs. In this section I show you some sites, list a few others, and make some suggestions.

The first jobs on the Internet were found in Usenet newsgroups, not on the Web. Performing a search in AltaVista (`www.altavista.digital.com`) on newsgroups instead of the Web using the keywords of your job specialty is still worth your time. The Web has big sites for employment, though. This section gives you five places to start.

JobBank USA

`http://jobbankusa.com/`

This site (see Figure 9-1) is huge and recommended by every personnel director I know. It has a reasonably well-designed search form as well, so you don't have to spend your whole life clicking through lists (see Figure 9-2).

Wanted: Computer folks

The job list is getting broader in scope, but it is still somewhat specialized at most of these Web sites. If you can write programs in Java or C++, manage an enterprise-wide Web site, or, better yet, actually have succeeded in selling advertising space on a site, hundreds of employers are just dying to hear from you. If you're the best Toyota mechanic in Los Angeles, hundreds of employers are just dying to hear from you — but most of them haven't posted offers on the Web just yet.

Here are two cases to illustrate this situation. I got a call from a friend who had worked in several advertising agencies representing computer companies and wanted a new job in Web-based advertising. And she wanted the job to start at $55,000 a year and be located within three miles of her favorite restaurant in Berkeley, CA. A quick search turned up *11* such jobs, and she took one of them.

Then I got another call, from a friend who has one of the best reputations on the West Coast as a furniture craftsman specializing in exotic hardwoods. When business around San Francisco was a little slack, he asked me to see what kinds of projects might be posted to the Web. I found in the U.S. a total of *one* project, located in Marblehead, MA. Jobs on the Web still tend to be mostly computer-related, probably for the reason that if you're looking on a Web site, you must at least know a bit about computers.

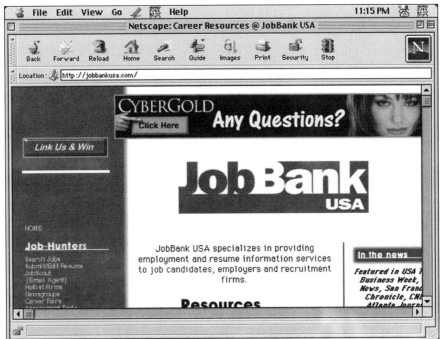

Figure 9-1:
A huge job bank.

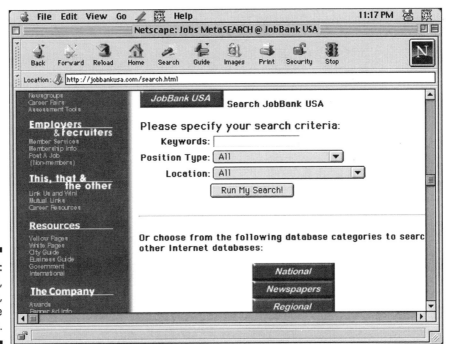

Figure 9-2:
And, fortunately, a key to the bank.

StudentCenter

http://www.studentcenter.com/

I hope that you already have a job you like, or if you don't, that you're a student. If you are a student, there's exactly one place to start a Web job search (see Figure 9-3). Search this site for two reasons: It offers the best help with drafting a first real resume, and it includes the most entry-level job listings.

Hard@Work

http://www.hardatwork.com/

Hard@Work isn't so much a job-search site as a career-counseling site (see Figure 9-4). It has lots of humor, advice, and discussions of strategies for getting along in the workplace. This site is at least as helpful as reading *Dilbert* every day.

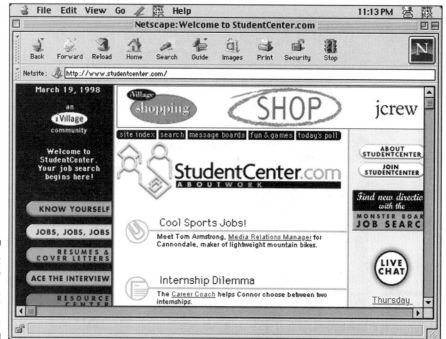

Figure 9-3:
After school, head over here.

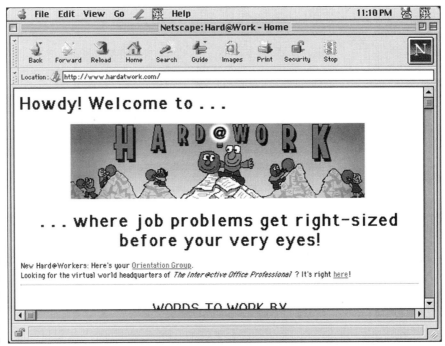

Figure 9-4:
Lighten up
at this job-
related site.

Career Mosaic

http://www.careermosaic.com/

This giant site is updated amazingly often (see Figure 9-5). Although it shares the Web's general bias in favor of computer jobs, this year the site has expanded to include significant numbers of regular jobs, as well.

CareerPath

http://www.workingsmart.com/careerp.htm

Last but not least is the wave of the future. This site logs the want ads from newspapers in most of America's big cities (see Figure 9-6). As papers begin to develop more elaborate Web sites, their content is migrating online. Because these help-wanted ads are searchable and take e-mail resumes, making a case for the ads in black ink is hard.

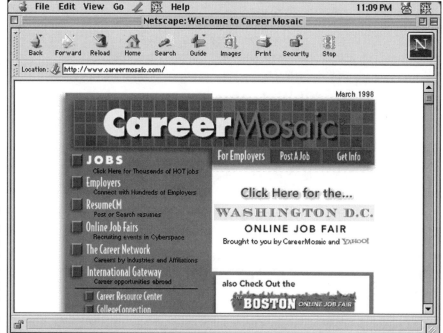

Figure 9-5:
Search this
site for
computer
jobs as well
as other
jobs.

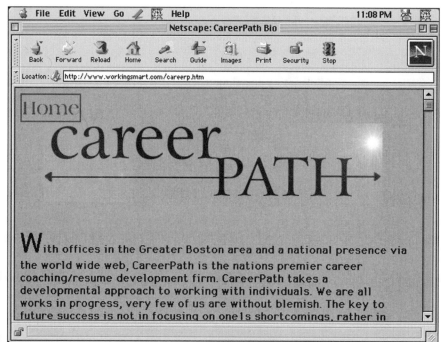

Figure 9-6:
Jobs all
over.

Other job sites

Here's a list of the other job sites rated most helpful by not only Web organizations but real-life job counselors as well:

- ✔ www.occ.com
- ✔ www.careermag.com
- ✔ www.techweb.com
- ✔ www.hightechcareers.com
- ✔ www.jobsmart.org
- ✔ www.adone.com
- ✔ www.jobcenter.com
- ✔ www.intellimatch.com

The Web and Education?

An author faces this subject with considerable trepidation. In the early 1950s, many writers were so enthusiastic about the educational potential of the exciting new medium called *television* that they predicted it could replace traditional schooling in most cases. They thought that people would just sit around at home and watch brilliantly designed educational programming until we were the most cultivated people on earth. Instead, we got *Funniest Home Videos*. A tiny amount of real educational programming is available on the shrinking, under-attack, now-semi-commercial PBS network. And many critics would argue that television is a powerful force for promoting sheer illiteracy.

Later, in the 1980s, attempts to teach online courses sprang up in many university extension programs. The majority of these courses didn't work out, partly from problems with courseware design and slow modem speeds. But even now, in a world of much faster modems and more powerful computers, online courses are making pretty slow headway against traditional courses and extension services. The World Wide Web is not only graphics-oriented but more instantly interactive than earlier online schemes, and therefore looks like an ideal way to teach remote courses. But only the next decade will tell whether the Web becomes a key medium for transfer of serious information, or whether commercial pressures will distort its content exclusively toward advertising-based information, goofy personal Web pages, and sleazy adult sites.

Real Education on the Web

In high school, you typically take a geometry class that's recognizably the same subject you would have taken in Alexandria in 200 BC. In chemistry, topics are similarly presented in order of discovery, with the late-eighteenth century taking up the first few months. Education is a very conservative domain, and although lots of people have set up resources on the Web, it's not time yet for a comprehensive catalog. This survey will therefore look at a few outstanding examples.

Providing resources

The first educational function of the Web is to provide online resources for remote users. If you think about it for a minute, you'll realize that every class handout, every textbook, and every presentation you ever saw in school can be duplicated on the Web. The audio-visual resources of the best high school in North America are pathetically modest in comparison to the resources of a good Web site. For example, the Cool Student Resources site at

```
http://www.teleport.com/~burrell/
```

has links outward to every useful resource for K-12 education. The material at this site (see Figure 9-7) has also been screened for quality — all of it is first rate.

Another general directory for online educational resources, again aimed more or less at the K-12 set (face it — K-12 education has to be done right in the first place) is the index site at

```
http://k12.school.net/
```

This service (see Figure 9-8) is the education-only equivalent of a high-powered resource like Yahoo!.

Continuing education

Of course, the real promise of Web educational material is in *distance learning,* as it's called in the trade. Whatever education you may have obtained, you can nearly always use a bit more. Maybe you need to finish a college degree, maybe your new job requires you to know a bit of accounting (and you were an English major), or maybe, like most engineers, you need to have your skills retooled every few years (the information lifetime in electrical engineering is like the date stamp on a yogurt container these days).

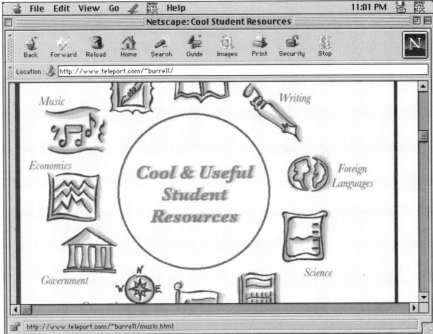

Figure 9-7:
K-12
education —
a big
resource.

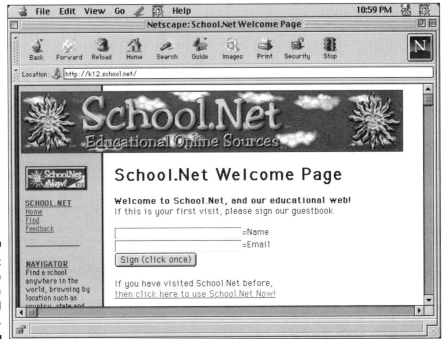

Figure 9-8:
A one-stop
online
educational
resource.

College courses offered online, by the way, don't have to suffer at all in comparison to classroom courses. Especially because the content can be designed interactively by a group of teachers, online courses tend to be richer in content and have better sets of examples than standard textbook courses. The statistics course on the Chance page (see Figure 9-9), for example, is better than any statistics course you took and is not only rigorous but easier to follow and more entertaining:

```
http://www.geom.umn.edu/docs/snell/chance/welcome.html
```

If you don't believe that online courses will ever be more than a sort of night-school replacement, consider the institution in Figure 9-10. If Harvard is interested in selling online courses, you confidently may expect that everyone else will be interested, too. The big issue here is that expenses for college education have been growing much faster than the general inflation rate, which is itself something of a disaster. An eighteen-year-old, facing the prospect of paying off $100,000 in college loans with a job that starts at $28,000 per year, may justifiably be curious about finding ways to collect at least some credits by means other than the standard and expensive classroom instruction.

```
http://www.harvard.edu/
```

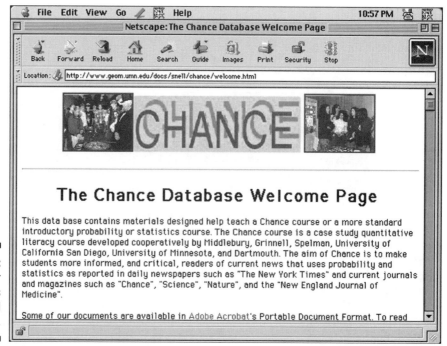

Figure 9-9:
A better statistics world online.

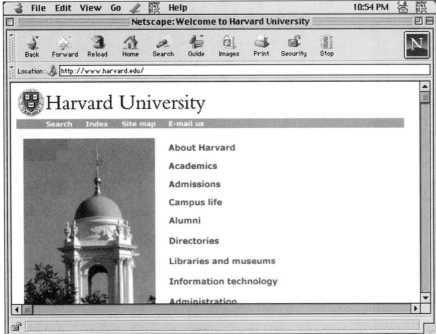

Figure 9-10:
Visit
Harvard
online.

Figure 9-11 is an example of the direction that continuing education is taking. The University of Vermont lets you finish your degree work or start a new one, conveniently online. By the way, a search on *continuing education* in your own state is now likely to turn up a similar program somewhere near you.

```
http://uvmce.uvm.edu:443/
```

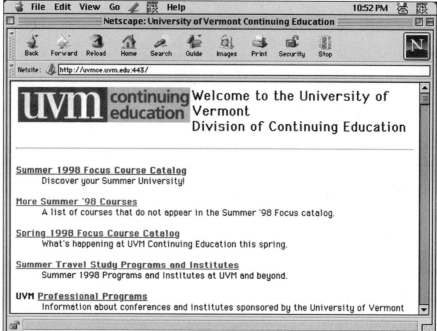

Figure 9-11:
Stay in
school
forever!

Health

Health has always been a hot area on the Internet. There were thousands of newsgroups and mailing lists on health topics even before the Web became popular. These got converted into Web sites at lightning speed, and thus health is one of the biggest information exchanges on the Web. As a category, "health" includes straight medicine and lots of fringe areas as well. The following modest listing of URLs and comments is at least a reasonable starting place.

Acupuncture.com

```
http://www.acupuncture.com
```

This site is not only a very complete acupuncture resource, but it's rapidly developing links to all sorts of alternative-medical sites (see Figure 9-12). You can download your own map of all these little places that you're supposed to stick needles for particular results, and for that matter you can order your own set of needles.

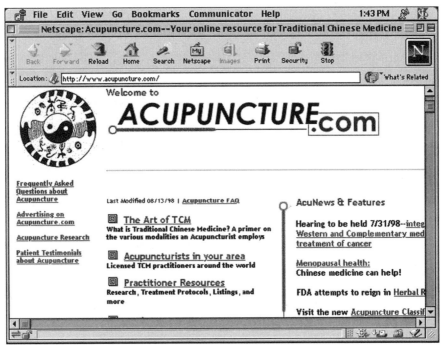

File Edit View Go Bookmarks Communicator Help   1:43 PM

Netscape: Acupuncture.com--Your online resource for Traditional Chinese Medicine

Back Forward Reload Home Search Netscape Images Print Security Stop

Location: http://www.acupuncture.com/   What's Related

Welcome to
ACUPUNCTURE.com

Frequently Asked Questions about Acupuncture

Advertising on Acupuncture.com

Acupuncture Research

Patient Testimonials about Acupuncture

Last Modified 08/13/98 | Acupuncture FAQ

The Art of TCM
What is Traditional Chinese Medicine? A primer on the various modalities an Acupuncturist employs

Acupuncturists in your area
Licensed TCM practitioners around the world

Practitioner Resources
Research, Treatment Protocols, Listings, and more

AcuNews & Features

Hearing to be held 7/31/98--integ Western and Complementary med treatment of cancer

Menopausal health: Chinese medicine can help!

FDA attempts to reign in Herbal R

Visit the new Acupuncture Classif

Figure 9-12:
Get stuck!

AIDS

http://www.teleport.com/~celinec/aids.shtml

This one stop has all the information on AIDS that's available online, which in fact is everything (see Figure 9-13). The HIV-positive community has been connected by bulletin boards for a decade, and all that material migrated to the Web.

The Alexander technique

http://none.coolware.com/health/alex_tech/FlyerBody.html

The Alexander technique is a form of bodywork that actually dates back to earlier in this century and has been in much favor with actors and other performers. It amounts to a reeducation of your habitual patterns of muscle tension.

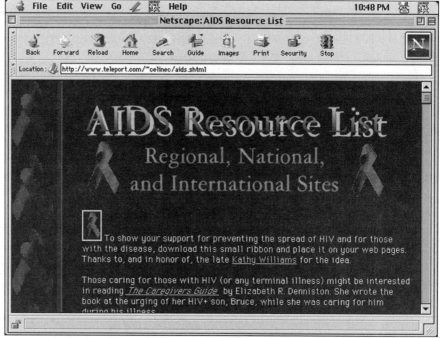

Figure 9-13: At long last, some realistic hope for those living with HIV.

Save your own life

The health resources on the Web are not only extensive. In many instances, these resources are more up-to-date than those in your friendly family physician's mind. The reason that this third edition of *The Internet For Macs For Dummies* got finished at all is a mildly interesting Web-related story.

Lying in a hospital with my second stroke in six months, my daughter (Mary Toth, a Web hotshot herself who started writing for *Macworld* at age fourteen) showed up for a visit. We decided to formulate a few simple Web searches to see if we could gain some insight into my condition. One of the searches was an AltaVista query on

+stroke +multiple +"under 50"

The search turned up a reference to a condition called homocysteinuria, which, despite the endless amount you may have read in the popular press about cholesterol and high blood pressure, is actually a prominent culprit in strokes and heart attacks in people of less-than-retirement age. Following a rather standard pattern in medical research, the physician who first brought attention to this condition was banished from Harvard for questioning the standard explanation of strokes, and today you still can't expect most non-specialists to know much about it. But it's what was happening with me, and luckily there's a fairly straightforward fix-up.

Anxiety

http://www.sover.net/~schwcof/

You can order a video on anxiety problems and get FAQs on anxiety disorders (see Figure 9-14). You can also find a lot of information on the controversial topic of repressed memory (this site strongly backs most cases).

Asthma

http://www.cco.caltech.edu/~wrean/asthma-gen.html

Here's the main Frequently-Asked-Questions file on asthma, with links to subtopic pages. You also can find lots of information about new kinds of treatment.

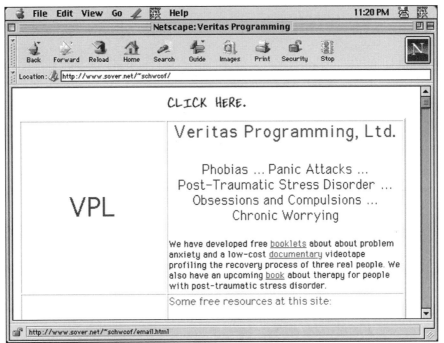

Figure 9-14: Anxiety and related problems.

Autism resources

```
http://web.syr.edu/~jmwobus/autism/
```

You can find long lists of information resources on this baffling disorder. If you want to convince yourself that cognitive psychology doesn't have all the answers yet, check out some of the discussions in these FAQs.

BIO Online

```
http://cns.bio.com/bio.html
```

This site is a serious research-data exchange center. It includes an employment center with dozens of major sponsors, all kinds of industry investment and regulatory information, and online journals.

Cybercise

```
http://www.cybercise.com/
```

If you've started to slump over permanently from working day and night at a keyboard, or if your wrists are starting to feel odd, you may want to order some exercise equipment from these people.

CyberShrink

```
http://www.cybershrink.com/
```

This site is one of many e-mail psychological counseling services (see Figure 9-15). The evidence proving the efficacy of this system isn't necessarily in yet, but it's hard to believe that it will be much worse than the efficacy of standard office-based "talking cure" practice. Maybe people are more willing to go into more depth with someone they can't see.

Deaf World Web

```
http://dww.deafworldweb.org/
```

This single, unified, well-organized site (see Figure 9-16) has everything for deaf people online, and it's available in four languages. If you consider for a moment, you'll realize that the Web is one of the best resources for deaf people that's ever been developed.

Chapter 9: Looking Around in Cyberspace

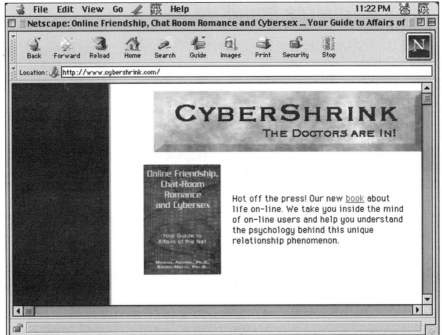

Figure 9-15:
Tell the cybershrinks your problems.

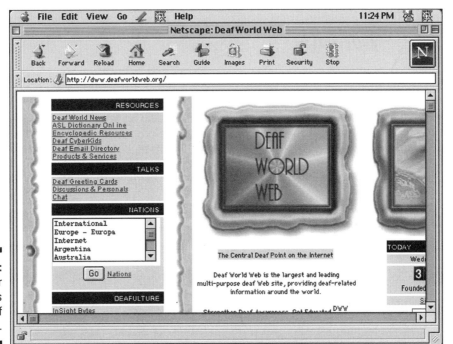

Figure 9-16:
Superior resources for deaf people.

Diabetes home page

http://www.nd.edu/~hhowisen/diabetes.html

Lavish use of graphics and searching over other diabetes resources make this an award-winning site. The graphics mean that this site is better with a very fast connection.

Diabetes knowledgebase

http://www.biostat.wisc.edu/diaknow/index.htm

This site provides a searchable database on all diabetes topics, so you can look up details on particular types and complications.

Disabilities Access Online

http://www.pavilion.co.uk/CommonRoom/DisabilitiesAccess/

Similar to Deaf World Web, this site is a central directory for all sorts of disability issues — medical, physical, and legal.

DocTalk

http://www.indirect.com/user/cnewhall/

This service provides online medical advice, and it's pretty good advice at that. The developer, Clark Newhall, is also an attorney, so it's a good bet that he's thought through the legal implications of handing out this kind of advice to strangers online. One interesting feature of this service is called SkinFlix, which offers QuickTime movies and JPEG stills. These are not, however, what you may think from the name — these are x-rays and MRI scans.

Feldenkrais Method

http://www.cbima.com/Gabriel/feldenkrais.html

This is a bodywork method developed in Israel that bears remarkable resemblance to Alexander methods (see the earlier section, The Alexander technique). Maybe it turns out there are actually just a few ways to get the same kinds of body results after all. Once again, if you work at a keyboard for hours every day, sooner or later you'll need this stuff.

Good Health Web

http://www.social.com/health/

Good Health Web is a sort of directory-within-a-directory. From this site, you can find almost all the Web's health-related material.

Health and healing from ConsciousNet

http://www.consciousnet.com/

This site is a very big resource for all kinds of stuff, including directories of online stores and so forth. If you're looking for hypnotists, or aromatherapy consultants, or holistic practitioners, you can find them here.

Health Technologies Network

http://www.ieway.com/business/max/welcome.html

Connoisseurs of late-20th-century American business practice will want to check this site — it's more or less an Amway-type business. Will this approach work on the Web, or does the whole premise of so-called multi-level-marketing depend on face-to-face contact with friends and relatives that you can guilt-trip into buying things? Stay tuned as we all find out.

Index of mental health pages

http://www.sover.net/~schwcof/links.html

Everything indexed at the other mental health sites is recapitulated here. This site is exceptionally well maintained.

Medicine OnLine

http://www.meds.com/

If you're going to get any kind of medical services, check this site. The information quality is higher than you usually get in the photo-copied handouts from a hospital or doctor.

OncoLink

```
http://www.oncolink.upenn.edu/
```

This site is especially worthwhile (see Figure 9-17). It contains lots of good explanations of cancer issues in laymen's language rather than medical jargon.

Physician Finder Online

```
http://msa2.medsearch.com/pfo/
```

This site offers a keyword search for finding a doctor by specialty, region, language, or six other criteria. So far, it still needs a larger assortment, but it's filling in fast.

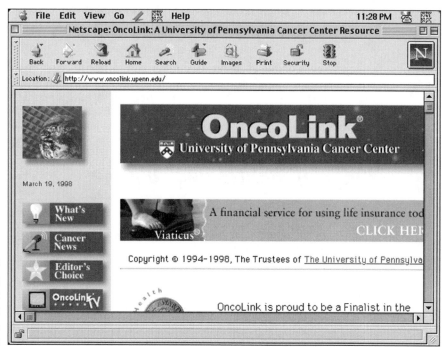

Figure 9-17:
Excellent
advice on a
scary topic.

Physician's GenRx

`http://www.icsi.net/GenRx.html`

This site is good for finding any sort of drug equivalents — you'll be amazed at the welter of trade names that exist for even the simplest pharmaceuticals. The service used to be open to anyone. Now, mostly for security reasons, you have to sign up for the service.

Present Moment

`http://www.presentmoment.com/`

This is a gigantic informational site. It's almost odd that the warp-speed world of the Internet is becoming a resource for meditation and philosophy, but maybe Web-heads can use some help appreciating the "present moment."

Relax The Back

`http://www.relaxtheback.com/`

According to recent research, back ailments are second only to colds and flu as a reason people miss work. Here's a big catalog of ergonomic products and a little online 60-second exercise drill.

Walker's Dynamic Herbs and Botanicals

`http://www.txdirect.net/kombucha/`

Kombucha is an Asian fungus/mushroom that will grow from a starter culture in a pot of tea with sugar. You then drink what's left, and devotees of this stuff claim that it has many amazing medical properties. It has many adherents among people for whom standard medical practice has failed to produce results. Generally, people just pass around the starter cultures for free. But, if you don't know anyone doing this, you can get some starter cultures from the company at this site.

Science

Science is an enterprise with a unique need for exchanging large chunks of information among sites all over the globe. The Web has changed the old meetings-once-a-year situation and made the world one big laboratory. Here's one way to gauge the importance of science on the Web: This category is bigger than entertainment!

Just for fun, check out the absolute original, first-ever Web site (see Figure 9-18) in history, the physics research site CERN, at

```
http://www.cern.ch/
```

You can even find some interesting stuff for laymen.

In March 1997, I came across the incredible statistic that the number of students majoring in computer science in the U.S. has dropped by about 40 percent *in the last decade*. Sciences in general are also losing students and funding. What does it take to develop a little interest in science of all kinds? I don't know, but I'm willing to predict that rabid interest in basketball is not the key to a 21st-century growth economy. Following is a little directory as an appeal to the curious, at least.

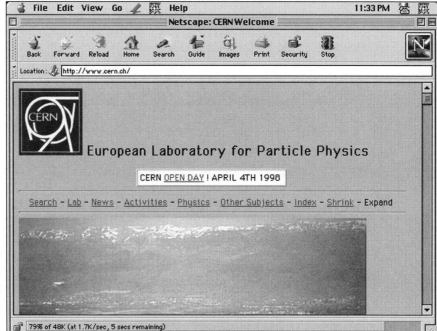

Figure 9-18:
The first
site on
the Web.

Agriculture Online

`http://www.agriculture.com/`

This is *the* source for commercial agriculture information. There's an old joke, "How do you make a small fortune in farming? Start with a large fortune and keep farming till it's nearly gone." Those days are gone, and besides that, they're now wired down on the farm. Even if the next house is a half-mile away, we're all neighbors on the Web.

Alternative Energy

`http://www.nando.net/prof/eco/aee.html`

This index site shows you how to find information on generating your own power. It's more useful perhaps for non-city folks, but it's interesting reading even for Manhattan apartment dwellers.

American Mathematical Society

`http://e-math.ams.org/`

The Godzilla of math sites (see Figure 9-19). It leads everywhere, but everything is already here anyway. Journals, jobs, papers — you name it. And most major university programs are cataloged here.

Artificial Life

`http://www.fusebox.com/`

If you need to show a friend what's cool about the Web, check out this site (see Figure 9-20). It displays running simulations of the key artificial life programs, demonstrating why this subject is so fascinating. Boids, the bird flock simulation, is irresistible, as is its progeny, Swarm.

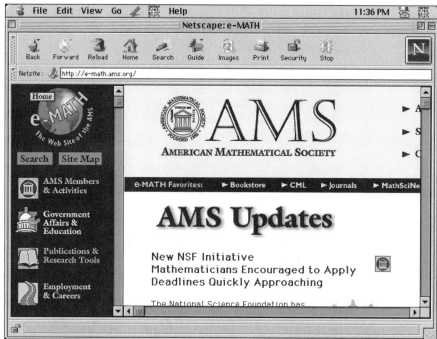

Figure 9-19:
Math. Lots
you can
even use.

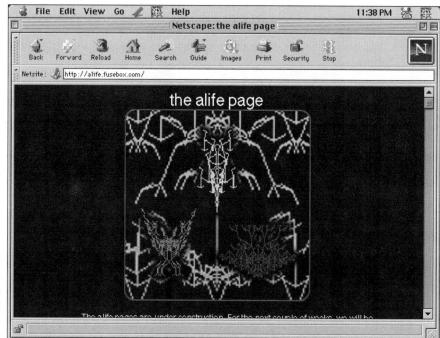

Figure 9-20:
The strange
world of
alife.

Astronomy Cafe

`http://www2.ari.net/home/odenwald/cafe.html`

"For the astronomically disadvantaged," this site has all sorts of friendly materials. An ideal place to point a young person for a science project.

AstroVR

`http://brando.ipac.caltech.edu:8888/`

Although this site is really for professionals, it gives you a glimpse of the way the Web is changing things in science. It's a collaborative, interactive, virtual-astronomy laboratory, with access to main research databases and sky catalogs.

Auditory phenomena

`http://www.music.mcgill.ca/~welch/auditory/Auditory.html`

This site gives you a multimedia guide to all sorts of interesting psycho-acoustic phenomena. We still have a lot to learn about the way the brain processes sounds.

BioBox

`http://golgi.harvard.edu/biopages.html`

Wow! Biologists post their favorite URLs here (see Figure 9-21), and the duds are gradually weeded out by natural selection. This site leads outward to every important resource in modern biology.

BioSci

`http://www.bio.net/`

A professional resource that connects all the online literature in biology to databases. Formerly government sponsored, it now has commercial backers as well.

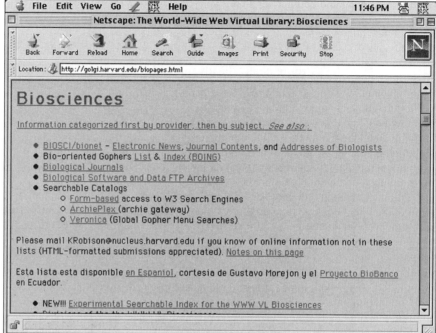

Figure 9-21:
The place
to start for
biology.

CHANCE

`http://www.statistics.com/`

The CHANCE project (see Figure 9-22) is a statistics course, freely distributed, that explains the stats behind the headlines in today's news. Your appreciation of the nonsense-level of so much of TV news will be greatly enhanced thereby. If you want to understand how the world really works, start here.

Complex Systems

`http://life.anu.edu.au/complex_systems/complex.html`

This truly great site not only has the best professional sources, but it also contains the beginner's tutorials in the core areas of complexity (cellular automata, fractals, fuzzy logic, and so forth). It's a real Web treasure for the intellectually curious.

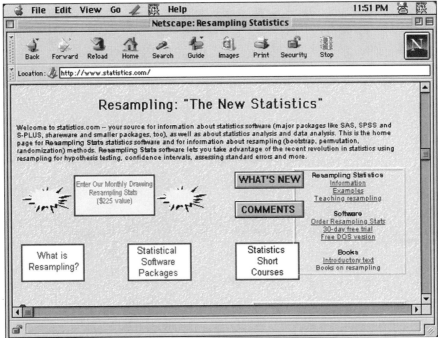

Figure 9-22:
One of the many cool topics on statistics.

DNA to dinosaurs

http://www.fmnh.org./

This site is an online museum organized by The Field Museum in Chicago, and it's an example of how this kind of site should be done (see Figure 9-23). You can also find links to other collections, as well. If you get to Chicago, visit the real thing.

Earth and universe

http://www.eia.brad.ac.uk/bt1/

A dazzling, spectacular, multimedia astro-extravaganza. Really, this site is a very cool collection of astronomical topics, with amazing photos and animations.

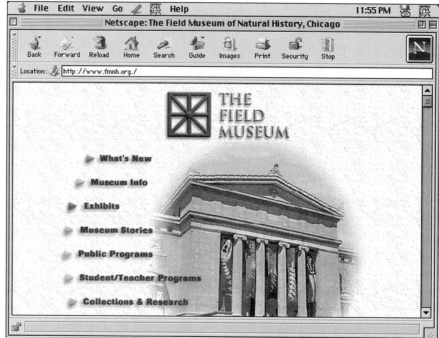

Figure 9-23:
Chicago's
Field
Museum
Web site.

EcoNews Africa

http://www.io.org/~ee/ena/

If you're interested in ecology, you may as well be interested in an area that has the worst, fastest-developing problems. This site is good for monitoring the forthcoming, apparently inevitable, demise of the black rhino.

EE Circuits Archive

http://weber.u.washington.edu/~pfloyd/ee/index.html

No point in reinventing the wheel, no point redesigning a circuit. This big library covers hundreds of circuits, all tested and practical.

The Electronic Zoo

http://netvet.wustl.edu/e-zoo.htm

Washington University has always been an Internet hotspot, and this zoo is a great, sophisticated attraction (see Figure 9-24). Stop by some afternoon. In fact, drop in while you're at work!

Engineering Design

http://class1.ee.virginia.edu/~tmo9d/Fall94/home.html

A very nice online review of things that work (Panama Canal) and don't work (Space Shuttle Challenger) and the reasons why. It's enough to make you wait a year or so before trying out newly built aircraft or bridges.

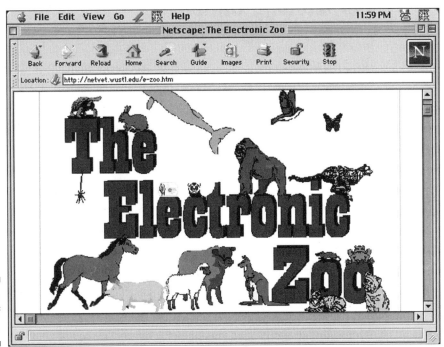

Figure 9-24:
The Zoo of
the Future.

Fractal Movie Archive

http://www.cnam.fr/fractals/anim.html

This site is a premiere archive for cool fractal movies. You get access to mind-boggling displays, whether you know any math or not.

Geo Exchange

http://giant.mindlink.net/geo_exchange/index.html

This is a good resource for people with amateur interests (in gems or volcanoes, for example) and also for Web links to professional information. Besides, you can see the cartoon Unreal Estate, one of the best on the Web.

Herpetology Gallery

http://gto.ncsa.uiuc.edu/pingleto/herp.html

Okay, it's a bunch of pictures of snakes and amphibians. But they're very good pictures, and there seems to be vast interest in this topic.

Holography page

http://www.hmt.com/holography/index.html

This site is an index page for commercial and experimental holography. Order holograms, get them made from your photos, or find out how to do it yourself.

Hubble Space Telescope

http://newproducts.jpl.nasa.gov/s19/hst.html

Since we're not getting off this planet any time soon, the next most exciting adventure is finally getting (after lots of trouble) a decent telescope that works outside of our own blurry atmosphere. Check here for the latest and greatest from the newly repaired HST.

Nanoworld

`http://www.uq.oz.au/nanoworld/nanohome.html`

One quick way to find out something about molecules is to see what they look like. This site has tons of atomic-scale pictures of chemicals in action, surfaces, crystals, and so forth.

NASA Spacelink

`http://spacelink.msfc.nasa.gov/`

The people who run NASA have quite correctly figured that the general public is bored with routine satellite-launching runs and telescope repair-bungling. But they have high hopes that WebHeads will be more sympathetic to their cause, so they've put together a Web site that's as good or better than a movie. This one's a must-see, even as an example of HTML design.

OCEANIC

`http://diu.cms.udel.edu/`

A pretty good guide to all sorts of oceanographic data, most particularly the large-scale oceanic circulation experiment. We know more about the moon than we do about most oceans.

Physics for Poets

`http://seidel.ncsa.uiuc.edu/Phys150/`

A remarkable course taught at the University of Illinois, and all the material, including slide shows associated with the lectures, is available here. If you'd like to take a dry run at a good, basic physics course before doing the real thing for a grade, this site is your best bet.

Physics News

`http://www.het.brown.edu/news/index.html`

This site is a bulletin board with links to all major physics research sites. Mostly, this site is for researchers, but it's good for students, too. When you're taking a course, seeing what real physicists do helps.

Rainforest Action Network

http://www.io.org/~ee/ena/

If anything, the rainforests are under more direct assault than the savannahs of East Africa. Check here for the latest on rainforest conservation, a difficult topic indeed.

Relativity

http://sunsite.unc.edu/lunar/geomet.html

This site is a self-paced multimedia course, advertised as "for trekkies." You can't do much about relativity, but everyone nonetheless finds it fascinating compared to agriculture (See Figure 9-25).

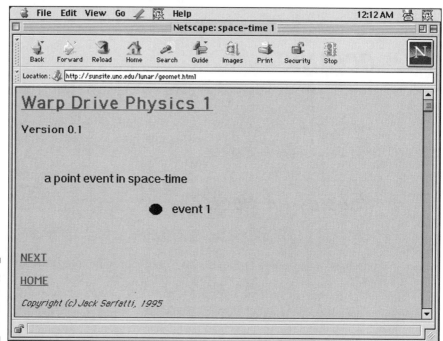

Figure 9-25:
Just you
and
Einstein.

Santa Fe Institute

```
http://www.santafe.edu/
```

And if it turns out that complexity theory produces nothing more than a bunch of conferences, most of them are here. This site is the main U.S. resource in complexity theory.

SkyMap

```
http://www.execpc.com/~skymap/
```

This site is a great online planetarium, essentially the equivalent of the commercial product of the same name on CD-ROM. See what the sky looked like the day you were born.

Visualization for Science

```
http://www.cs.brown.edu/people/art035/Bin/science.html
```

This site is an online classroom of phenomenally good animation on biology topics. It's a very nice place to spend an afternoon. It gives you hope that the Web will still be an educational resource after all the commercial businesses sign on and dominate the Web.

Web Advanced Research Project

```
http://www.hia.com/hia/pcr/
```

A way cool site for all sorts of interesting topics in The New Physics and other amazing things. Almost impossible to describe, you must visit this page for yourself.

Weird Science

```
http://www.eskimo.com/~billb/weird.html
```

This site is your one-stop shopping center and link farm for everything, from unlikely Tesla coil experiments to UFOs to ESP and everything in between (see Figure 9-26). When you're bored with *X-Files* reruns, stop here and make up your own show.

Location: http://www.eskimo.com/~billb/weird.html

PREV GUESTBOOK GOOD STUFF NEW HELP LINKS

Weird Research, Anomalous Physics

- SEATTLE WEIRD SCIENCE MEETINGS
- DISCUSSION GROUP freenrg-L: Unconventional projects, physics
- DISCUSSION GROUP taoshum-L: Taos hum speculation, research

WEIRD SCIENCE OF THE WEEK

- PEAR Labs, solid evidence that minds affect matter! (3/3/98)

Figure 9-26:
This site deserves its name, for sure.

These Sites Are Fun?

In the context of the Web, "fun" seems to mean looking at pictures of other people doing the things *you* want to do. Here's what I'll do, being on somewhat unfamiliar ground myself on this topic: I'll show you a few quirky samples, tell you something that you may need to know about pictures, and then show you the doors to fun. This area changes so fast that the doors are your best bet anyway.

SciFi

http://www.bestware.net/albatross/SCEFIIMG/scifiimg.htm

If you were to tour the Macworld offices and head for the lab, you'd find a veritable shrine of science fiction, with posters everywhere retailing the glories of Star Wars, Star Trek, and Star-Whatever. It's not my area of expertise. Twenty years ago, I was in fact thrown out of the movie *Star Wars* by my own friends (!) for mildly observing that in space you can't actually see laser beams or flaming explosions. Well, you can't, you know. For all I know, Jedi knights are out there, but there isn't much oxygen between galaxies. See Figure 9-27.

Figure 9-27:
Pictures of
things that
never were.

Disney

```
http://www.hiddenmickeys.org
```

Now, you may wonder whether the people who actually design the Happiest
Kingdom on Earth ever get bored with their cheerful task. They do indeed
(see Figure 9-28). As a result, they amuse themselves by smuggling so-called
"Hidden Mickeys" into the decor. You have to see this to believe it, but it'll
keep you awake nights, if you ever get to Disney World.

Fun door #1

The first place to look for fun and entertaining sites is Yahoo! Just think of
the name — of course these guys are fun-oriented, and this service started
life as a sort of silly hobby. One URL in particular (you can find a whole area
called Entertainment) gives a phenomenal number of links to follow:

```
http://www.yahoo.com/Entertainment/
```

Figure 9-28:
Can you
spot the
hidden
Mickeys?

If you've become a fan of anyone you ever saw on TV or in a movie, you can safely bet that someone else has put together a fan site for your enjoyment (see Figure 9-29). And since fan clubs mean pictures, it's now time to discuss, in this out-of-the-way corner of the book, the whole picture situation. Please consult the "Graphics and explicits" sidebar, and don't blame me if you get into trouble.

Fun door #2

```
http://my.excite.com/entertainment/academy_awards/
```

```
http://my.excite.com/sports/
```

The search service Excite has little subsections right on its start page that lead out to fun areas such as movies (see Figure 9-30) and sports (see Figure 9-31). The big advantage of Excite for these topics is that the reviewers have already filtered out the 95-percent-waste-of-time sites. Unfortunately, that's the case with most Web sites. Everything posted on Excite actually *is* good. Think about it: Your TV sure can't make the same claim.

Graphics and explicits

A few years ago, to collect pictures from the Internet you joined a newsgroup that featured the pictures (pictures from astronomy, pictures of Mt. Fuji, pictures of squirrels, pictures of model types getting spectacularly even tans), downloaded them as UU-encoded text files, ran them through a decoding program, and then checked them out in a viewer such as JPEGView (shareware available at www.shareware.com). The problem with this arrangement was that you didn't know if the picture was worth keeping before going through the tedious download-decode cycle.

Those days are gone. Here's what you do:

1. **Using Netscape Navigator or Internet Explorer, go to a search site, such as Yahoo! (www.yahoo.com).**

2. **Type in the object of your desires, from '73 VW Super Beetles to Julia Ormond, and click Search or press Enter to start the search.**

3. **Start looking through the links that result. If you see a picture that you like in the Web pages that turn up, move the cursor to it, hold down the mouse button (don't just click it), and select Save this Image as from the pop-up menu.**

You can check to see if the image was saved correctly by using JPEG View. The same command is available if you find a picture (which is automatically decoded and displayed) using the News window of Navigator 3.0.

The equivalent command in the Microsoft Internet Explorer 3.0 browser is Download Image to Disk, which doesn't ask you to produce your own name for the picture (which often is something on the site like 456.jpg). In practice, I haven't been as successful using MSIE as Navigator, and I suspect it's because most sites are still more likely to make themselves optimized for Netscape action.

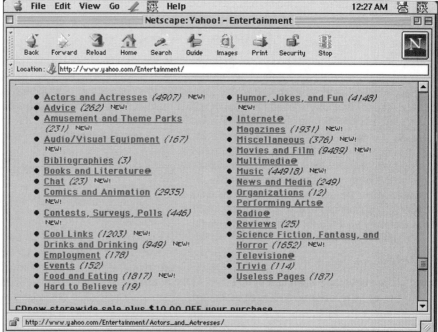

Figure 9-29:
Everyone
who ever
faced a
microphone
or camera.

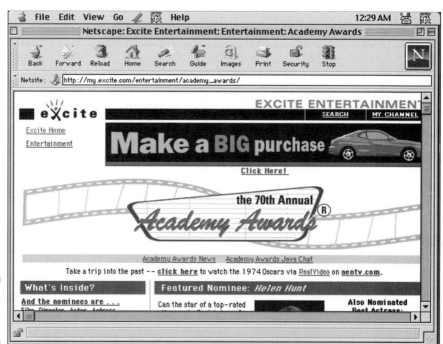

Figure 9-30:
Oscar night,
every night.

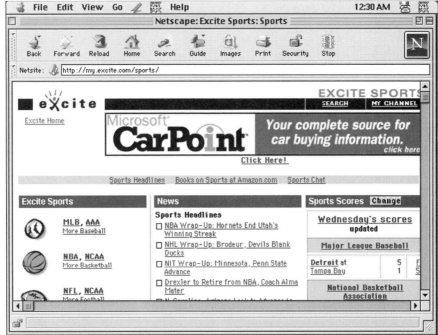

Figure 9-31:
A better
sports
source.

Chapter 10

Finding Anything

● ●

In This Chapter

▶ One-stop shopping: Starting with Netscape

▶ Giving your browser enough memory

▶ Fancier searches

▶ A Yahoo! example

▶ Looking for special topics

● ●

*W*hat are you going to do with the Web? If you're like most people, you're going to look up information — about health, car insurance, school assignments, Taoist mysticism, the Spice Girls, or about anything else on earth. To prove my point, I've included a list of the most-visited sites on the Web in early 1998. As you'll see in this chapter, most of these sites are *search engines*. A search engine is a Web site that's an abstract of other Web sites. For example, a typical search engine explores as much of the Internet as it can and gleans the body title or other special information available from any Web site it encounters. The search engine then catalogs the data in its search functions. If, by some miracle, you still don't have a Web browser, you can go to Netscape or Microsoft to download browsers.

Searching for Answers

Using a search engine isn't any different than answering a test question. The problem is that, like in the game of "Jeopardy!," you have to supply the best answer to get the proper question.

Most search engines use a basic search method known as *Boolean* math. To get the best results, I might want to try search terms that are as specific as possible. I talk more about these search methods later.

Well, I hope you've got some questions, posers, and queries. Let's begin.

Go to Netscape at `www.netscape.com` and check out the search function of the Netcaster welcome page (see Figure 10-1). Following is my little speech in favor of starting here rather than somewhere else.

Most popular sites

- ✔ Yahoo!   `http://www.yahoo.com`
- ✔ Netscape   `http://home.netscape.com`
- ✔ Microsoft   `http://www.microsoft.com`
- ✔ Excite/WebCrawler   `http://www.web-crawler.com` and
                              `http://www.excite.com`
- ✔ Infoseek   `http://www.infoseek.com`
- ✔ AOL   `http://www.aol.com`
- ✔ GeoCities   `http://www.geocities.com`
- ✔ ABC/Disney/ESPN   `http://abc.com`, `http://www.disney.com` and
                              `http://www.espn.com`
- ✔ MSN   `http://msn.com`
- ✔ Lycos   `http://www.lycos.com`
- ✔ AltaVista   `http://www.altavista.com`
- ✔ CNet   `http://cnet.com`
- ✔ Hotmail (bought by MSN)   `http://www.hotmail.com`
- ✔ WhoWhere?   `http://www.whowhere.com`
- ✔ ZDNet   `http://zdnet.com`
- ✔ CNN   `http://cnn.com`
- ✔ RealNetworks   `http://www.real.com`
- ✔ Wired   `http://wired.com`
- ✔ AT&T   `http://att.com`
- ✔ CompuServe   `http://www.compuserve.com`

Clicking the pull-down search menu gives you an impressive list of search services. For example, the Yahoo! link pursues your search through regular Yahoo! categories, but also invokes an AltaVista keyword search, shown in Figure 10-2. On the Web, you can get just about anywhere from just about anywhere else. A similar case is found by calling on AOL NetFind. AOL is too busy to program its own search engine, so it defaults to Excite.

Figure 10-1:
Netscape's
home page
is a central
search spot.

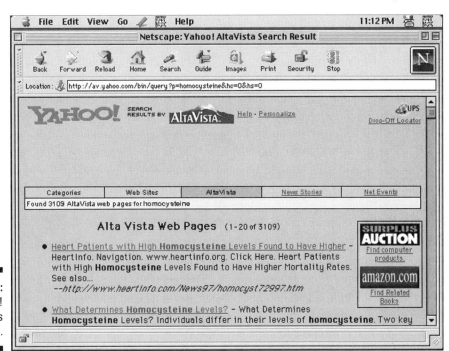

Figure 10-2:
Yahoo!
invokes
AltaVista.

Keeping up to date

When the Web first became popular, searching was often frustrating. People tended to rely on software utilities to manage their bookmark lists for fast Web navigation. Recently, I riffled through my giant collection of bookmark folders in Netscape Navigator (write Web books, and you really pile 'em up) and found that 10 percent of the month-old bookmarks were out of date (site moved or missing), and 22 percent of the two-month-old bookmarks were out of date. (Here's a fun publishing fact — the sites listed in a magazine article were typically put there three to four months ago.) Stale bookmarks are less useful than stale bread but more inevitable, thanks to the dynamic nature of the Web. Microsoft will probably still be found at www.microsoft.com in 2005, but most other current bookmarks by then will get you the dreaded 404 not found message, presumably in 3D with cool sound effects by then. So, it's more logical to go to a central location that's unlikely to change and that keeps itself updated with the latest and best places to go. Netscape Netcaster fits the bill.

And that's not bad. Excite, shown in Figure 10-3, has a nice compromise between Yahoo!-style category searching and AltaVista-style keyword/phrase searching. Rather than list thousands of hits, Excite has its own internal criteria for deciding which sites are most likely to be useful, and the criteria work pretty well.

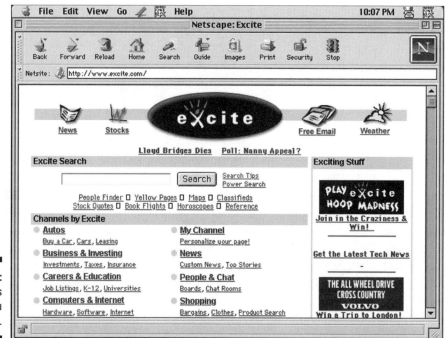

Figure 10-3:
Excite tries
to keep you
excited.

What can't be captured, without a large collection of examples, may be called The Uselessness of 5,000 Hits. Some search services simply return links to every page that matches your search term. As a result, if your term is tennis, you'll get a near-infinite pile of junk. However, checking out the first two or three links from the services to see how relevant they are can be interesting.

In Table 10-1, in order, are the hit list totals for a search on the rarer term *homocysteine*. In the results, look for something that makes sense to you about stroke or heart attack, as I explain in the "Homo- what?!?" sidebar. The results are shown in Figures 10-4, 10-5, and 10-6.

Table 10-1	Counting Those Hits
Search Service	*Results*
Excite	1,150 hits
AOL NetFind	1,150 hits
WebCrawler	86 hits
Lycos	66 hits
Infoseek	1,248 hits
Snap	1,193 hits
Looksmart	2,833 hits
AltaVista	3,117 hits
Yahoo!	3,117 hits
HotBot	3,743 hits

Homo- what?!?

Just to show how much I appreciate you for buying this book, I'm going to try to save your life. We've experienced thirty years of press releases about dietary cholesterol intake as the big factor in heart disease and stroke. Now, a growing body of evidence suggests that a formerly obscure variant amino acid (amino acids are what make up proteins) called homocysteine may be more relevant, in many cases, than the minor changes in cholesterol level we've been brooding about for decades.

Homocysteine is a big topic with me, because I personally spent two weeks in a hospital as a result of a stroke. The hospital then found that I was running the highest level of serum homocysteine ever reported at the main reference lab for Northern California. I was given plenty of wheelchair

(continued)

(continued)

time on the Net to research the subject. The current best guess from the largest British study is that more than half of early (under age 55) heart attacks or strokes can be traced to above-average homocysteine levels. Do yourself (or your parents) a big favor, and go to www.homocysteine.com, run the search shown in the figures here, or search on the name of the research physician (Kilmer McCully) who first identified the problem. What you find will make you glad you read this, because nearly foolproof preventive measures are quite simple and cheap. Wish I'd known them a few years ago, I can tell you that for sure.

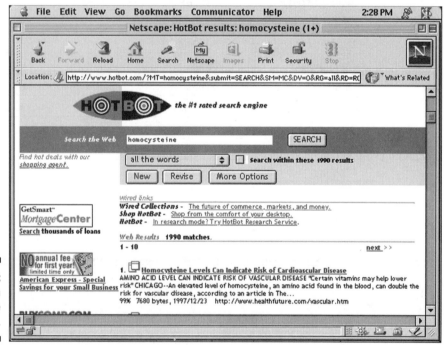

Figure 10-4:
HotBot, a mighty pile o' hits.

Figure 10-5:
WebCrawler
concentrates
results.

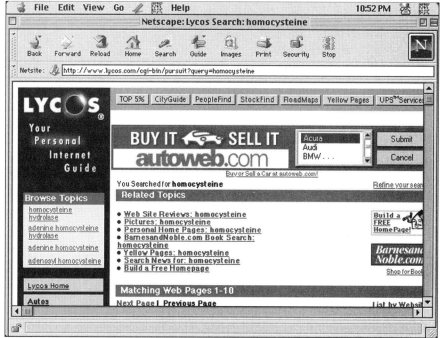

Figure 10-6:
The
updated
Lycos
service.

Advice to the Impatient

Happily, most Web search engines can find pages on the Web faster than FindFile can find one on my hard drive. Keeping small bookmark files and continually staying up-to-date with fresh searches makes sense. The main point of bookmarks is tracking the few sites that actually have what you want, for this week anyway.

You can find lots of information on the Web simply by clicking hypertext links in Yahoo! or other *catalog* sites. And nothing is wrong with surfing around to get yourself oriented. If you want to find a large amount of useful information in a hurry, however, you need a strategy. Dozens of different searching techniques exist. You can save yourself lots of online time (they don't call it the World Wide Wait for nothing) by leafing through the rest of this chapter before starting online searches.

Now stop for a minute, and think about what businesses and individuals have to communicate on the Web. You'll see that the overall information content of the World Wide Web is quite different from the content in traditional information providers, such as libraries. In the reference part of a library, you see the result of centuries of fact-checking, aimed at providing standard reference material that's been organized and screened by experts. On the Web, you see anything that someone wants to post. You have no guarantees that the Web material is correct, or even useful. Some of it is advertising (personal or corporate), and you probably have your own set of stories about the expected accuracy of advertising. Just something to keep in mind.

Memories, Memories

One thing you may want to do is give your Web browser as much workspace as possible. You can do this in two ways. First, when your browser is not running, click once on its program icon and choose Get Info from the File menu. In the box that appears, change the browser's preferred memory setting to 1000 or 5000 higher than the number you see. Also, while your browser is running, open the browser's preferences screen and increase the size of the disk cache (that's pronounced "cash"). The disk cache is the temporary spot where pages and their graphics are stored. If the browser detects that nothing has changed on a page you're revisiting, the browser will reload the page from the cache and not from the Internet, which allows you to use the page faster. Giving more RAM to the browser (using the Get Info box) improves the performance of the browser and reduces the likelihood for crashes, especially when working with complex pages.

A key point also to keep in mind is this: You don't know what you really want until you see it.

Very often, stuff that you turn up in the course of a search turns out to be more interesting than the topic you were investigating when you started. That's one of the great advantages of poking around a page at a time — the rate at which you see information is a rate at which you can actually evaluate it for yourself. You'll see that keyword searches are sometimes more difficult than manual searches to manage and evaluate information — a search can turn up all sorts of irrelevant pages, and often, too many of them. One interesting, relatively new service, with a unique cataloging scheme, is LookSmart, shown in Figure 10-7. Because it displays the different index levels on the screen at the same time, it's excellent for "Wait, I changed my mind" searching, which is often the most informative.

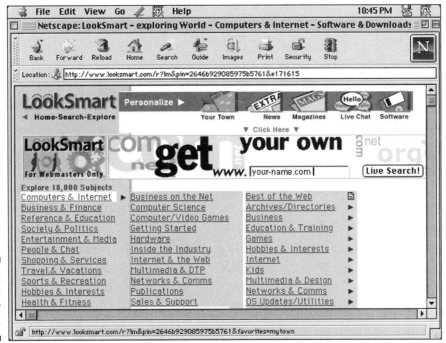

Figure 10-7: LookSmart's nifty indexing.

Advanced Searching

You can guess from the piles of links found for an obscure term like homocysteine that a main goal in Web searching is to avoid drowning in pages of not-quite-what-you-wanted.

Some services, notably AltaVista, in a truly international approach, serve up page after page of hits in Finnish, Dutch, and the odd ASCII scramble that means the site's in Japanese, so you have an option to restrict the search to English. Other services, such as Excite or Lycos, realistically assuming that few Americans are adept polyglots, filter the sites so that you get English-language sites only or English-language sites at the top of the list.

Of course, readability isn't the whole story. You also want to find the most relevant material with the least effort. To make this approach work, knowing what kind of results to expect from a few advanced searching tricks can help.

Getting specific — AND

The way to avoid drowning in keyword searches is by using logical (or Boolean, after the pioneering 19th-century logic expert George Boole) restrictors. The most useful restrictor is AND, which means the search should only return sites that have all the search terms. It takes several forms. The older mode, using a + sign for AND, is recognized by nearly all keyword search engines, because it's built into the UNIX operating systems. For example, a search for

```
+chess +".edu"
```

would find chess-oriented sites at universities in the U.S., on Infoseek (see Figure 10-8) and on AltaVista or Yahoo!. The point of the quotes is to make sure that exactly .edu is found instead of just anything containing edu, as in names such as Eduardo. Some services encourage you to write this as "chess AND .edu," because + means logical AND, but the computer at the search site translates +/AND internally anyway. In either case, it means that somewhere the site has to have both terms.

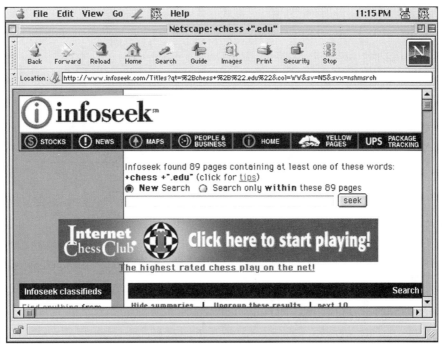

Figure 10-8:
Infoseek's
plusses and
minuses.

Narrowing your search — NOT and OR

The other important options are NOT, represented literally as NOT, if you
like, or equivalently as the – sign, and OR. For example, if you're interested
in recent Hollywood stars, you could try

```
+"pamela anderson" -"pamela anderson lee" -".jpg"
```

in your research seeking pre-tattoo pictures of that young lady's frequently
photographed upper arm. Perhaps a better typical use is to filter a list. If
you find, as can often happen, hundreds of irrelevant links from
www.(junksite).com, you can redo the search with

```
-www.(junksite).com
```

in the search line, and get rid of all the JunkSite contributions. Plenty of junk
sites are out there, too — you'll find that fast enough.

OR, by contrast, widens your search, which helps if you're not quite sure
what you want. OR usually turns up as a special option on services such as
Excite (see Figure 10-9) that have a form (usually under a link called Tips or
Advanced Searching) for specifying more complex searches. Services that

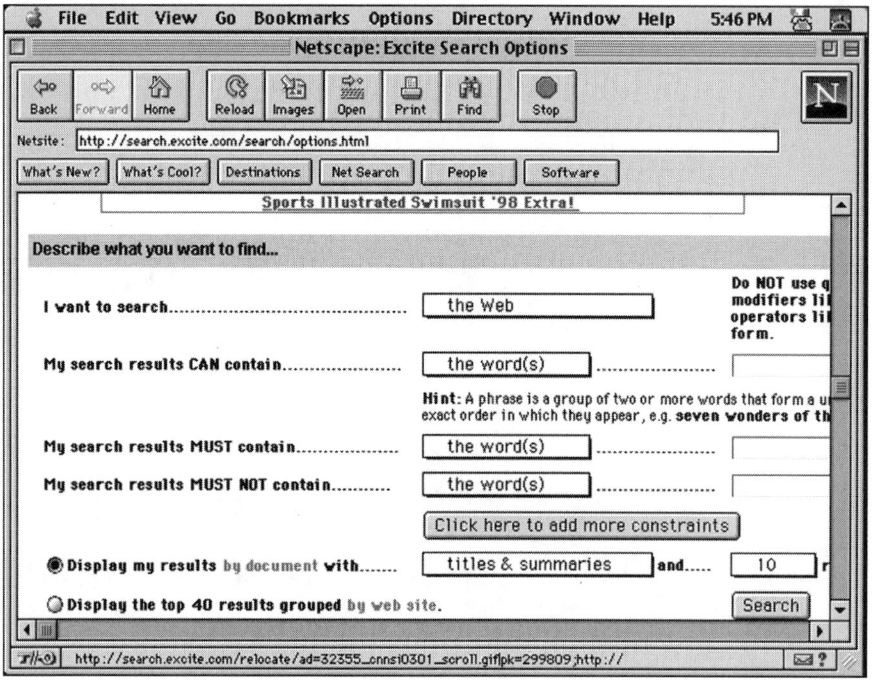

Figure 10-9:
An Exciting
search
form.

return heaping boatloads of sites typically put an automatic OR as the default connector (instead of +) between the search terms you enter. Apparently, these services are figuring that they look better by giving you lots of irrelevant sites, rather than the much smaller collection you'd see if AND were inserted between the terms. In many cases, if you decide on a general search topic, any other term you add with an OR simply produces deterioration in the quality of the hit list.

Working Yahoo!

In many cases, the Yahoo! service represents the quickest path to Web info. If you do a search over the whole Web on a vague keyword, you're going to get pointed to zillions of documents (well, actually, most search software mercifully only reports the first hundred documents at first pass). And in many circumstances, a search that returns hundreds of links (called *hits*) is almost as useless as a search that turns up nothing at all. And the growth of the Web is still aggravating the zillion-hit problem. So designing searches that return a usable amount of information is a big priority in Web searching.

Yahoo! is different from the standard keyword searches. Yahoo!'s tree directory structure has already been carefully designed to yield very fast results with almost no planning on your part. When you click a link in the directory, you get back only one or two pages of results. That means you're positively encouraged to click around at random. You won't be punished with an unstoppable twenty-minute download for clicking a vague topic.

Because Yahoo! is probably the fastest way to get an overview or a topic on the Web, its filtering mechanism is worth a close look. In a hierarchical set of choices such as Yahoo!'s (*hierarchical* means that the choices are arranged in layers rather than presented all at once), the first layer, shown in Figure 10-10, might contain fifteen choices. When you pick one of these choices, the next layer might offer thirty choices, and then the third layer might give you a list of fifty choices. This example is, in fact, very close to the way Yahoo! is arranged. Looking at the numbers, when you pick something at the third level, you have selected from

```
choices = 20 x 30 x 50 = 30,000
```

possibilities. When an option for a fourth layer of fifty choices appears after you pick something from layer three, you've negotiated your way at level four through one and a half million options.

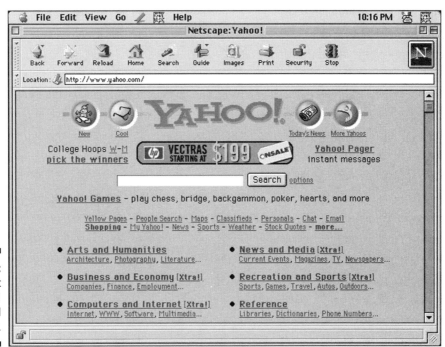

Figure 10-10: The first Yahoo! hierarchical layer.

What happens if you take a wrong turn at one of the forks in the search path? You probably won't find the information you wanted. That's exactly why all Web browsers since the earliest days have included icons for both Back and Forward navigation. You may have to back up a step, or two steps, or three steps, but backing up is not particularly time consuming. Usually, your Web browser has temporarily stored most of the pages on the backward path on your system. As a result, you can back out of a page a lot faster than you got there in the first place.

A *Yahoo!* search

To pick one search example that you would imagine to be childishly simple, try the case of finding a map of Washington, D.C. You sign on to Yahoo!, and the first thing you see is that screen in Figure 10-10. Yahoo! does some minor tinkering from time to time, and the numbers in the categories change, but this screen is the starting point for a topic search. In this example, you're looking for that map of Washington, D.C., so scrolling down the list and thinking about where such a document may be found is appropriate.

One of the items on the opening list, near the bottom, is called <u>Regional</u>. This sounds promising — after all, you're not going to find maps under Health, presumably. Click <u>Regional</u> and you see the screen in Figure 10-11, offering an assortment of geographical choices.

Figure 10-11:
Regions . . .
lots of
pages to
search.

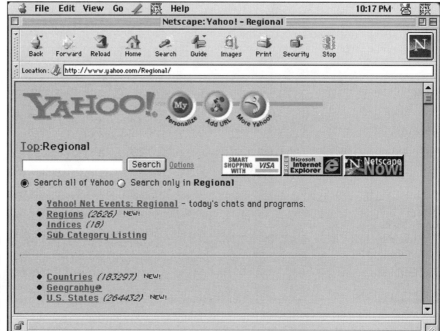

Regional hi-tech

One of the things you'll see, while poking around the regions of the world, is a lot of fantastically well-organized, high-tech countries, such as the Netherlands or Taiwan, that have a big-time Web presence. On the Web in 1998, Singapore is a bigger country than mainland China, mainly because Singapore is wired as a matter of government policy. You can find, at the Singapore Web site, design and engineering businesses that can turn around finished metal or plastic parts, in any quantity you want, within a week or so, from a faxed sketch. The global reach of the Web means than an appliance manufacturer in Beloit, Wisconsin, is competing with companies from Thailand to Norway, like it or not.

Now D.C.'s not really a state exactly, but you may well guess that Washington, D.C., will be filed under U.S. States. They have to put it somewhere. Although it may seem like a foreign country when you're lost there at night, it's more like a U.S. state than anything else. It's worth keeping in mind that the people making all the decisions for classification at Yahoo! are just like you, except perhaps that they get less sleep because they're always at work. But your guesses about the way Yahoo! has organized things will be right more often than not.

Click <u>U.S. States</u> and see what happens. You find a page of state site listings, but also one for Washington, D.C. The obvious choice is to click the D.C. site and see what happens. You guessed it — you get a whole raft of D.C. possibilities, as shown in Figure 10-12. The gang's all there, from the White House to the Smithsonian to dozens of places you may not know. But there's also a link for a D.C. map, shown in Figure 10-13. Bingo!

This particular map, as it happens, is an amazing little item that enables you to zoom in, zoom out, rotate the map, and perform all sorts of tricks, simply by clicking the points around the map border. The zooming function is crucial, since the sheer dots-per-inch resolution and size of a $2.49 map from a gas station can put to shame the picture on a your Mac's monitor. Also, a complete map of D.C. that enables you to pick out 501 K Street easily takes a half hour to download with a fast modem. This map, at any rate, enables you to zoom down to individual big buildings.

Keywords, for comparison

Finding the map of D.C. takes a little bit of intelligent decision-making on your part, and a few clicks. But perhaps finding things with the standard Yahoo! search form is a faster way to find things on Yahoo!. Several options are built into this form. But for now, just type **Washington D.C. map** in the search field and see what the HotBot search engine finds (see Figure 10-14).

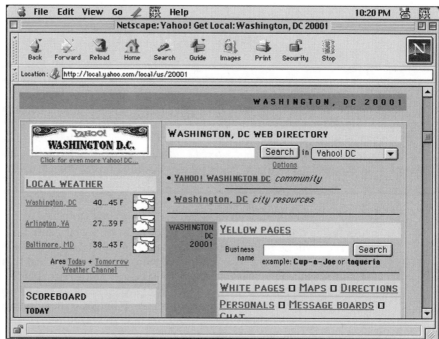

Figure 10-12:
The DC site,
a local mini-
Yahoo!.

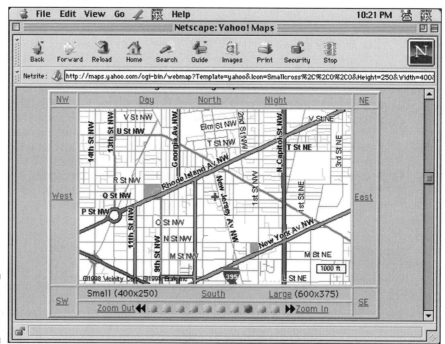

Figure 10-13:
The glorious
D.C. map.

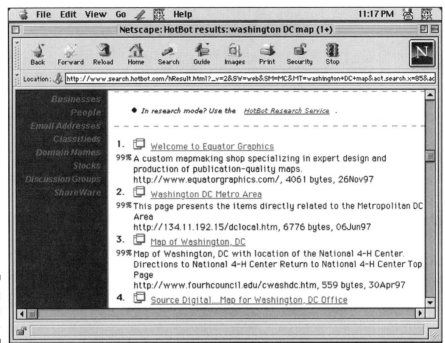

Figure 10-14:
Searching
with HotBot.

Well, HotBot finds some things, but nothing as cool as the Yahoo! map. Also, you get to observe that the contents of all Web index sites are registered in a database that may or may not have the exact keyword you expect. Most services index all the text in Web pages, not just titles and keywords. At times, you may want as much data as you get from an indexed-everything search, and other times, you'd rather have less.

To see more Web research in action, having a fancier search goal than just a map is helpful. Using asthma as a search topic turns up a goodly amount of information, because medical data is a huge area of the Web, both for companies and for nonprofit organizations. Yahoo! gives you a nice, manageable set of choices, one of which is health. Near the top of the selections on the Health page, you find a choice called Diseases and Conditions — a reasonable place to look (see Figure 10-15). It's an odd list, too. Asthma is an entry, with a really nice set of listings, shown in Figure 10-16. Personally, I was a bit taken aback that AIDS and Jock Itch are both categories at the same level.

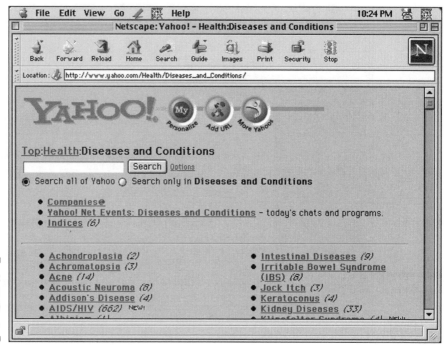

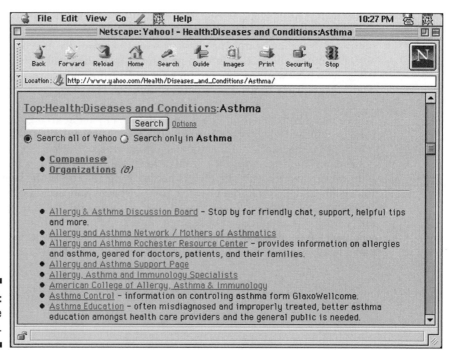

Looking for Special Topics

Lycos, shown in Figure 10-17, is similar to WebCrawler, HotBot, and AltaVista. All of these services are automated operations that search the whole Web for sites to index. As a result, you'll find more asthma references than searching the Yahoo! directory. But Yahoo! hires people to review sites and keeps only the good ones. If you're interested in the Maritime Archaic culture of the shores of Labrador and Maine; or you want to look up references to maximum-entropy signal processing in nuclear magnetic resonance spectroscopy; or you wonder if texts in Etruscan are available somewhere on the Web, you're going to find Lycos and these other prodigious indexers your most valuable resource. They index every scrap of every Web site, so material too obscure for a Yahoo! category is nonetheless covered.

For dealing with real obscurity, your best bet is a technique called *metasearching.* In a metasearch, one site sends your request out to a whole collection of search services (see Figure 10-18). This idea is insanely bad if your keyword is golf or Microsoft. But using Metasearch makes great sense if you want to determine whether any Byzantine empress had her face on a coin, or if your uncle Hadley Cadwallader is listed in a genealogy database. Some services present you with a whole menu of all possible search sites, and when you click your favorites, the metasearcher crawls through the whole group. (See Figure 10-19.)

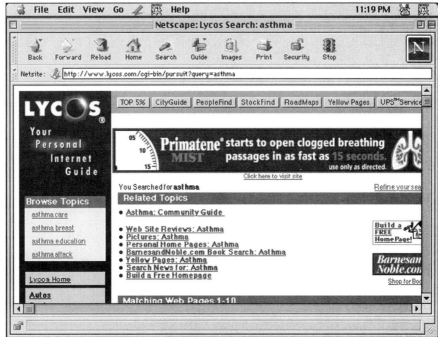

Figure 10-17: Asthma according to Lycos.

Figure 10-18:
Meta-searching.

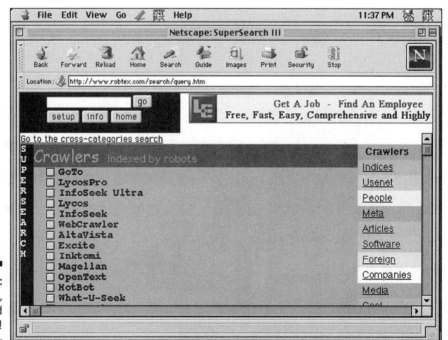

Figure 10-19:
Click, pick, and stand back!

One service that Metasearch provides is called Highway 61 at www.highway61.com, shown in Figure 10-20. Being brilliantly organized and efficient, Highway 61 is one of the few places on the Web with a reasonable sense of humor. And the results, shown in Figure 10-21, are terrific — a search on pictish language (a mysterious language of northeastern Scotland that apparently comes from pre-Celtic tribes with their own distinct culture) turned up. I can assure you, every reference is worth considering. To make this point simple: On Scottish topics, go to Yahoo! for golf, go to a metasearch for the Picts. That's about the size of it.

Figure 10-20:
Highway 61
is a truly
great
service.

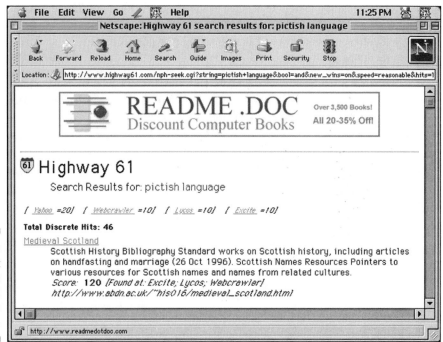

File   Edit   View   Go   ✎   ▦   Help   11:25 PM   ▦ ▦

Netscape: Highway 61 search results for: pictish language

Back   Forward   Reload   Home   Search   Guide   Images   Print   Security   Stop

Location: http://www.highway61.com/nph-seek.cgi?string=pictish+language&bool=and&new_wins=on&speed=reasonable&hits=1

README .DOC
Discount Computer Books

Over 3,500 Books!
All 20-35% Off!

🛣 Highway 61

Search Results for: pictish language

[Yahoo =20]   [Webcrawler =10]   [Lycos =10]   [Excite =10]

Total Discrete Hits: 46

Medieval Scotland

Scottish History Bibliography Standard works on Scottish history, including articles
on handfasting and marriage (26 Oct 1996). Scottish Names Resources Pointers to
various resources for Scottish names and names from related cultures.
Score: **120** *[Found at: Excite; Lycos; Webcrawler]*
http://www.sbdn.ac.uk/~his016/medieval_scotland.html

http://www.readmedotdoc.com

Figure 10-21:
More about
the Picts
than you'll
even need in
Dundee.

Chapter 11

Your Own Web Page! The World's Easiest Guide

*1*n Chapter 13, you get a look at Microsoft Office 98's "automated" Web-page production. But if you really want to do a bit of Web work (or understand why Office doesn't always give you exactly what you want), you ought to look at more advanced, but still easy to use, Web page creation tools and how to get the most out of them without taking a class in HTML or graphics design. Interested? Then read on!

So, Where Do Web Pages Come From?

Web pages come from people, of course. Hypertext Markup Language, HTML, is the language of Web pages. HTML prevents us from having to follow only one company's rules for how text and graphics are displayed. HTML, like all Internet data, is nothing more than a bunch of text that, when fed into any Web browser on any kind of computer, is formatted into a nice, orderly group of words and pictures. So long as the HTML given to the browser is formatted in such as way that the browser understands, the page comes up the same on every computer that asks for the page.

Knowing just a little bit about HTML's *tags* will help you to understand how Web pages work. Ever used the old program WordPerfect, the word processor? It used tags in much the same way. Tags are markers that you usually put just before and after the item(s) you want to format. For example, the bold tag, which looks like this: <B>, could be put at the beginning and end of the word "Jabberwocky," like this:

```
<B>Jabberwocky<B>
```

Now, that's what you would see if you were using an HTML editor. Think of an HTML editor as a plain-jane text processor that does not allow any formatting in the conventional sense. To format the text, you need to use the HTML tags. Viewing the tag's formatting only happens when the page is viewed in a Web browser. So, when you look at your text in a browser, you see this:

Jabberwocky

The browser interprets the tags and makes them invisible, and applies the formatting as you would expect to the word between the tags.

Other tags, like `<Heading 1>`, `<I>` (that's italic), and `<P>` (for paragraph) become clearer to you as you get familiar with the English inside the tags.

It would be nice if all HTML tags were as easy to use. But, sadly, some use different rules.

Fortunately, there is some good news:

- ✔ Most tags are self-explanatory. I bet you can tell roughly what `<Title>` and `<Heading1>` are all about just by guessing.

- ✔ Literally millions of examples are on the Web that you can download and copy to learn fancier tricks for your own pages.

- ✔ You really don't need to remember all the HTML details, because "Save as HTML …" is a File option in most current word-processing programs.

You might want to grab a copy of *Creating Web Pages For Dummies*, Second Edition, which talks more about HTML basics, or you can fall headlong into HTML with *HTML 4 For Dummies* (both from IDG Books Worldwide).

Hyperlinks: The one big new thing

The one big new thing Dr. Berners-Lee invented was a convenient tag format for hyperlinks. A hyperlink in a document is a special tag that tells the software interpreting the page to open another file. Look at the underlined words in Figure 11-1. And it doesn't matter if the other file is on your hard drive, on one of Apple's Web servers in Cupertino, or anywhere else.

In the first version of HTML, the "other file" was just another page of text. But even the earliest HTMLers realized that the page could include references to any type of file (sound, video, pictures, and so on), and that meant that all content was exchangeable between any computers connected to the Web. For the first Webbers, that meant fast exchange of physics papers between labs. For you, it means shopping online for sweaters at L.L. Bean, listening to audio clips from a remote CD, checking the weather, or a thousand other things.

You can shop online and listen to music, among other things, because Marc Andreesen, a graduate student at the University of Illinois (who became one of the founders of Netscape) wrote a simple program that could easily handle picture files in HTML documents as well as plain text. That program, as the free Web browser Mosaic, was basically the kickoff of the giant Web scramble. Andreesen made a fortune at Netscape, Mosaic spun out to several other companies, and Microsoft finally got scared enough about the Web encroaching on its desktop turf to start copying what Netscape did.

Understanding how it all works

The page shown in Figure 11-1 (displayed in Netscape Navigator) looks like Figure 11-2 in the original HTML. Every element on the browser screen is put in place with a pair of tags, always in the format $\langle tag \rangle$ at the beginning and $\langle /tag \rangle$ at the end. Keep these points in mind:

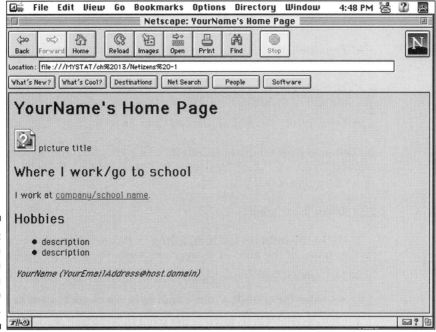

Figure 11-1:
The underline indicates a Web hyperlink.

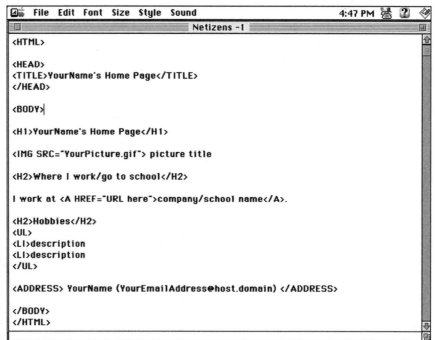

File   Edit   Font   Size   Style   Sound   4:47 PM

Netizens –1

```
<HTML>

<HEAD>
<TITLE>YourName's Home Page</TITLE>
</HEAD>

<BODY>|

<H1>YourName's Home Page</H1>

<IMG SRC="YourPicture.gif"> picture title

<H2>Where I work/go to school</H2>

I work at <A HREF="URL here">company/school name</A>.

<H2>Hobbies</H2>
<UL>
<LI>description
<LI>description
</UL>

<ADDRESS> YourName (YourEmailAddress@host.domain) </ADDRESS>

</BODY>
</HTML>
```

Figure 11-2:
The HTML
that defines
Figure 11-1.

✔ The whole document starts with an ⟨HTML⟩ tag and ends with an
⟨/HTML⟩ tag.

✔ The main section, everything but the page title, starts with a ⟨BODY⟩
tag and ends with a ⟨/BODY⟩ tag.

✔ Every other element on the page has its own pair of tags, too.

In the home page template shown in Figure 11-3, the little bulleted lists (they
begin with the ⟨UL⟩ tag) are left for you to fill by replacing the word *description* with some actual text.

Just follow these steps:

1. **Fill in the hobbies list first, filling in for this example the actual
   hobbies of the kind of people who write these ...*For Dummies* books.**

   Just replace the text in SimpleText to get the page shown in Figure 11-4.

2. **Save the file (give it a name ending in .html, just to get in the habit).**

3. **Choose File⇨Open to view the page in Netscape Navigator.**

   Now you can see the magnificent results proudly announcing your
   favorite leisure activities to the world. (See Figure 11-5.)

```
I work at <A HREF="URL here">company/school name</A>.

<H2>Hobbies</H2>
<UL>
<LI>description
<LI>description
<LI>description
</UL>

<H2>Personal Hot List</H2>
<UL>
<LI><A HREF="URL here">description</A>
<LI><A HREF="URL here">description</A>
<LI><A HREF="URL here">description</A>
</UL>

<ADDRESS>
YourName (YourEmailAddress@host.domain)
</ADDRESS>
```

Figure 11-3:
HTML for a
little list.

```
<HTML>

<HEAD>
<TITLE>YourName's Home Page</TITLE>
</HEAD>

<BODY>

<H1>YourName's Home Page</H1>

<IMG SRC="YourPicture.gif"> picture title

<H2>Where I work/go to school</H2>

I work at <A HREF="URL here">company/school name</A>.

<H2>Hobbies</H2>
<UL>
<LI>I catch wild goats!
<LI>I make kazoo noises in my throat.
</UL>

<ADDRESS> YourName (YourEmailAddress@host.domain) </ADDRESS>
```

Figure 11-4:
Changing
description
to real stuff.

I use SimpleText to edit HTML pages instead of a real word processor or one of the many great editors (BBEdit, QUED/M) with special HTML features because everybody has SimpleText, and because for most people the next step up is going to be Internet Assistant for Microsoft Word, which is free with Word 5.1 or higher. The other fancy stuff is for pros — for this book I look for the easy way out every time. Also, the SimpleText approach lets you create usable HTML on any old Mac you may have lying around — you don't need a 300 MHz G3 just to stick together a Web page.

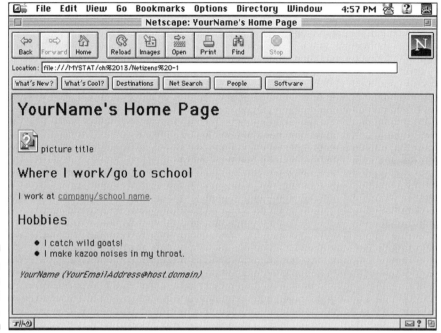

Figure 11-5:
Viewing the
real stuff in
a browser.

However, it turns out that the fancy stuff, namely hyperlinks to other files or other Web sites, just fills in the same way. The tag ⟨A HREF= *fill in the stuff*⟩ *The stuff* ⟨/A ⟩ marks the spot. Figure 11-6 shows an example. When you see what this looks like in a browser (see Figure 11-7), you see that the HREF= part of the tagline is just used to tell the browser software what site to visit when the user clicks this link. The user doesn't see this part, just the description before the ⟨/A⟩ tag.

```
I work at <A HREF="URL here">company/school name</A>.

<H2>Hobbies</H2>
<UL>
<LI>description
<LI>description
<LI>description
</UL>

<H2>Personal Hot List</H2>
<UL>
<LI><A HREF="www.yahoo.com">search on Yahoo!</A>
<LI><A HREF="www.macworld.com">Macworld OnLine</A>
<LI><A HREF="www.idgbooks.com">The IDG Site</A>
</UL>

<ADDRESS>
YourName (YourEmailAddress@host.domain)
</ADDRESS>
```

Figure 11-6:
You fill in
links and
descriptions
at ⟨A⟩.

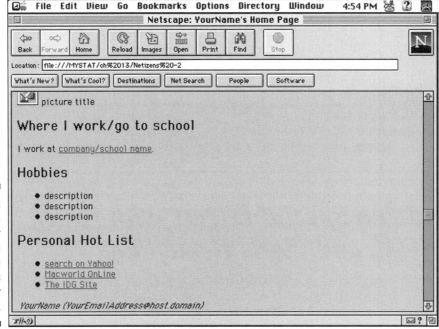

Figure 11-7:
The browser uses the links; the user sees your description.

Getting mail through links

You can also use links for getting e-mail based on your home page. After all, you'll have plenty of questions to answer about your hobby of goat-roping after your relatives find the page ("How come you never invited ME?!"). As far as HTML is concerned, e-mail is just another link in the `<A HREF=>` family. Here's what the HTML looks like:

```
<ADDRESS><A HREF="mailto:name@yourservice.com">yourname
      </A></ADDRESS>
```

Just to make sure you get it right, here's the same line, with the parts that don't change in **bold**:

```
<ADDRESS><A HREF="mailto:name@yourservice.com">yourname
      </A></ADDRESS>
```

That is, `"mailto:` and `">` have to be there for the tag to work. When the user looks at your page in a browser, only *yourname* shows, as an underlined link. Click the link and the browser opens a mail window with the message correctly addressed to you. Making mail this simple is just another one of the ways the Web became the center of Internet activity.

Learn by borrowing

One of the problems with books on HTML is that they assume responsibility for taking you through the language step-by-step and providing examples (actually, *HTML For Dummies* is well worth buying). As professional programmers can tell you, real-world programming most often means taking over an existing pile of code and tinkering with it. That's what I'm doing here; this sample home page was posted to the public domain by AOL. If you find something on the Web that impresses you, choose File⇨Save As Source in your browser and check out the HTML in SimpleText for elements to borrow for your own pages.

Adding Special Effects with Fancy HTML and Claris Home Page

As you make more elaborate pages, you may find that it becomes tiresome to keep track of all the little ⟨ ⟩⟨/⟩ tags in your documents. You could actually still do all your Web page work in a plain editor like SimpleText, but it's just too time-consuming to be much fun.

I recommend turning to our ever-friendly software vendors for help. Although Adobe makes a fine HTML product (PageMill), Netscape Communicator has a good Web page creator (Composer), and dozens of shareware packages for HTML are available on the Web, I've had the best results from Apple's Claris Home Page, Version 3.0 or higher. By "best results," what I mean is this: I recommend it to people in my own little town, and the next thing I get is an e-mail saying "hey, check out my cool Web page." When recommending most other products I get a phone call, typically at 10:30 p.m., asking "How come I can't make this look right?" Case closed, as far as I'm concerned.

Claris Home Page and its brethren are Web page creation programs that hide the HTML part of Web page design away from you. These programs offer you tools (like a word processor does) from graphical palettes that allow you to literally draw up your pages.

Using pretty pictures

Okay, mine aren't really pretty. Look at Figure 11-8, and you'll see some logos I've stuck into a single GIF format picture in a Claris Home Page window. In Home Page, you just set up a page as if you were in a word processor — typing in text, picking out fonts, inserting graphics, and so forth. But the program lets you switch to Edit HTML Source mode, where you can see the underlying HTML that corresponds to the pretty viewable page you created.

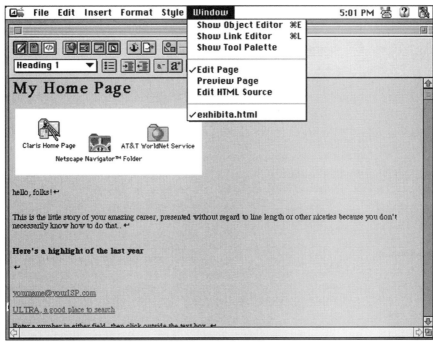

Figure 11-8:
Artwork at
last, in
Claris Home
Page.

But look at the HTML for the page shown in Figure 11-9. The line <H1>My Home Page</H1> is clear enough — you are just setting up a heading. The tag set for the GIF file is considerably gooier:

```
<P><IMG SRC="pic.GIF" WIDTH=274 HEIGHT=95 X-SAS-
        UseImageWidth X-SAS-UseImageHeight
        ALIGN=bottom></P>
```

Now all you really need to put my little pic.GIF into the page (the browser would manage to read it) is the following line:

```
<IMG SRC="pic.GIF">
```

The <P> tags are there for tidy spacing, and the other business about WIDTH, HEIGHT, and ALIGN is Home Page's effort to force the browser displaying the page to make it look *exactly* the way you want. If you have a page with lots of little images, exact spacing in the display becomes critical, and you have two choices:

✔ Let Home Page figure it out, as you simply drag figures around.

✔ Spend the rest of your life (or at least several tragic hours of it) working out HEIGHT and WIDTH numbers.

```
<HTML>
<HEAD>

    |<TITLE>My home Page</TITLE>

    <HTML>
</HEAD>
<BODY>
<FORM action="" method="POST">

<H1>My Home Page</H1>

<P><IMG SRC="pic.GIF" WIDTH=274 HEIGHT=95 X-SAS-UseImageWidth
X-SAS-UseImageHeight ALIGN=bottom></P>

<P>hello, folks!<BR>

</P>

<P>This is the little story of your amazing career, presented without
regard to line length or other niceties because you don't necessarily
know how to do that..<BR>

</P>

<P><B>Here's a highlight of the last year</B></P>

<P><BR>
```

Figure 11-9:
A nice long
`IMG SRC`
line.

GIF, JPEG, and you

GIF is just a picture format, like PICT or TIFF or any other — it just happens that browsers expect your artwork to be either a GIF or a JPEG format file. These days, almost any program you can use to create or scan a picture gives you these formats as Save options, so it's not a problem.

If you have a program that runs a scanner, usually it will let you save picture files as JPEGs at different levels of compression. You will find out that you can really stomp on files (using 60-to-1 compression or more) before

the picture quality viewed in a browser looks bad. Check out the lovely pictures of a classic B&B at `http://www.camelliainn.com`. Those pictures are 800K PICT files squished down to 12K JPEGs, and they look great! Remember, faster downloads of smaller pictures make everyone happy. Also, look at `http://www.shareware.com` for a copy of GIFConverter, a graphics program that can do nearly any kind of compression or conversion you're likely to need.

Adding sound

Sounds are added to files pretty much the same way as pictures. After all, a file is just a file.

You link up an `<A HREF= >` tag to a sound file like so:

```
<A HREF="boom.AIFF">Boom!</A>
```

In this case, the file extension AIFF, a common Mac format, tells a Web browser that it's looking at a sound file, and the browser then calls up the right helper application to play the sound. You don't have to worry too much about details; the helpers are usually installed when you install the browser itself.

Posting movies

The Web also uses several video formats: The Windows AVI format and the Apple QuickTime movie format are popular, along with the full-motion video format MPEG. To post movies on your Web pages, you use the same tags as you do for sound files, except that you make an `<A HREF= >` to a video file, as in the following:

```
<A HREF="birthday.mpeg">Here's my birthday party!</A>
```

Digital video files are almost always huge, so let readers know how big the file is in your link so that they can decide whether they want to spend the time to download the file. For example, you might try this:

```
<A HREF="birthday.mpeg">Here's my birthday party!(6850K)
        </A>
```

I think the really thoughtful thing to do is suppress the urge to post movies until we all get cable modem, but the media pioneers disagree.

The Special Case of AOL

It turns out that good old AOL is not a bad place to learn some HTML. The service runs a contest for member Web pages (see Figure 11-10), offers a special page-creation tool (as this was written, they were still working on a newer version, as shown in Figure 11-11), and maintains bulletin boards full of helpful advice, often from the contest winners themselves (see Figure 11-12).

Figure 11-10:
AOL's
member
Web page
contest.

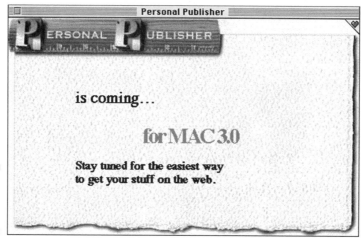

Figure 11-11:
Easy page
setup.

One odd feature of AOL is that its own browser (a modified version of last year's Microsoft Internet Explorer) isn't very helpful. You can look at a contest-winning page (see Figure 11-13), but you can't really check out the HTML details online. But if you find a page you like, you can save it and then open it in another browser, such as Navigator or Internet Explorer, to examine the details (see Figure 11-14). You can learn all the HTML you need simply by copying cool features from other Web pages.

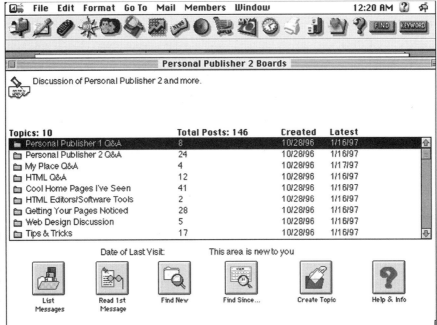

Figure 11-12:
Helpful tips
from other
AOL
members.

Figure 11-13:
A contest
winner on
AOL.

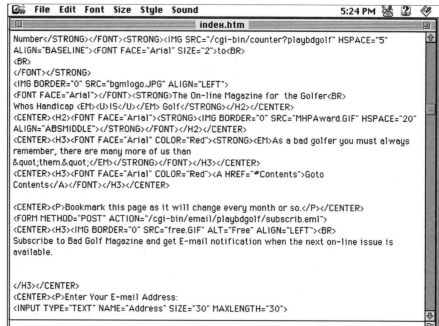

index.htm

```
Number</STRONG></FONT><STRONG><IMG SRC="/cgi-bin/counter?playbdgolf" HSPACE="5"
ALIGN="BASELINE"><FONT FACE="Arial" SIZE="2">to<BR>
<BR>
</FONT></STRONG>
<IMG BORDER="0" SRC="bgmlogo.JPG" ALIGN="LEFT">
<FONT FACE="Arial"></FONT><STRONG>The On-line Magazine for  the Golfer<BR>
Whos Handicap <EM><U>IS</U></EM> Golf</STRONG></H2></CENTER>
<CENTER><H2><FONT FACE="Arial"><STRONG><IMG BORDER="0" SRC="MHPAward.GIF" HSPACE="20"
ALIGN="ABSMIDDLE"></STRONG></FONT></H2></CENTER>
<CENTER><H3><FONT FACE="Arial" COLOR="Red"><STRONG><EM>As a bad golfer you must always
remember, there are many more of us than
&quot;them.&quot;</EM></STRONG></FONT></H3></CENTER>
<CENTER><H3><FONT FACE="Arial" COLOR="Red"><A HREF="#Contents">Goto
Contents</A></FONT></H3></CENTER>

<CENTER><P>Bookmark this page as it will change every month or so.</P></CENTER>
<FORM METHOD="POST" ACTION="/cgi-bin/email/playbdgolf/subscrib.eml">
<CENTER><H3><IMG BORDER="0" SRC="free.GIF" ALT="Free" ALIGN="LEFT"><BR>
Subscribe to Bad Golf Magazine and get E-mail notification when the next on-line issue is
available.


</H3></CENTER>
<CENTER><P>Enter Your E-mail Address:
<INPUT TYPE="TEXT" NAME="Address" SIZE="30" MAXLENGTH="30">
```

Figure 11-14:
The gory
HTML
details of
the winning
page.

The Future of HTML: JavaScript

Officially, the future of HTML is in the hands of a standards committee, deciding the design of future versions of the XML (extensible markup language) standard. The reality is, however, that both Netscape and Microsoft tend to keep adding non-compatible tweaks to standard HTML, and they both have more clout than the standards committee.

But the interesting development for Mac HTML fans is really JavaScript, anyway. JavaScript is a way of putting commands (based on the syntax of the serious programming language Java, which is much harder to use) into standard HTML pages. Just as with stock HTML for formatting, you can find hundreds of great examples of JavaScript in use out there on Web pages, just begging to be stolen.

What does it look like? Figure 11-15 shows a little example of a Fahrenheit-to-Celsius temperature converter in JavaScript, and Figure 11-16 shows the way it looks in a browser. Even this tiny example (by the way, doesn't it some-times strike you as odd that in the Wired U.S. of The Year 2000 we still use Fahrenheit, inches, and gallons?) is interactive, in the sense that the user enters numbers and the script then does a little math. It's a small extension of this example to loan calculators, order forms, and the other nuts and bolts of online business. So you can expect more JavaScript in HTML pages. Lots more. Soon.

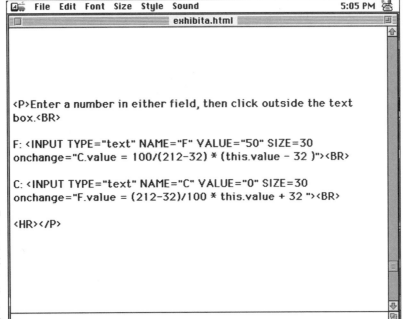

File Edit Font Size Style Sound   5:05 PM

exhibita.html

```
<P>Enter a number in either field, then click outside the text
box.<BR>

F: <INPUT TYPE="text" NAME="F" VALUE="50" SIZE=30
onchange="C.value = 100/(212-32) * (this.value - 32 )"><BR>

C: <INPUT TYPE="text" NAME="C" VALUE="0" SIZE=30
onchange="F.value = (212-32)/100 * this.value + 32 "><BR>

<HR></P>
```

Figure 11-15:
A
JavaScript
Fahrenheit-
to-Celsius
converter.

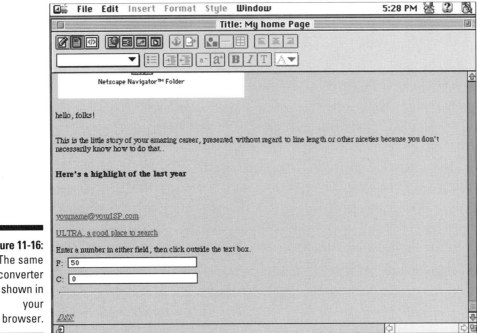

File Edit Insert Format Style Window   5:28 PM

Title: My home Page

Netscape Navigator™ Folder

hello, folks!

This is the little story of your amazing career, presented without regard to line length or other niceties because you don't necessarily know how to do that..

Here's a highlight of the last year

yourname@yourISP.com

ULTRA, a good place to search

Enter a number in either field, then click outside the text box.

F: [50]

C: [0]

DSS

Figure 11-16:
The same
converter
shown in
your
browser.

Ten Web page tips

1. Steal from the best. Anything that impresses you on another page can be part of yours. OK, I don't *really* mean steal. Web pages are copyrighted material, and people have been sued for plagiarism. Just visit some of sites and create something yourself, based on anything you saw that inspired you.

2. Keep it simple. Studies show that Web pages work more like magazine ads and less like encyclopedias.

3. Download browsers from both Microsoft and Netscape to make sure that your page looks right in either browser. If possible, have your pages viewed on a friend's Windows PC to check the look, too.

4. Try compressing all figures until they actually get blurry, then just back off a bit. Compression doesn't hurt quality very much.

5. Remember that tons of Web users are still working at 33.6 Kbps or slower.

6. Think twice before you post something stupid or embarrassing — it'll be all over the planet in a couple of hours.

7. Although movie files in Apple's QuickTime VR format aren't too bad (for size), posting lots of movies can clog your own Web site pretty badly.

8. Check out the HTML freeware at `http://www.macworld.com`.

9. Old advertising guys used to say, "Don't do bulleted lists with more than five items." They were right.

10. Get *JavaScript for Dummies,* Second Edition (IDG Books Worldwide, Inc.). It's your next step in becoming a Web hotshot.

Chapter 12

Special Effects: Web Audio and Video

● ●

● ●

*T*his is a guest chapter by Jim Heid, who has been *Macworld's* authority on audio and video since they first appeared on the Mac. He's produced loads of professional multimedia work, and his *HTML and Web Publishing Secrets*, also from IDG Books Worldwide, is the main current reference on using video and sound on the Web.

It's impossible to show it adequately in a book, but the Web is now booming with sound and dazzling with movies. To get started on this chapter, take a little break now and check out two sites. First, go to neworleansonline.com/rfno.htm, shown in Figure 12-1, and listen to the cool radio station from New Orleans. Then look at www.heidsite.com and have a peek through the Weathercam, shown in Figure 12-2. At both sites you'll find detailed instructions for downloading plug-ins for your browser to make the audio and video work. You're likely to find, though, that the browser you're using now already had the appropriate plug-ins when you started it.

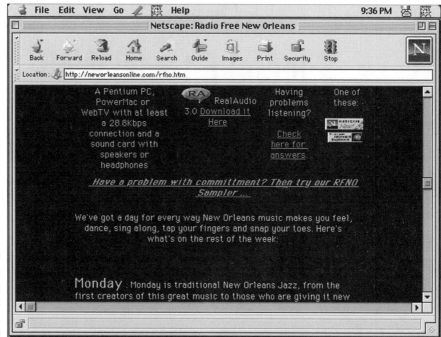

Figure 12-1:
It's always
Mardi Gras
at WNOR.

Figure 12-2:
The lovely
Mendocino
coast,
featuring
whales (no
kidding!) in
the spring.

The Internet's mostly modem connections rule out any surround-sound, high-resolution, audio-video extravaganzas, but they can certainly accommodate some audio-video seasoning. And if the experts are right — if, several years down the road, we will have virtually unlimited bandwidth — now is the time to start learning how to apply audio and video.

This chapter takes a look at ways to put audio and video on a Web site. Innumerable technicalities exist behind audio and video production, ranging from choosing microphones to lighting a scene to buying sound cards and video-digitizing hardware for your computer. I skip most of those details and concentrate on issues that affect you as a user: file formats, quality issues, compression, and HTML. If you don't have any audio or video experience, I recommend consulting the resources near the end of the chapter to learn more about details of the actual production process.

Sounding Off: Adding Sound to a Web Site

Audio's transmission speed demands are significant, but they're pretty modest compared to those of video. That's one good reason to start this brief tour in the audio realm. Here's another: Unless you're looking at silent movies on the Web, you can use some grounding in audio concepts for your move up to video.

To understand how a computer can record and play back sound, think first of a movie. By taking 24 photographs per second, a movie camera captures a reasonably accurate sampling of the action in front of it. When those samples are played back, the illusion of smooth motion is created.

Digital audio also samples motion — the moving air molecules that make up sounds. Vibrating objects — whether strings, saxophone reeds, vocal chords, or slamming car doors — produce *sound waves,* variations in air pressure that travel outward from the sound source like the ripples from a stone dropped into a pond.

A computer equipped with sound-recording circuitry can sample these sound waves thousands of times per second. Each sample is a digital image of the sound at a given instant. The samples, each recorded as a series of bits, are stored on a computer disk and can then be modified. Each modification alters the overall image of the sound wave, so when the samples are played back, you hear a different sound.

With movies, taking too few pictures per second results in jittery, unrealistic motion. With sound, taking too few samples per second results in a distorted recording that doesn't faithfully convey all the frequencies present in the original sound. Fortunately, most current Macs can record at 44.1 kHz, the same rate used by familiar audio CDs. Another factor that influences digital sound quality is the *sampling resolution* — a compact disc player has a 16-bit sampling resolution, as do most current Macs.

So-called *CD-quality* audio — 44.1 kHz, 16-bit sound — may be commonplace in music stores and even within computers, but it's a rarity on the Web. The reason is limited Web transmission speeds (bandwidth). One minute of 16-bit, 44.1 kHz stereo audio uses 10MB — *ten megabytes!* — of disk space. A Web surfer with a 14.4 Kbps modem would get old waiting to hear that clip.

Shifting audio gears

Web audio producers must digitally compress their audio tracks with sound editing software to reduce the sound file's size, thus reducing download times and bandwidth demands. The resulting sound file is usually something a great deal less than CD-quality. If you'd like the gory production details, look at www.rfspec.com/index.htm, a great resource for audio product information. Another terrific resource is Sweetwater Sound's Web site (see Figure 12-3) at www.sweetwater.com/. Sweetwater Sound is a major retailer of not only audio equipment, but also electronic musical instruments and music software.

Figure 12-3: An audio playground of digital tools.

Tools for soundworkers

Waves (www.waves.com) offers a family of state-of-the-art audio-processing utilities, most of which originally debuted as plug-in modules for high-end audio hardware systems from Digidesign (www.digidesign.com/). Most of the Waves family is now available for software-only Mac audio and video applications, including Adobe Premiere, Macromedia's Deck II, and SoundEdit 16.

Waves's L1 Ultramaximizer, a plug-in for Digidesign audio hardware, boosts a soundtrack's volume and shapes its waveform for optimal quality. Waves' WaveConvert utility also packs sophisticated level-optimization features that yield the best possible audio quality for the sample rate and bit depth you choose. WaveConvert can process batches of files, and it provides presets that are optimized for RealAudio. It's terrific.

If you want to put sound clips on your own Web site, you need a sound-editing program to cut, paste, and modify audio clips. Macromedia's SoundEdit 16 (www.macromedia.com/) and Bias Systems' Peak (www.bias-inc.com/) are excellent editing tools. All waveform-editing programs display a recorded sound as a waveform.

Using the sound-editing program, you can zoom in on the waveform display and select part or all of the waveform and cut or copy it to the Clipboard to rearrange the notes in a musical passage or the words in a phrase. You can also modify the sound, adding reverb to simulate a concert hall, or filtering certain frequencies to improve the sound quality. You can even reverse the sound to make it play backwards. Finally, you save the clip in a common audio file format. Just as a variety of graphics formats exist — GIF, JPEG, PICT, BMP — a large selection of audio file formats also exist — WAV, AIFF, AU, and more. As with graphics, your goal is to choose the format that retains the most quality and assures the broadest compatibility.

The three most popular formats for downloadable Web audio clips are AU, WAV, and AIFF. Netscape Navigator and Microsoft Internet Explorer (Version 3 or higher) now come equipped to play all three formats — no external helper application is required. Navigator's audio talents come from its LiveAudio technology, which debuted in Version 3.0. Microsoft Internet Explorer relies on Microsoft's ActiveMovie technology (which also debuted in Internet Explorer's 3.0 release) to play these formats as well as MPEG clips.

Which format is best? For voice, AU is a good bet. For music (or higher-quality voice), either WAV or AIFF are safe. Given that Windows machines make up the majority of the computers on the Web, you might stick with WAV. Doing so won't lock out any Macintosh users: The Mac versions of Navigator and Microsoft Internet Explorer can play back WAV files, as can popular Mac helper applications for audio, such as SoundApp and SoundMachine.

Audio etiquette

Here are a few things to keep in mind if you put Web audio clips on your own page:

🗸 **Consider multiple versions.** Because Web surfers may have anything from a 14.4 Kbps modem to a 10 Mbps cable modem, consider providing each audio file in a compact, low-fidelity form and in a larger, high-fidelity form. This means more work for you, but it will allow visitors to choose the format that best suits their connection speeds.

🗸 **Tell 'em what they're in for.** For most audio formats, include the file size and format within parenthesis near the clip. For example:

Fingernails on a chalkboard (45K WAV file, 50K AIFF file).

Here's a brief listing of file types for reference:

🗸 **AU** is one of the most common audio file formats on the Web. AU files of 8 kHz have a fidelity — if you can call it that — roughly equivalent to that of a telephone.

🗸 **WAV** is the standard file format in the Windows world. WAV files, whose names end with the file extension *.WAV,* are also extremely common on the Web. Most Mac and all Windows sound programs can open and save WAV files.

🗸 **AIFF** stands for Audio Interchange File Format (commonly referred to as either AIFF or Audio IFF). It's the Mac equivalent to the WAV file.

🗸 **QuickTime** isn't an audio file format, strictly speaking. But because both Netscape Navigator 3 and Microsoft Internet Explorer 3 (and later versions of both) can play QuickTime movies, you'll see audio clips in QuickTime format.

🗸 **RA** is the format used by Progressive Networks's RealAudio technology, which allows for real-time *streaming audio* over the Internet. You'll see more on RealAudio later in this chapter.

🗸 **MPEG** is a data-compression standard most commonly associated with digital video, but it's also gaining popularity for distributing audio on the Web.

Understanding sound and HTML

You have several ways to get sound clips on a page (see Chapter 13 for more on HTML). You can create simple hyperlinks to the sound clips using the ⟨a⟩ (anchor) tag, as in:

```
<a href="loudsound.wav">Hold your ears!</a>
```

This is the simplest method and it provides the broadest browser compatibility. You can also use the `<embed>` tag, which has the benefit of enabling the sound's controller (its playback buttons) to appear within a page — that is, with text, graphics, and other elements around it. For example, to embed a QuickTime movie in a Web page, a line of HTML may look a bit like this:

```
<embed SRC="//movies/mymovie.mov" NAME="My Movie" WIDTH=300
       HEIGHT=200>
```

Incorporating streaming audio

Instead of waiting a minute or more while an audio file downloads from the Web, a newer method called streaming audio starts up almost immediately as the rest of the file downloads. Debuting in 1995, RealAudio (`www.realaudio.com`) was the first streaming audio technology (see Figure 12-4). It sounded scratchy, but it worked, and the advantage of streaming audio become immediately apparent: Major networks and media outlets added RealAudio content to their sites, and news magazines ran articles about "Internet radio."

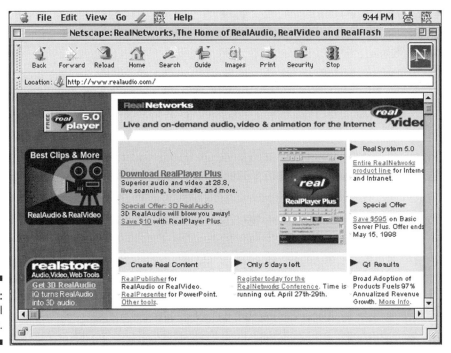

Figure 12-4:
It's real, all
right.

RealAudio clips begin life like every other sound clip: as ordinary WAV-, AU-, AIFF-, or PCM-format audio files. You process them into RealAudio format using Progressive Networks' RealAudio Encoder. The encoder applies filtering to the original clip, compresses it, and stores it as a RealAudio RA file. This RealAudio file is downloaded and played on a visitor's system by the RealPlayer application or the RealPlayer plug-in.

RealPlayer Plus also enables visitors to record incoming RealAudio or RealVideo content to their hard drives so they can replay it later — the basic, free-download RealAudio Player and RealPlayer don't permit this. This is the *selective record* feature, and you can enable it for a given clip by checking the Encoder's Enable Selective Record button. Note that doing so makes it possible for unscrupulous listeners to pirate content.

To get a RealAudio file to stream, Web site developers use a tiny file, called a *metafile,* that references the RA file. They then reference that metafile in your HTML page using a standard <a> tag. When a visitor clicks the link, the metafile causes the visitor's RealPlayer to launch, and the player then accesses the server and begins retrieving and playing the RealAudio file.

Using Video on Web Sites

Of all the data types that go into a Web site, the one that imposes the greatest playback demands on a computer and its network connection is, of course, video. As the previous section has shown, streaming audio is a reality now. But audio is easy compared to video, where every second of content is made up of 30 frames, each containing thousands of pixels — *plus* audio. In case you skipped your computer manual's techie section, a *pixel* is a graphic point on your monitor. Group several hundred or thousand pixels together of various shades and colors, and you have a picture on your screen. Imagine trying to manage millions of pixels on a screen. It's a lot of work.

For most World Wide Web users, smooth streaming of high-quality digital video just isn't a reality yet:

- The Internet, the phone system, the modems — the entire Web infra- structure — can't provide the bandwidth of even a double-speed CD-ROM drive.

- High-speed connections, particularly cable modems and satellite links, have the potential to make high-quality streaming video real, but only for a select few users at first. Cable modems are just becoming avail- able to a scant few who (guess who?) have cable television, and satellite links are still too expensive for the average Joe.

- Even a high-speed connection can't overcome the performance vagar- ies of the Internet itself.

But these are today's limitations. A faster Internet infrastructure, more efficient video-compression techniques, and other advancements *will* make high-quality streaming Web video practical. However, video streaming is available today:

- ✔ If you're willing to sacrifice image and sound quality, lower-quality video streaming technology is available now.

- ✔ Plenty of Web sites contain downloadable video clips that weigh in at a megabyte or much more, and plenty of Web surfers seem to be willing to download them.

- ✔ The latest video technologies, particularly Apple's QuickTime 3.0 plug-in for Netscape Navigator and Microsoft's ActiveMovie, can provide some of the immediate-gratification advantages of streaming video.

If you're a video beginner, you may want to pay a visit to my Web site (www.heidsite.com/), where you'll find background and tutorials on video (and audio) basics.

Answering the video format question

There's no question: It's QuickTime (www.apple.com/quicktime/), as shown in Figure 12-5. Apple's digital video technology dominates the personal computer world on both Mac and Windows platforms. Using QuickTime for your video clips gives you the broadest platform and browser compatibility. Apple's QuickTime plug-in module for Netscape Navigator provides a *fast-start* feature that even provides for *pseudo-streaming*: If the combination of movie size and connection speed allows, the movie plays back while it downloads.

Beyond these advantages, QuickTime is simply superior to Microsoft's Video for Windows (AVI). Basics such as sound synchronization are better, and QuickTime also allows for advanced features, such as text tracks that can display closed-captioning text beneath a video. Microsoft's ActiveMovie shows promise, but for now at least, it's geared more to consumer-level video playback than to video production. MPEG is another option for Web-based video. Windows and Mac OS machines alike can play back MPEG video with no additional hardware. (Windows machines need Microsoft's ActiveMovie; Power Macs can use Apple's MPEG Extension for QuickTime.) But encoding MPEG video is time consuming and difficult, and slower machines may not be able to play it back smoothly. Indeed, 680X0-based Macs can't use the Apple MPEG playback extension. For these reasons, QuickTime is a better format.

Figure 12-5:
QuickTime
is cool and
free.

Understanding video and HTML

Many of the same comments about HTML for audio (that is, including sound sources in your page that play on both Windows and Mac OS systems) also apply to video clips. Pages should post video clips in both QuickTime and Video for Windows format to improve cross-platform compatibility. And pages should *always* tell visitors how large a movie file is before displaying an embedded movie.

The basics of the `<embed>` tag are the same for video as they are for audio, but height and width tag attributes are required for embedding video. If you don't know the dimensions of a clip, you can find out using the Apple MoviePlayer utility, which comes with every Mac as part of the QuickTime software.

Normally, a QuickTime movie doesn't begin playback until a visitor explicitly clicks its play button. If you'd rather have the movie begin playback automatically, add `autoplay=true` to the `<embed>` command. As soon as the visitor's QuickTime plug-in determines that enough of the movie has downloaded to allow for smooth playback of the entire movie, it begins playback.

Looking around the Web, you'll see a variety of video formats. Should you decide to create video content, remember that browsers and helper applications (see Chapter 4) currently rely on these file extensions to identify the video file format. Table 12-1 lists the extensions for each format. This table can also help you identify what type of movie format you find online, and guide you to what utility is needed to view the item.

Table 12-1	File Extensions for the Most Popular Video File Formats
For This Format	*Use This Extension*
QuickTime	.mov
Video for Windows	.avi
MPEG	.mpeg or .mpg
VivoActive	.viv

Streaming video with VivoActive

Streaming video is what's happening at the leading edge on the Web (with the corresponding sacrifices in image and sound quality) and on intranets (where quality is okay because bandwidth constraints aren't as significant). An *intranet* is a scaled-down Internet-like network that's accessible by only a select group, such as an office building. Several streaming video technologies are available, including VDO's VDOLive (www.vdo.net/), RealNetworks' RealVideo (www.real.com/), and as shown in Figure 12-6, Vivo's VivoActive (www.vivo.com/).

VivoActive's features, ease of use, and results are impressive. You can view VivoActive clips on such high-profile sites as CNN's site (www.cnn.com/) and, as shown in Figure 12-7, Home Box Office's site (www.hbo.com/).

VivoActive is cross-platform. The VivoActive browser plug-in is available for the Windows and Mac (PowerPC only) platforms. VivoActive Producer, the software that compresses video into VivoActive format, is also available for both platforms. It doesn't require any special kind of Web server. And VivoActive Producer software makes it easy to compress QuickTime or Video for Windows files into VivoActive format. From there, a simple <embed> command puts your video on the Web.

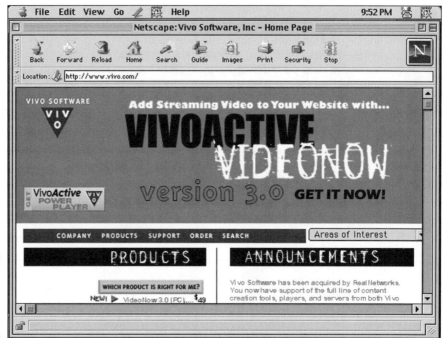

Figure 12-6:
VivoActive,
sharp tools
for video.

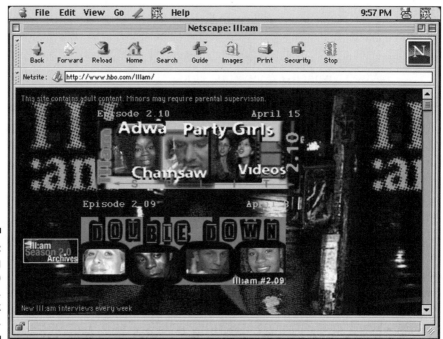

Figure 12-7:
Moving
Web
pictures.
Just click
for pix.

Another strong contender is RealVideo, from the RealAudio people. It has most of the same virtues as VivoActive, plus a few tricks of its own. On a Mac, developers encode RealVideo clips using Progressive Networks' RealVideo Encoder plug-in for Adobe Premiere. As with RealAudio files, site builders can't add a RealVideo clip to a page by simply referring to the clip's name in a URL. If they did, the entire clip would download to a visitor's hard drive, thus defeating RealVideo's streaming talents.

As with RealAudio, developers create a text file that references the RealVideo clip and then call that text file in HTML. They also use the `<embed>` tag to play back video clips using the RealPlayer plug-in instead of the RealPlayer helper application.

Chapter 13

Microsoft Office and the Web

● ●

● ●

*T*his is a guest chapter by Tom Negrino, an old friend and co-author of *Macworld Web Essentials* (IDG Books Worldwide, Inc.) who has prepared a magnificent volume, *Microsoft Office 98 For Dummies* (IDG Books Worldwide, Inc.). If you want the complete story on the new Macintosh Office, easily the best Mac product from Microsoft in a decade, order Mr. Negrino's book directly from www.idgbooks.com.

What a difference a few years makes. When version 4.2 of Microsoft Office was released, the Internet was used mainly by a fairly small group of people, mostly in universities. Since then, the World Wide Web has been invented, practically everyone and their grandmother has an e-mail address, and the Internet has been the subject of a seemingly endless torrent of complaints, praise, and hype. In the real world, the Internet is neither the savior of humanity nor the destroyer of Western Civilization; it's just a bunch of computers hooked up to one another over really fast phone lines.

Microsoft has responded to the rise of the Internet by building Internet integration features into all the Office 98 programs. Word, Excel, and PowerPoint can now all save their documents as Web pages. And you can put *hyperlinks* into any Office document. A hyperlink connects one part of your document to a Web page, a different location within the same document, or to a different Office document on your hard disk. For example, you can have a table of contents at the start of a long document, with each heading hyperlinked to the appropriate part of the document. Clicking a heading in the table of contents takes you to that part of the document.

Using Hyperlinks

Hyperlinks enhance the usability of your documents by enabling the reader to easily get to related or supporting information. To insert a hyperlink, you need to tell whichever Office application you're working in where the link starts and its destination. By convention, the hyperlink is formatted blue and underlined, but Office 98 enables you to customize that style if you want.

Linking to Web pages or Office documents

To insert a hyperlink that points to a Web page or another Office 98 document, follow these steps:

1. **In your current document, select any text or picture that you want to turn into a hyperlink.**

2. **Choose Insert⇨Hyperlink, click the Insert Hyperlink button on the Standard toolbar, or press Cmd-K if you're using Word or PowerPoint.**

   The Insert Hyperlink dialog box appears, as shown in Figure 13-1.

3. **Choose one of the following:**

   - If you're hyperlinking to a Web site, type the URL of the Web page in the Link to file or URL box and then click the OK button.

   - If you're linking to another Office document, click the Select button next to the Link to file or URL box, find and double-click a file, and then click the OK button.

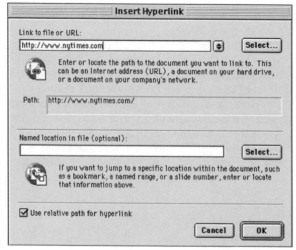

Figure 13-1:
The Insert Hyperlink dialog box.

The Office program you're using creates the hyperlink, formatting it blue and underlined. This formatting makes seeing the links in your document easy.

Adding hyperlinks as you type

Word 98 is smart enough to recognize all the standard forms of URLs (Universal Resource Locators — Internet addresses) and can format them automatically as hyperlinks as you type them. To turn on this automatic hyperlink formatting, follow these steps:

1. **Choose Tools⇨AutoCorrect and then click the AutoFormat As You Type tab.**

2. **Under the Replace as you type section, click the Internet paths with hyperlinks check box. See Figure 13-2.**

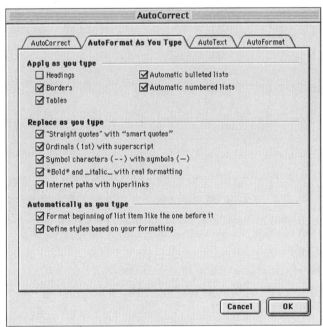

Figure 13-2:
Turning on automatic hyperlinking.

3. **Click the OK button.**

Whenever you type a URL into your document, Word 98 turns the URL into a hyperlink. If the URL is for a Web page and you're reading the document, clicking the hyperlink launches your Web browser (Internet Explorer or Netscape Navigator), connects to the Internet, and loads the Web page. If the URL is an e-mail address, your e-mail program starts up and a new e-mail message is created and addressed.

Internal links

An internal hyperlink jumps the reader from one part of your document to another part of the same document. Follow these steps to create an internal hyperlink in any Office document:

1. **Select the text or picture that is the destination of the hyperlink; in other words, where the reader ends up after they click the hyperlink.**

2. **Choose Insert⇨Bookmark.**

   The Bookmark dialog box appears, as shown in Figure 13-3.

Figure 13-3:
The
Bookmark
dialog box.

3. **Enter the name for your bookmark and then click the Add button.**

4. **Select the text or graphic that you want to define as a hyperlink.**

5. **Choose Insert⇨Hyperlink, click the Insert Hyperlink button on the Standard toolbar, or press Cmd-K if you're using Word or PowerPoint.**

   The Insert Hyperlink dialog box appears.

6. **Click the Select button next to the Named location in file (optional): box.**

   The Bookmark dialog box reappears.

7. **Click the bookmark that you want to be the hyperlink's destination and then click the OK button.**

8. **Click the OK button in the Insert Hyperlink dialog box.**

Removing hyperlinks

After working with a document for a while, you may want to eliminate a hyperlink. To remove a hyperlink, follow these steps:

1. **Select the offending hyperlink.**

2. **Choose Insert⇨Hyperlink, or press Cmd-K if you're using Word or PowerPoint.**

   The Insert Hyperlink dialog box appears.

3. **Click the Remove Link button.**

Using the Web Toolbar

The Web toolbar (see Figure 13-4) is available in all the Office 98 applications, and it enables you to integrate Web browsing with your work. You use the Web toolbar when you're working on a document and you want to look something up on a Web site. Basically, the Web toolbar is a condensed set of the same buttons found in a Web browser, like the Back and Next buttons, a Stop button, and a place to type in a URL (a Web site address).

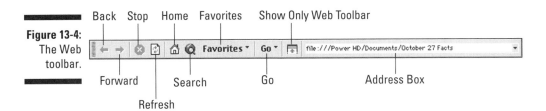

Figure 13-4:
The Web toolbar.

Back Stop Home Favorites — Show Only Web Toolbar

Forward — Search — Go — Address Box

Refresh

Showing the Web toolbar

To display the Web toolbar, do one of the following:

- ✓ **Choose View⇨Toolbars⇨Web.**

- ✓ **Control-click any toolbar, and choose Web from the resulting pop-up menu.**

- ✓ **Choose Tools⇨Customize, click the Toolbars tab, and then click the checkbox by Web. Click the Close button.**

Browsing with the Web toolbar

After you make a choice from the Web toolbar, the Web page isn't displayed inside the Office program that you're using. Rather, Office sends a message to whatever Web browser you've set up in Internet Config or the Mac OS 8.5 Internet control panel (see Chapter 4 if you're scratching your head at this point) as your default browser, which then launches and loads that Web page.

The Web toolbar has most of the same navigation buttons as Internet Explorer. As in that program, Office uses the various settings that you've made in Internet Config, so it inherits your home page and your preferred search engine when you click the Search button. Office also contains the Favorites menu with all your Internet Explorer bookmarks.

To browse the Web with the Web toolbar, use the toolbar in the same way that you would with Internet Explorer (see Chapter 6 if you need to review the details).

Creating Web Pages with Office 98

All the Office programs can save their documents in HTML, which is Web format. Word 98 does a much better job of it than Excel or PowerPoint, however. Word 98 has many features that help you create Web pages, and considering that it's a word processor, you can use it to create surprisingly credible Web pages. You probably won't turn to Word 98 as your main Web page creation tool, but it's definitely worth using to convert your Word documents into Web pages. After converting, you may want to touch the pages up a bit by using a true Web page editor such as Claris Home Page, Symantec's Visual Page, or GoLive CyberStudio.

Excel and PowerPoint aren't nearly as capable as Word because they lack the editing capabilities needed to create Web pages. You're best off to use the HTML export capabilities of these programs as a starting point, knowing that you'll be editing the resulting pages with Word 98 or another Web site building program.

Building Web pages in Word 98

Basically two ways exist to create Web pages using Word 98. One way is to use Word from scratch to build the page, perhaps using Word's templates or Wizards for assistance. The other way is to take an existing Word document and save it as HTML.

What's this HTML stuff?

HTML is an acronym that stands for HyperText Markup Language, which is the format used to create Web pages. Nothing is really special about an HTML file; it's just plain text surrounded by *markup tags,* which tell the Web browser how to interpret the text inside the tags. For example, I want to display the phrase "Office 98" in boldface on a Web page. The HTML code to do that looks like this:

```
<B>Office 98</B>
```

The first tag, <B>, starts the boldface formatting, and the end tag, </B>, ends boldface.

The nice thing about using Word 98 to build Web pages is that you generally don't have to mess with HTML. But nothing is stopping you from editing the HTML pages that Word creates, either. If you'd like to find out more about HTML, pick up any of the three billion books on the subject. You may want to start with one of two books, however: *HTML and Web Publishing Secrets,* by Jim Heid, or *HTML 4 For Dummies,* by Ed Tittel and Stephen Nelson James, both published by IDG Books Worldwide, Inc.

Using the Web Page Wizard

The Web Page Wizard produces a variety of pages that may be all that you need for a simple Web site. Similar to all Wizards, it walks you through a number of steps and ends up with a page that's mostly finished. You just need to add your text and (sometimes) graphics to finish the page.

To use the Web Page Wizard to create a Web page, follow these steps:

1. **Choose File⇨New and then click the Web Pages tab.**

   The New dialog box opens, as shown in Figure 13-5.

2. **Click the Web Page Wizard and then click the OK button.**

   The Web Wizard dialog box appears, as shown in Figure 13-6. A new document also appears, behind the dialog box.

3. **From the Web Wizard dialog box, click which kind of Web page you want to create and then click the Next button.**

   You'll notice that as you make choices, the page behind the dialog box changes to reflect your choice. The next screen of the Wizard enables you to choose the visual style of the page, as in Figure 13-7.

4. **Click the Finish button.**

   The Wizard dialog box goes away, and you're left with a document template ready for customization, as shown in Figure 13-8.

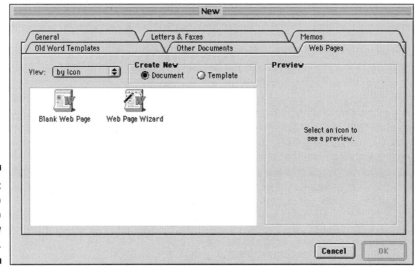

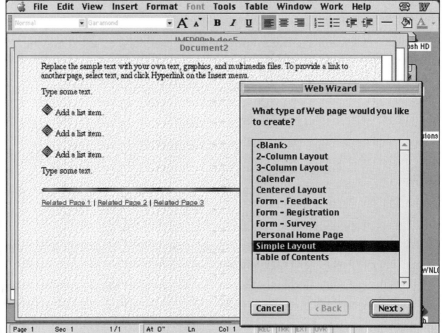

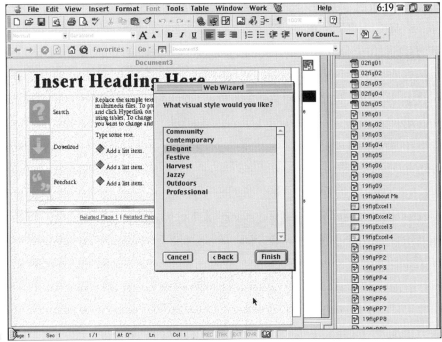

Figure 13-7:
Choosing
the look of
your Web
page.

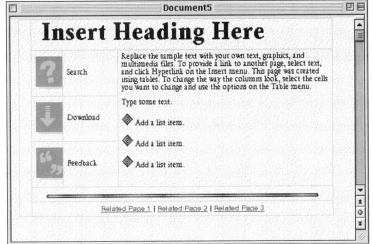

Figure 13-8:
The Web
page
template.

5. **Replace the sample text in the template with your information. The final result should look something like Figure 13-9.**

The page template appears in Online Layout mode so that you can see how the page looks in a browser. But no substitute exists for looking at the page in a real Web browser. No exact correspondence exists between the way that Word 98 displays a page and the way it looks in a browser. Always preview your pages in a browser before you publish them to the Web.

Figure 13-9:
The
completed
page,
viewed in
Netscape
Navigator.

Saving a document as HTML

To save a document that you've already created as a Web page, follow these steps:

1. **Open the document you want to convert.**

2. **Choose File⇨Save as HTML.**

   The Save As dialog box appears.

3. **Type in the name of the new file. For most Web servers to recognize the file, you need to add the ".html" extension to the file name. For example, if you're writing about a bill moving through Congress, you may name your file porkbarrel.html.**

   Naming HTML files using no spaces or slashes is vital. Spaces and slashes confuse the heck out of Web servers. Using all lowercase is also a good idea (but not mandatory).

4. **Click the Save button.**

    The Office Assistant pops up a message warning you that some formatting may be lost in the conversion to HTML. That's because you can't do all the things on a Web page that you can within Word.

5. **Roll your eyes, mutter "yeah, yeah," and click the Yes button to complete the conversion.**

Adding flashy pictures to your Web pages

Most Word documents look pretty dull when you convert them into Web pages. One good way to liven them up is to add pictures to the page. The Office 98 CD-ROM comes with tons of clip art and photographs that you can use on your Web pages.

To add pictures to your Web page, follow these steps:

1. **Put the cursor where you want the picture to appear.**

2. **Choose one of the following:**

    • Insert➪Picture➪ClipArt to pick a picture from the Office 98 clip art library.

    • Insert➪Picture➪From File to choose another picture that's on your hard disk.

    • Insert➪Picture➪Browse Web Art Page to connect to the Internet and check out the Web art available from Microsoft's Web site.

3. **Find the picture that you want to put in your page and then click the Insert button.**

Turning Excel spreadsheets into Web pages

When Excel 98 saves a spreadsheet as HTML, it turns the file into a big, plain HTML table. This table can then be prettied up in a Web page editor or in Word 98. Excel uses a Wizard to step you through the process.

To save a spreadsheet as an HTML document, follow these steps:

1. **Open an existing Excel 98 spreadsheet, or create and save a new spreadsheet.**

2. **Select the part of the spreadsheet that you want to convert into a Web page.**

3. **Choose File➪Save As HTML.**

    The Internet Assistant Wizard appears, as shown in Figure 13-10.

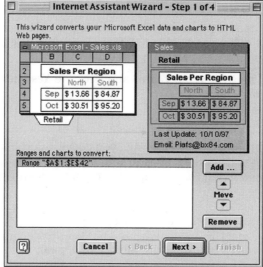

4. Click the Next button.

The second Wizard screen enables you to create a new Web page or insert the converted data into an existing HTML file, as shown in Figure 13-11. If you create a new page, remember that you can always cut and paste the data into an existing page later.

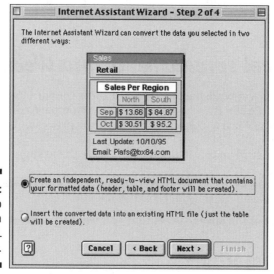

Figure 13-11:
Choosing to
create a
new HTML
page.

5. Click the Create an independent, ready-to-view HTML document radio button and then click the Next button.

The next screen, shown in Figure 13-12, enables you to add information to the HTML page, such as headers and footers, the name of the person updating the document, and an e-mail address.

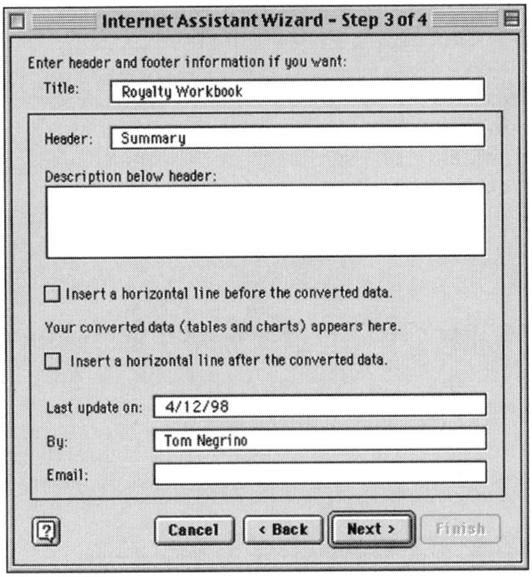

Figure 13-12:
Adding a title and other information to the Web page.

6. Enter the information you want on the Web page and then click the Next button.

The final Wizard screen tells Excel 98 where you want to save the converted file, as shown in Figure 13-13.

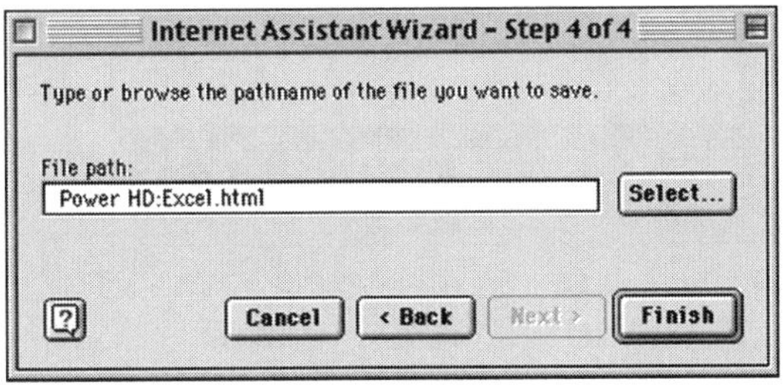

Figure 13-13:
Saving the HTML page.

7. Click the Select button to choose where you want to save the HTML file, and then click the Finish button.

Converting PowerPoint presentations into Web pages

Turning a PowerPoint presentation into a series of Web pages is certainly possible, and the process isn't that difficult. The trouble is that the results aren't great. PowerPoint exports each of the slides as a GIF or JPEG graphic, and the text on the slides tends to look jagged and unpleasant. And because each slide is one big graphic, you can't edit the results.

A better alternative to using PowerPoint's built-in HTML export is to use the $69 Terry Morse Myrmidon (http://www.terrymorse.com), a utility that gives HTML export capabilities to any program. Myrmidon does a superior job, and the pages it creates are completely editable.

To convert an existing PowerPoint 98 presentation into Web pages, follow these steps:

1. **Open an existing PowerPoint 98 presentation, or create and save a new presentation.**

2. **Choose File⇨Save As HTML.**

   The Save As HTML Wizard appears, as shown in Figure 13-14.

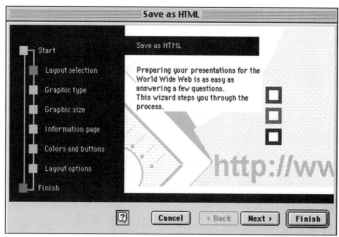

Figure 13-14: The Save As HTML Wizard starts the conversion of your PowerPoint presentation into Web pages.

3. **Click the Next button.**

   The Wizard gives you a choice of Standard or Framed page layouts, as shown in Figure 13-15.

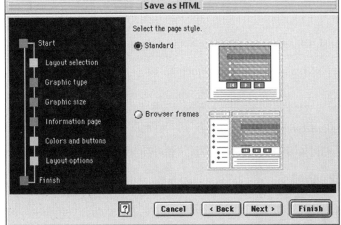

Figure 13-15:
Choosing
whether
you'll be
using
frames.

4. **Click the Standard or Browser frames button and then click the Next button.**

   Next you're asked if you want to save graphics in GIF or JPEG format, as shown in Figure 13-16. You're best off using the JPEG option, because it reproduces the colors in your slides more faithfully. The Compression pop-up menu enables you to choose between four quality levels of the saved graphics. Best Quality produces better images but creates larger files. On the other end of the scale, Best Compression produces smaller files of lower quality. Unless you're running an online art museum, Best Compression is your best bet. The results can be viewed on monitors at 72 dpi, so viewers see the same quality anyway, and the files load faster.

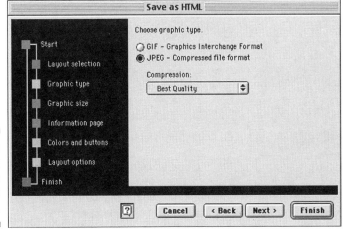

Figure 13-16:
Deciding
on the
graphics
format.

5. Click the GIF or JPEG button, and then click the Next button.

The next screen enables you to choose the resolution for the saved graphics. Because you're saving files for the Web, the best thing to do is to go for the lowest common denominator, which is the 640 × 480 resolution, as shown in Figure 13-17.

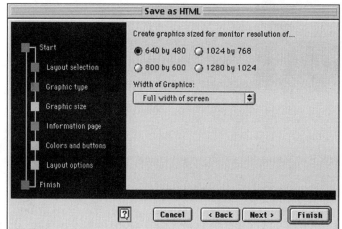

Figure 13-17: Choosing the graphics size.

6. Click the monitor resolution that you want to use and then click the Next button.

In the next screen, shown in Figure 13-18, the Wizard asks you for information that you can put on the Web pages, such as your e-mail address or the URL of your home page.

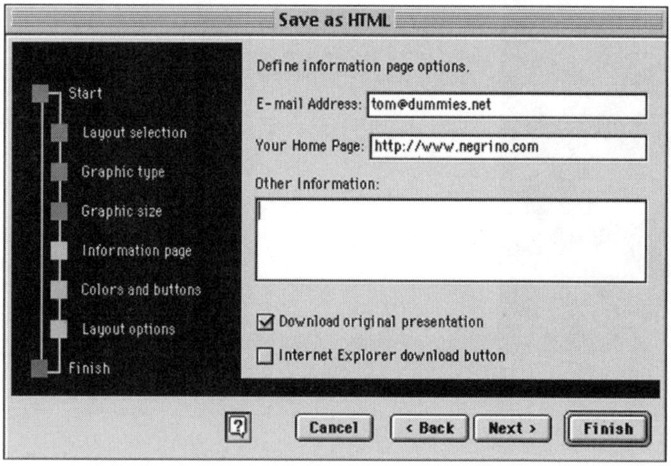

Figure 13-18: Adding your personal information.

7. Fill in the information that you want to include on the Web pages, and then click the Next button.

The next part of the Wizard enables you to customize the colors used in the pages, including the colors of the background, text, links, and visited links, as shown in Figure 13-19.

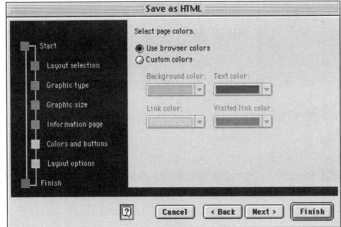

Figure 13-19:
Choosing the page colors.

8. If you want to go with the standard browser colors, leave the Use browser colors button checked and click the Next button. If you prefer to customize the colors, click the Custom colors button and fiddle away with the color choices.

On the next screen, shown in Figure 13-20, you get to pick the style of the navigation buttons the user will use to move through your presentation.

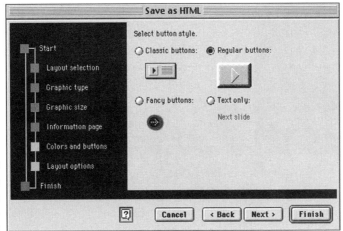

Figure 13-20:
Selecting a button style.

9. **Choose a button style and then click the Next button.**

Yes, this process is almost at an end. In this next screen you decide where the buttons you picked in the last screen appear; at the top, bottom, left, or right of the slides, as shown in Figure 13-21.

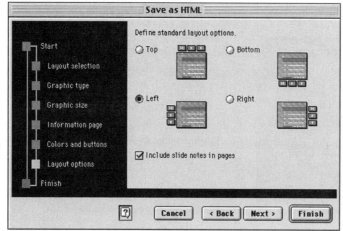

Figure 13-21: Deciding on the button layout.

10. **Click a button with the layout you want and then click the Next button.**

Figure 13-22 shows you the last choice you'll need to make. Choose the location where you want to save the files from the PowerPoint conversion.

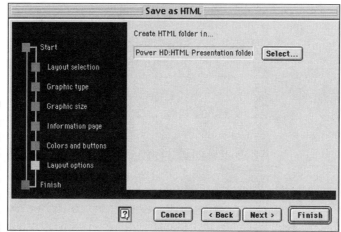

Figure 13-22: Telling PowerPoint where to save the presentation files.

11. **Click the Finish button.**

A Web Server of Your Own

Most of the time that you create documents for the Web, you upload them to your company or organization's Web server so that they can be viewed by anyone on the Internet. But you have another way of sharing those documents; you can fire up your very own Web server on your Macintosh. Sound complicated? Not at all! In fact, you probably already have the software that you need installed on your hard disk. The excellent Microsoft Personal Web Server (PWS) is installed along with the rest of the Easy Install of Internet Explorer 4.0. Take a look inside the Microsoft Internet Applications folder on your hard drive; you should see a Personal Web Server folder. If the folder isn't there, put in the Office 98 CD-ROM, run the Internet Explorer installer, and perform a Custom Install of the Personal Web Server.

Web serving with a personal touch

A personal Web server is designed for relatively light use, usually within a company's network. The Microsoft Personal Web Server (PWS) is easy to install and use, and surprisingly powerful. It runs in the background, so it doesn't slow down your Mac, and PWS only needs about 1.5MB of RAM. It can serve thousands of Web pages per day without breaking a sweat.

You can be up and running in literally just a few minutes with the PWS. And the personal site you end up with already has a home page, FTP upload capability, a visitor counter, a guestbook, a way for your site visitors to leave you private messages, and you can browse your hard disk over the Internet (don't worry; it's password-protected). This last feature enables you to transfer files from your office machine when you're at home or traveling on the road. People anywhere in the world can read Web pages running on your machine. So you can easily publish your travel schedule to the other people in your workgroup just by saving a file in Word 98 and putting it in your Personal Web Server folder.

An *intranet* is a private network running Internet-standard programs, such as e-mail, FTP, and Web servers. This means that people working at the company can use the same programs (Outlook Express, Claris Emailer, or Eudora for e-mail; Internet Explorer or Netscape Navigator for Web browsing, and so on) to access company information available on the company's intranet and other information from the Internet.

The fastest way to publish on your company's intranet is to use the Microsoft Personal Web Server software provided with Office. To use the Personal Web Server effectively, your Mac needs a full-time intranet connection. You can use the PWS for personal (non-company) publishing with a dial-up connection, but that means that people are only able to get to your

Web pages while you're connected. Most companies' Net connection is full-time; if you're not sure, ask your network administrator. If you connect to the Internet over the local area network rather than a modem, you almost certainly have a full-time Internet connection.

Setting up the Personal Web Server

It only takes a few minutes to set up the Personal Web Server. Follow these steps:

1. **Choose Apple Menu⇨Control Panels⇨Personal Web Manager.**

   The Main screen appears as in Figure 13-23.

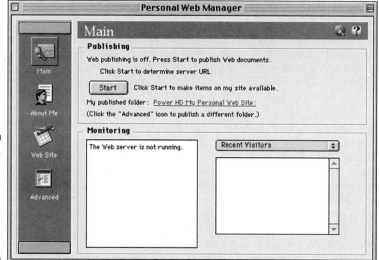

Figure 13-23:
The Main screen of the Personal Web Server.

2. **Click the About Me icon.**

3. **In the middle of the window is a pop-up menu that enables you to choose whether your Web site will be for your company, home, school, organization, or community. Choose one.**

   The fields in the bottom half of the window change to reflect the choice you made in the pop-up menu.

4. **Fill in the fields on the About Me screen, pressing the Tab key to move from field to field.**

   You don't have to fill in all the fields; for example, if you don't want to put your phone number on your Web site, leave that field blank.

5. **This step is optional.** If you want to put a picture on your home page, you can drag or paste a PICT, GIF, or JPEG file into either (or both) of the two picture fields on the About Me screen. When you're done, the About Me screen should look something like Figure 13-24.

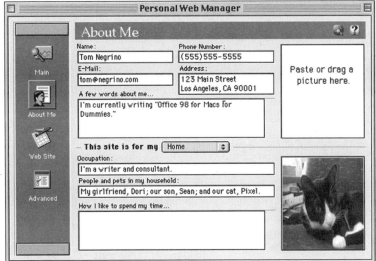

Figure 13-24:
The completed About Me screen.

6. Click the Web Site icon.

7. In this screen, type the title of your page into the Title field.

8. **This step is optional.** If you'd like to put links to other sites on your home page, fill in the Link Description and URL fields and then click the Add button. Repeat as necessary until you have all links you wish listed.

9. Click the Main icon.

10. Click the Start button. The Personal Web Server starts up, determines the URL for your server, and displays that URL in the Publishing section.

11. To view your Web page, click the server URL in the Publishing section. Internet Explorer starts up (if it isn't open already) and shows you your new page, which should look something like Figure 13-25.

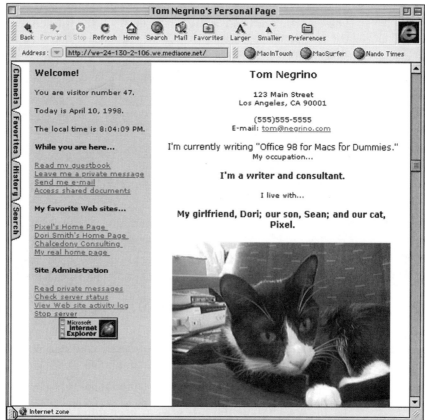

Figure 13-25:
Your new
Web page
should look
something
like this.

Adding to your personal Web site

One of the automatic links generated on your home page is *Access shared documents*. This link is the key to making documents easily accessible through the Personal Web Server. Clicking this link takes you to a listing of folders and files, as shown in Figure 13-26.

Here's how to add files and folders to your site. The PWS puts a folder called My Personal Web Site on the top level of your hard disk. Inside that folder is another folder called My Shared Documents. To publish a text, HTML, or picture file on the Web, all that's necessary is to drag it to the My Shared Documents folder. The PWS automatically indexes the files and creates the document list. If you have a bunch of files already organized in a folder as a Web site, just drag the folder to the My Shared Documents folder.

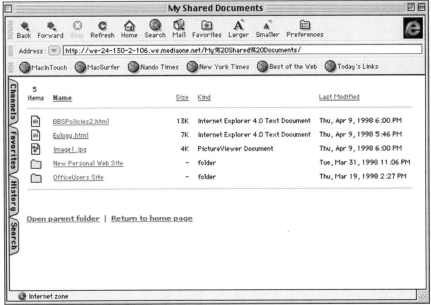

Figure 13-26:
Viewing
your shared
documents.

If you have text-only documents, the Personal Web Server can publish them without you needing to convert them to HTML first. The server converts text files to HTML on the fly.

The Personal Web Server has many more features, including some features usually found on industrial-strength Web servers. It's amazingly robust, and you just can't beat the price. To find out more about the PWS's capabilities, open the Personal Web Manager and choose Help⇨Personal Web Server Help.

Chapter 14

Web Business: As the Consumer

. . . .

In This Chapter

▶ Shopping around the world

▶ Shopping for specialty items

▶ Ensuring secure transactions

▶ Shopping for your Mac

. . . .

Some of the incredible explosion of the Web came about because people in universities saw the Web as an ideal way to distribute research results. Some of it happened because people at non-profit organizations found the Web an ideal way to communicate with people interested in good causes.

Something like 97 percent of the growth of the Web, however, by actual count of sites indexed by Yahoo!, has been caused by people who want to sell you something. You can buy this book on the Web, as well as the Mac I'm using to write it (an old 7100 with a G3 upgrade from Newer Technology), or, for that matter, nearly everything I'm wearing (shirt, pants, and shoes from Land's End — okay, the underwear I bought in a real store).

So let's do a little Web exploring, credit card in hand, and see how you feel about trudging around a mall parking lot in the rain after you see what you can do online.

Shopping Globally, Online

Five thousand years ago, at least according to historical records discovered so far, the first centers that had collections of stores with goods from far-away lands (sort of like the Nikes made in Vietnam at a mall near you) were found in small clusters on the shores of the Persian Gulf. For religious (can't buy Speedos for women in Iran) and economic (if you don't have oil, you can still be a duty-free zone) reasons, smaller communities in the same area are still hotbeds of consumer trade.

When you check this out, as shown in the site at the mall in Dubai (see Figure 14-1), you find that these exotic locales are no longer trading spices, silver ingots, and ivory — they're trading the same stuff you would buy in the suburbs of Pittsburgh. That's right, at the end of a fourteen-hour plane ride from the U. S., you can hop out and rush into a Burger King, and get yourself some Madras shorts at the Gap. Another bit of evidence that it's one world, like it or not, is that most of the overseas malls I'm showing here typically have the latest bits of Web-page flash written in Java. On the Web, the site Webmaster in Dubai can get the newest Internet software the same day the folks at Apple or Microsoft get it.

On the other side of the globe from Dubai, in a city that may be the biggest in the world (it's not clear whether Mexico City or Sao Paulo, Brazil, is bigger, but they're both over 25 million) is the shopping center Ibirapuera (see Figure 14-2). It's been a sentimental favorite of mine since I visited the place soon after it opened, twenty years ago. What makes it an interesting contrast to Dubai is content. Few goods are actually manufactured in Dubai, so the goods at that mall are mostly imports from elsewhere. Brazil, however, has some unique products, and if you're one of the most naive suckers ever born, you can actually order emeralds, sight unseen (NOT the emerald-buying method recommended by the pros) from one of the shops here. Actually, though, the Amazonian Indian artifacts are pretty good and priced right, too. Just keep that credit card handy!

Figure 14-1:
Different world, same old, uh, stuff.

Speaking of strange trips, I worked for a gentleman who was such a fanatic shopper that he once blew a huge pile of frequent-flier miles on a *weekend* trip to Singapore. That's eighteen hours flying out, eighteen back, and ten hours on the ground. And now, instead of thirty-six hours cramped in coach, you can just click through Yahoo! to Malls: Singapore and go to the same shopping center he visited, buy the same Rolex, and have the watch take the plane ride home instead of dragging your own rumpled, sweating (hey, it's the tropics) self back to your seat-back-upright-tray-tables-in-position place on the plane (see Figure 14-3).

Curious to see whether more sophisticated venues get themselves listed, I decided to try to find the stores in Donald Trump's fancy Tower in Manhattan, and sure enough, there they were. If you have a spare $2,100 and a burning urge to trade that cash in on a briefcase, people are there just waiting to help you. The surprise is that the Trump show is found indexed on a larger site, which also indexes a great variety of humbler operations, including (think of the indignity!) *regular old suburban malls* (see Figure 14-4).

Figure 14-3:
Exotic
Singapore,
as familiar
as a corner
store.

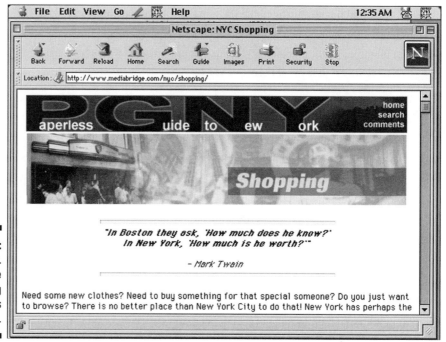

Figure 14-4:
New York.
Online
shopping
simplifies
parking.

Finally, a last bit of mall curiosity shows the power of American culture, at least in spreading itself like a virus. Our first exhibit is the pride of the upper Midwest, Minnesota's Mall of America, with approximately 600 stores and countless other attractions. The mall is so big that it presents organizational problems for the Web site designer. (See Figure 14-5.) After all, it has more businesses than a fairly large town. You may think of this kind of giant mall as a uniquely American thing, but other countries are ramping up at blinding speed. Merry old England, land of picturesque little tea shops on the local village High Street (in the U.S. travel poster version), has malls that could swallow your local shopping center in one mouthful and belch it out the service entrance. (See Figure 14-6.) Just for fun, go to the AltaVista search site and look up *Milton Keynes*. The old country is a bit more modern than the travel brochures tell you.

Shopping Realities

Let's face it — 90 percent of the things you use in daily life, you can buy just about anywhere. You don't have a problem finding milk, chips, or pens. But the last 10 percent of your purchases, the distinctive little touches that more or less make up your personal style, are a bit harder to acquire. That's where the Web becomes a truly astonishing resource.

Figure 14-5:
Visit
Minnesota,
at room
temperature,
in January.

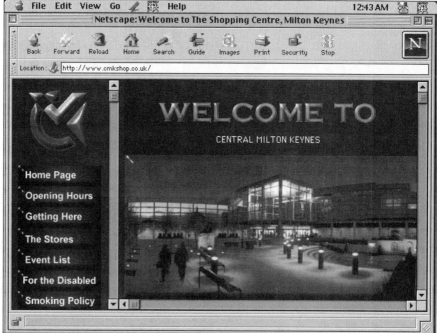

Figure 14-6:
The all-new
U.K.,
booming in
the '90s.

Here's a hint about the future — the first Web site to make serious money from Day One was 1-800-FLOWERS.

Want a perfect condition 1958 Patek Phillipe watch, tiny Roman numerals and no second hand? No problem. An Elizabethan costume to wear to the local Renaissance Festival? It's yours. Everyone wants special items from time to time, and you will find to your delight or dismay, depending on your finances, that all those special items are available.

It will likely come as no surprise to you that professional writers buy lots of funny writing-related stuff. Although writing isn't my main job (I design biotechnology equipment, lots of which turned up in laboratories featured in news reports on the O. J. Simpson trial; that was *my* restriction-fragment DNA analyzer you were seeing), I have the same obsession with books, pens, and fancy little notebooks that plagues all the pros. So take a shopping trip with me, and I'll show you how it works.

Book heaven

Normally, I wouldn't endorse any particular product or company, but for book-buying (trust me — all authors buy *tons* of books), it's hard not to be impressed with Amazon (http://www.amazon.com). I've placed close to thirty orders with these people in just the last year, and they not only

Is it safe to shop on the Web?

Yes. You bet. It's safe. Let me expand on that.

The browser you now use (assuming it's Netscape Navigator 3.0 or later, Microsoft Internet Explorer 3.0 or later, or America Online 3.0 or later) has a Secure Server mode, meaning that the credit card information and the rest of your order are encrypted. In other words, hackers won't get your VISA information, and overwhelming evidence shows that the Internet has NOT produced any documented cases of credit card fraud. In a case a few years ago, where the browsers of the time were non-secure, someone downloaded a lot of credit card numbers. Although he never actually used them, the case was headlined everywhere for weeks, in the breathless style TV news uses for non-events.

I was interviewed on this subject some time ago by a journalist for a Bay Area newspaper. We were sitting in the North Beach area of San Francisco, a neighborhood of Italian and Chinese restaurants, and when the check came the journalist popped out his credit card. The non-English-speaking waiter, a young gentleman of difficult-to-guess nationality, then disappeared for about fifteen minutes. I pointed out to the journalist that his card number, his name, phone number from the local phone book, and any other information he'd use in a Web order were now all in the hands of a complete stranger for quite some time, and could be jotted down in a notebook for reference. How's *that* for security? And it happens every day, with none of the spurious uproar people have made about Internet issues.

deliver standard items like *...For Dummies* books at a reasonable discount and next-day speed (if you want to pay a little more for fast delivery), but they also do an amazing job at locating obscure, rare, and out-of-print books. (See Figure 14-7.)

Shopping here is straightforward enough, producing only the problem that you will always be tempted by more titles than you can afford. When you find a page for a particular book (you can search on subject, author, or title), you also usually find reviews, comments, and often a little spiel by the author. You then have the option of clicking a button to add it to your "shopping basket." (See Figure 14-8.)

After you finalize your choices, you proceed to check out, where you specify c.o.d. or use a credit card. Here is where you see that your purchase is as safe or safer than it would be down at the mall, because you're almost certainly using either Netscape Navigator or Microsoft Internet Explorer, which have adequate support for security. The Amazon server recognizes that support in your browser, and the whole transaction is essentially encrypted so that no third party can snoop on your credit information. (See Figure 14-9.)

Unless you've turned the settings off, both Navigator and Internet Explorer will display an alert screen when you enter or exit a secured page. Just to be safe, you can verify that a Web page you are viewing is secure and that your

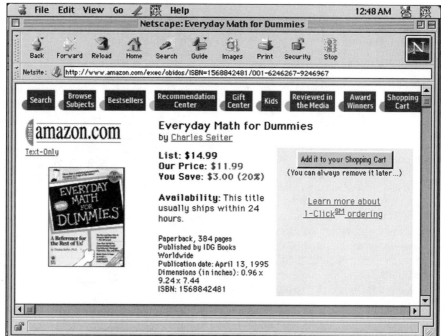

Figure 14-7:
An Amazon
sample.

Figure 14-8:
Note the
Proceed to
Checkout
button.

Figure 14-9:
The security question answered, more or less.

browser's security is working. A secure page uses a slightly different URL (that's the Web page address in the field just below the navigation buttons in your browser, remember?) than an unsecure page. In Figure 14-10, notice the URL begins with "https," not "http." The "s" stands for "secure" and activates your browser's security. In Navigator, you can also verify that things are secure by looking at the tiny lock symbol at the bottom left corner of the browser window. If the hasp on the lock is open, you're not in a secure page. If the hasp is closed, you're secure. Simple as that.

Dramatic proof that Amazon is onto a good thing is offered by Barnes & Noble. It took these guys about two months to realize that many people don't care about in-store Starbuck's coffee and other would-be amenities — they just want a title without looking for parking first. Figure 14-11 shows Barnes & Noble's page, which seems a bit similar to Amazon's, don't you think? The same design simplicity applies to buying music. If you just want a CD that's not on the current hit list, head to `http://www.cdnow.com`, and the odds are greatly in your favor that you can find it there. (See Figure 14-12.)

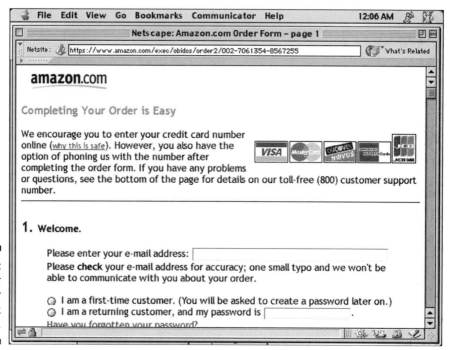

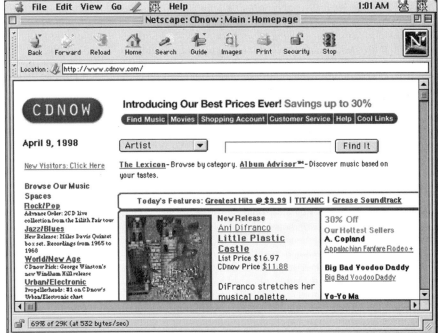

Figure 14-12:
Same idea,
but music
instead of
books.

. . . *and pens*

At Amazon, you can find books that are difficult or impossible to find
anywhere else. For the latest John Grisham novel, you can probably check
the paperback rack at the Safeway checkout; for out-of-print reference works
on statistics, go directly to Amazon or search directly for the title on the
Web using AltaVista or Infoseek.

Pens, however, are another matter. Although only a handful of publishers are
left who would accept a written manuscript (the text before you is obviously
a Mac keyboard product), writers as a group tend to be obsessed with pens.
A personal search for the elusive Namiki retractable fountain pen led me to
the lush Levenger site (http://www.levenger.com), where this elusive
writing instrument was actually on sale. (See Figure 14-13.) If you do a
search on *Namiki*, by the way, using one of the standard services, you find
some rather startling options — high-end Namiki fountain pens cost about
$6,000. Personally, I think I'd rather have a PowerBook 3400. For one thing,
it's cheaper, and it's a lot harder to lose.

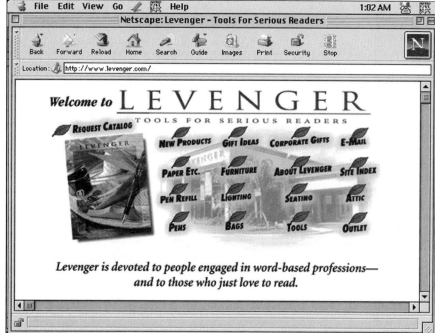

Figure 14-13:
The new
way to buy
the old way
to write.

. . . and paper

As the last obscure item on my Internet shopping list, I needed to find some refills for a Filofax-brand organizer. Once again, this wouldn't be a problem if I lived in a big city, but I'm out in the hinterlands on the fabulously interactive Russian River flood plain, where the local stores feel they're doing you a favor if they stock legal pads.

But here's something to consider: On the Web, we all live in New York, except with better parking and worse delis.

Filofax stuff? No problem. A simple search turned up the site shown in Figure 14-14 , which stocks everything the dedicated English designers of the over-elaborate little system have ever developed, from alligator-skin calendar holders for one thousand dollars to tiny expense-report envelopes for receipts. (Want your own map of the Paris Metro? Actually, it looks pretty cool.) With the usual repertoire of shipping options and credit-card choices, you can get anything you need in a day or so, which ought to give you plenty of time, even if you procrastinate, to get your hands on next year's calendar.

Figure 14-14:
A classic
product
enters the
computer
age.

Buying Mac Stuff on the Web

Your Macintosh is full of extremely standardized parts. SIMM or DIMM modules for memory, to take just one example, are as identical objects as human technology knows how to make. The same is true for 24X CD-ROM drives, Apple 17-inch monitors, ZIP drives, and the software, also. I've been reviewing monitors, scanners, and other complicated hardware for more than a decade, and although magazine reviews try to point out differences between products, such as three competing 4.2GB hard drives, I can prove that, statistically, they're more alike than the bananas in a bunch.

You have three different ways to shop for Macs or upgrades on the Web — from absolutely guaranteed safe, to great deals with perhaps a little more risk, to deals with a fairly large random component.

The first place to look is Apple's own online store (`http://store.apple.com`), which has been a roaring success in selling system upgrades and the G3 Mac line. (See Figure 14-15.) Apple finally woke up (actually, Steve Jobs poked it with a sharp stick) and realized it could model its hardware operation after Dell's highly successful site for peddling Wintel boxes.

Power Macintosh G3
Desktop and Minitower
Speeds up to 333MHz
Starting at $1,599.00

PowerBook G3
Speeds up to 292MHz
Screen sizes up to 14"
Starting at $2,299.00

iMac
The most revolutionary
Macintosh since, well...
the Macintosh! $1,299

The Apple Store

Store Menu   Your Order   Find   Help   The Apple Store

Figure 14-15:
Macs, fast
and cheap.
Finally.

The second category means consulting the Web sites of national distributors, the same ones who almost certainly pester you with catalogs every few months if you subscribe to *Macworld* or *MacAddict*. MacZone, shown in Figure 14-16, MacWarehouse, and MacConnection, among other national distributors, all have Web sites (`http://www.zones.com`, `http://www.warehouse.com`, and `http://www.macconnection.com`, respectively), and at most times of day it's easier to place an order using their Web sites than their 800 numbers. One of the main issues to consider is that the Web site is also totally passive (it won't try to talk you into anything) and also tends to feature a handful of specials at lower prices than the printed catalog reports. The major national vendors also have an additional critical element, a guarantee. The three vendors mentioned previously have all honored their returns policy several times in their dealings with me, at least.

As this book was prepared, the relative speed of a new Power Mac G3 soared past the Pentium-equipped Wintel machines and prices were dropping everywhere. Your best bet for getting the latest Mac at the best price was, by long odds, at a Web site instead of a dealer (dealers tend to have older inventories they feel obliged to unload). If you're absolutely clueless about Mac hardware, you may prefer the comfort factor you get from buying at a local dealer that you trust, but if you've opened up a Mac before with good results, you'll find that Web prices can't usually be matched anywhere else.

Figure 14-16:
In the Mac
Zone.

Another way to shop for your Mac on the Internet, with significantly more risk but great potential savings, is to go to a search service, such as AltaVista, that supports Usenet searches. Just type in what you want, and then see what happens. (See Figure 14-17.)

For this example, I needed a new hard drive for my PowerBook. (DON'T spill coffee into the keyboard. It's just spooky how much can go wrong.) I just tried the following search terms

```
Powerbook +drive +"for sale"
```

and started poking through the long list of e-mail messages to Usenet newsgroups (`comp.sys.mac.hardware` turns up a lot). Many of the messages are from small Mac dealers or repair shops, but many are from individuals, too. The deals are often very good, because you're looking at classified ads with a national basis. Your small town may not have someone with a good condition Power Mac 4200 for sale, for example, but somewhere in the U.S., somebody else does.

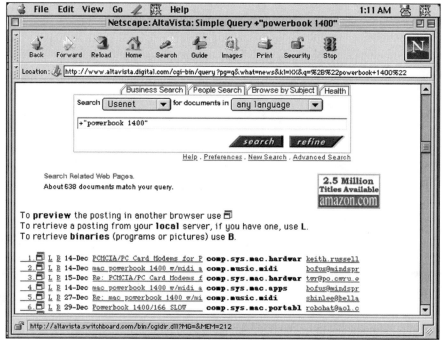

I got a used replacement hard drive for $40 from a guy in Utah, and I turned down my local Apple dealer's offer to solve my problem for $500. I installed the drive myself (the inside of a PowerBook is *really* crowded), it worked fine, and everyone was happy. The point to watch here is that you can find bargains, but you don't necessarily have much recourse if you buy a dud part from an individual in another state. So far I've been quite lucky, merrily popping "used" memory into my main desktop Mac and scrounging up cheapo CD-ROMs. But the Usenet approach obviously has all the risks involved in buying from the want ads, with a distance factor thrown into the mix.

Chapter 15

Web Business: As the Boss

● ●

In This Chapter

▶ Deciding on the right Web page for your business

▶ Putting your page on the Web

▶ Making your page work for you

▶ Choosing a service provider

● ●

*T*he Web, to many businesses, is a gold mine waiting to be discovered. But before you commit your company's coffers to a Cecil B. DeMille-ish epic of a Web site that draws so much energy that city lights fade, remember that planning is the first step to avoiding disaster. Web sites are just dialing in on what makes money online, so learn from the lessons of the failures as well as the successes.

Deciding What Works for Your Business Web Page

As late as March 1994, large parts of the Internet were a sort of electronic party for computer graduate students. I used to give Internet talks where business topics were handled in the question session at the end. Then I had to add a twenty-minute section on business, and now weekend seminars on Internet business can't cover the topic. Whether there's gold out there or not, the Gold Rush has definitely happened.

Because all large businesses have already signed up for fancy Web sites, I assume that you're looking into a site for a small business. You won't have much trouble making up a Web page, even if you don't know HTML (see Chapter 13 for more details). If you make up a text-plus-pictures document about your business using ClarisWorks (4.0 or higher) or Microsoft Word (5.1 or higher with Internet Assistant), you can also generate Web pages automatically. Dozens of firms near you are just dying to help you in this endeavor. Just pick up your regional version of *MicroTimes* or *Computer Currents*, or look through the business section of your local newspaper on Sunday.

The big issue you need to confront is the central issue about any business tool: What can the Web do for you? An alternative question worth asking is: What happens if you do nothing? In other words, what's the actual opportunity here, and how much is it worth?

The answer is often surprising. Consider the charming country inn shown in Figure 15-1. You might think this kind of business, being strongly traditional, wouldn't have much business on the Web. But because the inn is located in a prime wine-country vacation area for the hard-working denizens of Silicon Valley, the Web site, in fact, began paying for itself in its first month. By contrast, I would have expected office supplies to be a Web natural, but I must know a half-dozen businesses in that trade whose Web sites are a dead loss.

The sites that are trying to sell you Web storefronts often feature useful guidelines (check out `http://www.mercantec.com/merchants/aob.htm` for an example) to help you determine whether you have reasonable prospects of making money on the Web. A few important questions to consider include:

- ✔ Are you trying to sell something that people usually like to inspect, feel, or try out in person?

- ✔ Are you selling something that usually calls for personal contact (consulting or other services)?

- ✔ Will you be competing with well-organized competitive existing sites? (Selling books against Amazon is a tough one.)

- ✔ Are you reasonably familiar with credit-card transactions and merchant accounts in your current business?

One fast Web design lesson

If you take the relaxing trip to `http://www.camelliainn.com`, as shown in Figure 15-1, you should check the bottom edge of your browser window to check the size of the lovely figures. They're quite compact in kilobytes by Web standards, but they look great.

The lesson to be learned here is that scanners can resolve pictures to 300 – 600 dpi (dots per inch). Magazines print color pictures at about 150 dpi. However, the monitors people use to view your Web page display at 72 dpi. That means you can apply shocking amounts of

JPEG compression to Web pictures, such as 40-to-1 up to 80-to-1 (the scanner software supports compression, as does Adobe PhotoShop, and a number of shareware compression utilities are available).

The bottom line is that Web visitors — most of whom are using standard modems — will like you a lot better if they can download graphics chunks that are 5KB to 10KB in size, instead of 140KB. Whether you do Web-page design yourself or contract it out, test different compression levels for graphics. You'll be amazed what you can get away with.

Figure 15-1:
The Web
meets the
nineteenth
century.

Using a Service to Create Your Business's Page

Before 1996, getting a Web site usually meant dedicating a fast Mac to act as a server, figuring out the wiring and connection-software details, and maintaining the site yourself, after getting a site name and address from InterNIC, the organization that handles registration. However, times have changed. Now, thousands of companies want to design a site for you and host it on their own Web servers for a modest monthly fee. Competition in this area is fierce beyond all description; I tell you about a handful of national service/host/providers, but it's also a good idea to check at Yahoo!'s business category to watch the rapidly evolving face of Web commerce (see Figure 15-2).

Check out Viaweb

Several good places exist for you to start examining Web commerce for your own business, but one of the best is Viaweb (see Figure 15-3). This service assumes you don't know HTML, don't know much about Web commerce details, but do have some understanding of your own market. This service guides you through constructing your Web site just by pointing-and-clicking

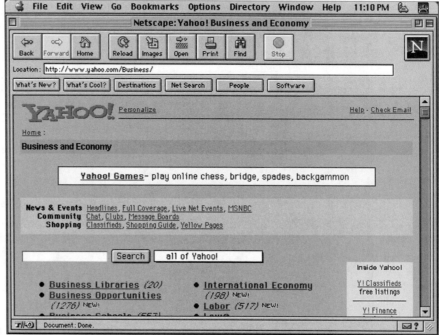

Figure 15-2:
Yahoo!
business,
updated
daily.

elements using a browser, then posts the site, handling order-taking from the Web (it can e-mail you the transactions for processing at your business, and also handle the credit-card charges if you like). Viaweb also sees to it that your site gets properly indexed on all the major Web search services.

You might expect that this style of site creation would be painfully limiting compared to real free-form HTML-based site creation. In some ways it is, compared to the flashiest work available, but it allows enough scope for creativity for plenty of major businesses. If it's good enough for these people (see Figure 15-4), it may be good enough for you.

Follow the directions using Virtual Spin

Another complete package that also lets you assemble a site following instructions using only your browser is provided by a company called Virtual Spin. (See Figure 15-5.) As easy as it is to create Web pages using plain old Microsoft Word and other tools, the Virtual Spin approach has three advantages:

✔ The simplicity forces you to confront the real "message" issues on your site instead of adding chirping mice with JavaScript.

Figure 15-3:
Everything
for a
storefront.

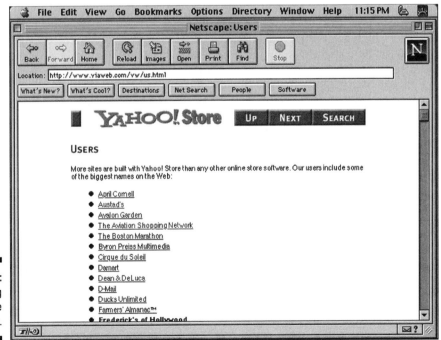

Figure 15-4:
Rolling
along the
e-way.

✔ Using Virtual Spin eliminates shopping for a Web consultant, some of whom have been in the business about one month longer than you.

✔ After the site is set up, all the links will work correctly and the orders will get entered correctly. This last point is far from trivial.

Take a look at Mercantec and SureSite

Two more services worth serious attention are Mercantec (see Figure 15-6) and SureSite (see Figure 15-7). These services require a little more work and a little more sophistication about the Web on your part than Viaweb and Virtual Spin, but they each have their own payoffs.

Mercantec's SoftCart system can attach a flexible order/inventory system to your Web pages — it's a highly developed automated business package with some unique bells and whistles. SureSite offers a more pedestrian but equally strong appeal — for most shops it's the lowest-cost national hosting service, and it requires no actual programming on your part.

Frankly, having suffered through the early days of the Web where order-taking from a Web page called for programming in UNIX-based command languages, I'm impressed with the success of these services in making Web commerce really accessible for mere non-tech mortals.

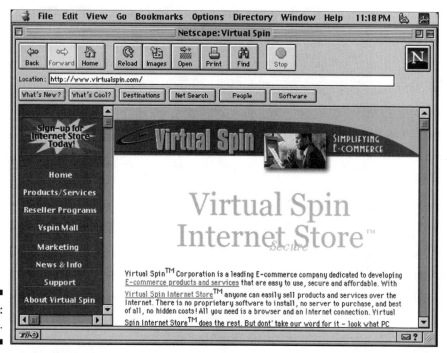

Figure 15-5:
Virtual Spin.

Figure 15-6:
Mercantec, supplier of SoftCart.

Figure 15-7:
Being sure of your site.

NetBits

This is just a little digression on terminology. It's stuff the service providers have to know. But if you wind up in a conference room at work and the higher-ups are discussing Net hardware details, you want to sound like you know what you're talking about:

✔ A *gateway* lets you connect two different kinds of network. The typical Macintosh network runs along rules specified by the AppleTalk standard, and the Internet uses, appropriately, Internet protocol (IP). You need software to translate messages designed for one network into messages that the other network can read properly. That's a gateway.

✔ A *bridge* is typically hardware and software that connects two local networks of the same kind. You may have two different AppleTalk networks in different parts of a building or in different departments. If you want the two networks to look like one big network to users, you have to buy a bridge, usually from the company that sold you the two networks.

✔ A *router*, for Internet purposes, sends IP messages from one Internet network host to another. Most commercial routers also know how to translate messages coming from other (non-IP) kinds of networks. Zillions of tricks are involved in making routers efficient, and if you're reading this sidebar, it's somebody else's job to learn them.

Following the Experts' Advice about Content

Technically, you won't have much of a challenge getting some sort of Web page together and having it posted somewhere online. At this point, dozens of firms stand ready to help you with network connections, server support, and page design. Just to make the design point vivid, one service vendor called Right Angle Design (http://www.rightangle.com), shown in Figure 15-8, shows before-and-after Web pages to illustrate its prowess in visuals.

What the service vendors can't do, necessarily, is tell you what to say in the text blocks on your page to make something happen (an order for your products, for example). For the best advice I have found on this exact topic, I refer you to three books, written well before the development of the World Wide Web. As it happens, I have done tons of advertising copywriting, with record-breaking response rates for both direct mail and magazine print ads, simply by slavishly following the advice in these books:

Figure 15-8:
More
helpful
advice.

✔ David Ogilvy's *On Advertising* (Vintage Books, 1985) is worth reading because it's based on several decades of research, rather than an opinion about last-year's-fad-that-worked. The issue clearly highlighted by Ogilvy is, "How do you keep someone's attention long enough to get your message across?" I should also tell you that Ogilvy's book is about a hundred times more entertaining reading than any of the dozens or so "Make Money with a Hot Web Page" books currently cluttering the shelves at a mall near you.

✔ If you read Ogilvy, you will notice that practically every third page or so he acknowledges his debt to Claude Hopkins and his books *My Life in Advertising* and *Scientific Advertising* (NTC Business Books, 1993). These works were actually written in the 1920s by the man generally acknowledged as the all-time advertising copy-writing champion. You might imagine that a book from the roaring '20s wouldn't have much to say to the Internet generation. But human nature has not changed much (it hasn't had enough time, genetically), and coffeehouse Gen-X hipsters turn out to have hopes, dreams, and insecurities remarkably similar to those of the wild youth after World War I or World War II, and playing to these emotions (along with a hard-hitting emphasis on product benefits) is by all accounts what actually sells products.

✔ NTC Business Books puts out another slender volume that will enable you to determine whether you have a reasonable judgment of ad effectiveness before sinking your ad funds into the Web. It's called *Which Ad Pulled Best?* (by Dr. Philip Burton and Dr. Scott Purvis, and updated almost yearly) and consists of 50 matched ads that, to the untrained eye, look fairly similar. But in each pair, one ad was a whopping success and the other one was a dud. The authors carefully point out the key features responsible for the difference in response. The people who manage Web index sites (Yahoo!, for example) have done enough research to show that some business Web home pages can get 20,000 to 25,000 hits per day with no sales at all, while some other pages with the same hit rate get hundreds of sales.

All the principles underlying this difference were thoroughly understood decades ago, and you can find them out in the work of Dr. Burton and Dr. Purvis. Steal a march on your competitors — while they're all reading the latest dorky book on the Web, you can read this trio of classics and find out how to make your own Web page bring in results. Trust me, the latest jiggle in Java-based animation is not as important as understanding why some ads work in the first place.

Survival of the Fattest: Local versus National ISPs

The future of the Web in business is clearly going to be driven by economics, as it has been since the Net left the confines of universities. Two years ago, it made some sense to dedicate your own Mac to be part of the Web explosion; now site-hosting has become so cheap you almost certainly have better uses for your money and hardware.

This same phenomenon works on a larger scale, too. Almost none of the local service providers I recommended in the first two editions of this book are still in business. Just as a service provider can likely make more efficient use of server hardware than you can, a bigger, national ISP can usually operate more efficiently than a smaller regional ISP, especially if it's also a phone company.

Having looked over the "automatic storefront" services mentioned previously, you may still be inclined to make up your own site and get it hosted by an ISP. So for third-edition recommendations, I'm inclined to say that, while a search may turn up a local or regional ISP that's a great choice, I want to list a few that I believe will still be with us past the year 2000:

✔ The first service you should know about, whatever you decide to do, is at `http://superpages.gte.net` (see Figure 15-9). After all, there isn't much point in having a Web page for a business if it doesn't get listed.

✔ You should also go to the search services Yahoo!, Excite, and AltaVista and read their advice on getting yourself indexed so that you'll be easy to find. Having experimented, I can tell you that after you're indexed with these search services, the other services will soon find you, too.

✔ Finally, phone companies are slugging it out for your business and want to handle everything from designing your Web page and hosting it, to tracking site statistics and helping you handle Web-based transactions. In the course of preparing this edition, MCI (see Figure 15-10) dropped prices and upgraded its service offers six times. In the long run, MCI has the resources to make it difficult for smaller local operations to compete, especially if you don't need much hand-holding or on-site assistance.

Figure 15-9:
Get yourself
listed.

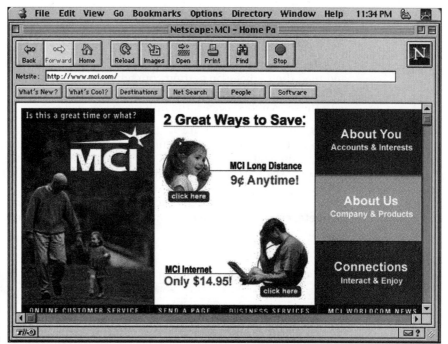

Figure 15-10: MCI sees you.

And, of course, someone even bigger than MCI is waiting in the wings. In retrospect, it's fairly amazing that AT&T took so long to wake up and smell the Java, but the logic of performing an additional service that they could just *tack onto your phone bill* couldn't be resisted (see Figure 15-11). Despite the leisurely approach, which in fairness is pretty much to be expected from such a giant operation, there's a thoroughness to the results that suggests that AT&T will do whatever it takes to be a major provider, on phone lines or cable or wireless modems or satellite receivers, as long as the Internet runs. (See Figure 15-12.)

Mac OS 8.5 offers one of the few national ISPs that have existed longer than three years. EarthLink Network offers not only a strong business package, but has recently joined forces with Sprint (the pin-drop telephone company) to reinforce its telecommunications power.

Figure 15-11:
The major
presence of
AT&T
WorldNet
Service.

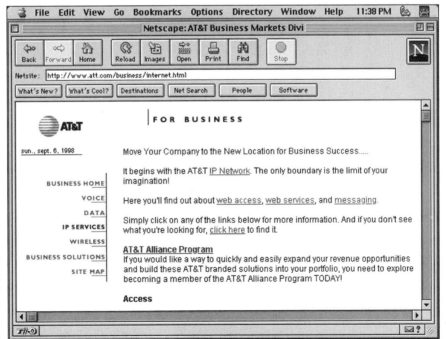

Figure 15-12:
AT&T
wants your
business.

Part V
The Part of Tens

The 5th Wave   By Rich Tennant

"I don't mean to hinder your quest for knowledge,
however it's not generally a good idea to try to
download the entire Internet."

In this part . . .

The Part of Tens, a patented Dummies feature, is a concentrated dose of Internet trivia, serious matters, and convenience.

I provide some alternate ways to find information so that as you and I use the Net, we can avoid colliding at peak times.

Chapter 16
Ten WWW Sites to See

. . . .

In This Chapter

▶ Ten great sites to check out

. . . .

*T*he Web has plenty of cool and useful sites, but they are often drowning in a sea of junk. Because I want you to get cruising on the Web, and because I'm also relentlessly serious, the sites I've listed here are *both* cool and useful. Try every one of these! You won't be sorry.

Shareware.com

www.shareware.com

Because it has the most diligent updating service and thus the newest stuff, you just can't beat Shareware.com. Also, you can restrict your search to Mac shareware. Many of the most popular programs, such as the window appearance changer Kaleidoscope, and demos of games such as Quake, are available. Its cousin site, Download.com, also offers additional software to download. Remember, you have to pay for shareware eventually if you continue to use it, so feed those starving programmers and send a check.

Morningstar

www.morningstar.com

You can find tons of investing Web sites, but the clearest, most authoritative is Morningstar. If you ever have a few thousand bucks to park somewhere, look here for advice.

The Perseus Project

www.perseus.tufts.edu

This site is just amazing. The Perseus Project has the entire world of ancient Greece and Rome on the Web — the literature (every scrap of it), the art, and the architecture. Just think — it took two thousand years to prepare the material — and probably just two years to post it.

The Great Outdoor Recreation Pages

www.gorp.com

If you've been to summer camp, you're probably enjoying the pun of this page's name (GORP is an acronym for "good ol' raisins and peanuts — a snack while hiking). For the world according to GORP, check out the Great Outdoor Recreation Pages, which has links to sites about vacations where you're not mostly sitting down.

College Board Online

www.collegeboard.org

The name of this site might be familiar to you — the College Board is the facilitator of the SAT high-school proficiency exams many of us took over the years. If you think college is expensive, you're right — college fees have outpaced inflation every year for two decades. This site has information on college admissions and also a great set of links to scholarships.

Scientific American

www.sciam.com

Scientific American magazine has a wonderfully rich electronic version of its publication on the Web. It seems to me that the Web may be a last best hope for science education in the U.S., a country whose children are encouraged to think, against all odds, that their careers lie in sports.

Mr. Showbiz

`www.mrshowbiz.com`

Having made my plea for science, I can now tell you that Mr. Showbiz has the greatest collection of entertainment industry news, trash, gossip, and reviews you're ever likely to need. Once you've had your fill, you can jump to its parent Web site, `ABCNews.com`.

The New York Times

`www.nytimes.com`

You can check out the online version of this venerable daily newspaper to find out right away what The People Who Run Everything want you to believe. This site is updated every ten minutes, so it's more current than the TV news you saw an hour ago.

The Louvre Museum

`www.louvre.fr`

Are you surprised to learn that France has an amazing art site? Check out The Louvre, and avoid the long plane ride, crowded museums, and $7.50 espressos. Don't be put off when you first view the site's content in French; just click the English, Japanese, or Spanish link on the home page to get the version for your preferred tongue.

Nolo Press

`www.nolo.com`

This site is the wonderful Web site of a legal self-help publisher. The site is loaded with FAQs on topics that will be of keenest interest to you at crucial moments in your life, believe me. Nolo also makes software that makes recordkeeping and preparing legal documents a breeze.

Chapter 17
Ten Mac Sites

In This Chapter

▶ A bunch of great Macintosh Web sites

*T*he Mac is still responsible for more than half of all Web sites, and Macintosh software is still a big deal in the universities that maintain software archives. If you want Tibetan fonts, Mac golf software, or a suite of free Web utilities, it's all out there. The Web's also now an excellent place for Mac hardware shopping.

Apple Computer

www.apple.com

Recent versions of Apple's Web site were flashy but filled with a pointless morass of self-indulgence; it was difficult to navigate or find what you needed. Now Apple's site is truly useful, and you can even design your own Mac online through the Apple Store. Like him or not, Steve Jobs makes things happen.

TidBITS

www.tidbits.com

Adam Engst offers the most objective Mac Internet news anywhere in his newsletter, posted on www.tidbits.com. His Internet book competes with this one, but TidBITS is an essential resource. Hey, I like the guy.

MacAddict

www.macaddict.com

For a little less objectivity, but more enthusiasm, surf to www.macaddict.com, the Web site for the popular magazine *MacAddict*. This magazine debuted in mid-1996, just as Apple's real business problems were showing. *MacAddict* sports colorful editions with personable staff, very useful articles, and lots of laughs at the Wintel juggernaut's expense. Each magazine comes with a CD filled with software from Apple, games, utilities, and an ongoing video journal from the MacAddict staff. These people are fun!

Webintosh

www.webintosh.com

If your main Mac interest is Internet-related news, you can't do better than the Webintosh site. In addition to news, you'll find software reviews, insightful commentary, and more about Macintosh Internet resources.

Macintouch

www.macintouch.com

Mac hipster Ric Ford runs a great Web site with the latest Macintosh news and links at www.macintouch.com. I check it myself every few days, and I write for the other magazines. Ric also writes for the weekly publication *MacWeek*, which recently transmogrified into the new publication *eMediaWeekly*.

Macworld

www.macworld.com

Ziff-Davis Publishing merged the flagging Mac magazine *MacUser* with IDG's *Macworld* in 1997. Subsequently, a big chunk of all Mac publishing, including most of my reviews, shows up at Macworld. Jim Heid and Tom Negrino are also regulars here. *Macworld* is the oldest of the Mac-based magazines today.

Absolute Mac

www.absolutemac.com

Before you buy anything related to Macintosh, check out the Absolute Mac site for the latest price information, advice, and reviews. This unique site claims to glean its data from over 300 Web sites. Absolute Mac is especially helpful with RAM memory, where prices change monthly.

Apple Software Mirror Site

mirrors.apple.com

The Apple mirror site should be your first destination when you need any software or updates from Apple Computer. You'll find Mac OS updates, utilities, and even unsupported but very fascinating beta software to try out. If you have an older Mac, you'll find your system software for free here (up to System 7.0.1, after which Apple began to sell its software). You can also reach this site more efficiently using an ftp program (such as the Fetch program from Dartmouth University) at ftp://mirrors.apple.com.

PlanetMac, Inc.

www.planetmac.com

PlanetMac is an Apple Authorized Sales and Service Provider that sells new and refurbished Macs and accessories. Its Web site is also quite appealing to the eye. Sometimes, you're just looking for a bargain. I've done pretty well buying used peripherals at this site. They also give quite objective recommendations, having no overstock axe to grind.

BizProWeb's Shareware for Web Page Development

www.bizproweb.com/pages/shareware/mac_webdev.html

If you're interested in getting some inexpensive but powerful software to help you churn out and maintain a Web site, then the BizProWeb site probably has everything you need to get started. Any program you find here is shareware, so if you like it and keep using it, be sure to pay the fee for the program to keep the software updated by its talented (and possibly hungry) programmers.

Chapter 18

Ten Communications Tips

Communications software is full of bugs. The fact that shareware programs still compete seriously with commercial applications indicates the unsettled state of things. If Apple had any sense of shame, it would have distributed a trouble-free Internet communications program as part of system software long ago.

Anyway, give thanks to the clever people who write shareware, or to the companies that now give Web browsers away. And be a good sport: Send in the modest registration fee if you use some shareware regularly.

Calling for Cable

Cable modems may be the likely Big Thing to Have in the near future if you have a love for the Internet. Cable modems will allow you to connect to the Net at incredible speeds — downloading several megabytes of data might take a few seconds! Look up area code 707 on a map. It's where I live — an area about the size of New England with maybe 300,000 inhabitants. If I'm going to get cable-modem access to the Internet in this rural zone, so are you. But call your local cable TV company and see whether someone can detail the plans for your area.

Checking Out No Back Roads

Anyone really living way out in the country and with a taste for the Internet should check Jim Heid's "No Back Roads" site at `www.nobackroads.com`. It's a documentary of a trip he and two others took to explore the effect that the Internet has had on the rural community in America (Jim's neighborhood makes mine look like West Fifty-Seventh Street). You will find that many small towns in Iowa have better Internet access than half of Silicon Valley.

Looking into ISDN

Don't bother. Hope that helps.

The long answer is that ISDN was a promising connection scheme in the mid-1990s, but cable modems and perhaps ADSL/DSL (kind of like ISDN Lite) is going to make it too expensive and slow by the end of the century.

Upgrading to a 56K Modem

Do it.

At first, it made little sense, as many Internet service providers hadn't adapted to accommodate 56K (that's a modem speed that's up to twice as fast as the modem speed that most people use today), mostly because there weren't too many versions of the software that drives the modems, each of which had its drawbacks. But most of the big ISPs today have something to offer you for these modems, which are much cheaper, and if you can't get cable yet, it's your best alternative. Besides, the new "language" that the modern 56K modems speak (V.90) is pretty reliable and will pull every bit of speed it can find to make your Internet experience speedier.

Choosing an Internal or External Modem

External.

Internal modems are a bit cheaper, but external modems are easier to manage. For example, when your Web browser tells you that it can't find a DNS entry for `www.apple.com`, you can look at the little lights on the front panel and see that your line has just dropped, and that Apple probably still has an Internet address. Most importantly, should you need to remove your modem (say, if you want to attach it to another Mac), it's a lot easier to do.

Choosing a Connection for AOL Downloads

With America Online, you can connect with an AOL local number or through your ISP.

For long downloads, use AOL's own number. I really can't tell who's at fault, but an ISP connection to AOL frequently disconnects after half an hour. Being disconnected can be very frustrating, especially if you're trying to collect an 8MB file with a 28K modem.

Then again, if you're using AOL for long downloads in any case, maybe you'll find it cheaper and more reliable to use an ISP alone (compare your ISP's monthly rate to AOL's hourly rate after you use up your allowed free time).

Scheduling Your E-Mail

Sure, you can check your e-mail at any time, but checking your mail while the rest of planet is also doing it makes for a slow Internet. But, checking mail during the off-hours on the Internet is likely a time that you'd prefer to be very soundly asleep, like 3:00 a.m. The good news is that virtually every e-mail program has a provision for e-mail scheduling, which lets you set the time you get your e-mail in advance. You can do the poor old overcrowded Net a big favor by using such a feature. Even if you feel like checking at peak times, the automatic script can dial in, get the mail, and clear out much faster than you can. You can then read your mail offline, which makes the Net that less crowded.

Using a Local Number to Connect

You've just installed AOL or the software from your ISP. You've picked out a local number, you're connected, and everything's humming away.

Even if you run a big phone bill every month anyway, you may find after a few months that the bill is somehow higher than you expected. Check the bill and make sure that you have selected a local access number that's truly not a long-distance number for your particular area. This problem is espe-cially true if you live in an area where a lot of area codes are assigned within a small region, like large cities such as New York or Los Angeles. It is also possible that the phone company has gotten things mixed up, so you might want to verify with them that the number you have is toll-free. I must know a hundred people who have been burned on this issue.

Naming Your Files Creatively

Don't get lazy when you save Web pages or images as Netscape Navigator bookmarks (or, in Internet Explorer-ese, "Favorites") in your Web browser. Sometimes the header of the page that the Webmaster uses for a page is almost never going to have much mnemonic value for you when you're viewing your bookmarks list. You may end up with a thousand files called "index.html" after you surf the Web for a month. Every time I've accepted a page default filename, I've regretted it. Be sure to edit your bookmarks to add a useful name to find later.

Trying Eudora

Although currently most people just use the e-mail software that shipped with their browser, you owe it to yourself to check out www.eudora.com and download the latest version of Eudora Light, or if you have a few cents and would like a few power features, Eudora Pro. Eudora Light is free and is a better e-mail program than what's bundled with browsers.

Chapter 19
Ten Good Causes

In This Chapter

▶ A list of ten good causes found on the Web

Y̲ou own a Mac. That means you're an idealist, at least in the sense of wanting to live in a world where things work the way they should. Even printers. Well, computers are easy; society is hard. Look through these sites and find a way to give a little of yourself to helping out the world!

Idealist

```
www.idealist.org
```

You can take the name "idealist" in two ways: *idea list* or *idealist.* Either way is right — this is a wonderful organization.

Empower Web

```
www.slip.net/~scmetro/empower.htm
```

This site is an encyclopedic list of non-profit organizations that could use some volunteers for good causes. This site provides information about all aspects of non-profit organizations, including fundraising, writing proposals, and networking.

MedSupport FSF International

```
www.medsupport.org/
```

The people at MedSupport do lots of good work for people who have any of a great variety of afflictions.

Independent Living USA

www.ilusa.com

If you know anything about the independent-living program for people with disabilities, you should also know about Independent Living USA. The people act more like a helpful organization than a business, bless their hearts.

Environmental News Network

www.enn.com

Environmental News Network carries up-to-date environmental news. If you think huge forest fires in Indonesia aren't really *your* problem, just wait a few years.

A Forum for Women's Health

www.womenshealth.org

No quips on this topic. U.S. firms have spent more research money on male pattern baldness than on breast cancer. Go to this site and get some facts. Talk online to women doctors, too.

The Lucien J. Engelmajer International Organization

www.oilje.com

The Lucien J. Engelmajer International Organization is a 25-year-old humanitarian enterprise engaged in a variety of activities throughout the world. Principal among these activities are drug treatment, drug prevention, AIDS prevention and care, youth programs, programs for the elderly, and disaster and famine relief, in addition to agricultural and construction projects in needy countries.

Amnesty International

www.amnesty.org

It's hard to argue with the aims of Amnesty International, unless you're actually a fan of prison camps.

Resistance

www.peg.apc.org/~resistance/

This site reminds me of my childhood, so I thought I'd include it. Decide for yourself whether it's a good cause or your worst nightmare.

Project Censored

www.sonoma.edu/ProjectCensored/

This site is an extremely interesting record of the news that TV and newspapers ignore to avoid offending commercial interests. That makes this site a good cause in my opinion.

Chapter 20

Ten Web Services for Businesses

*W*ell, no one seems to know yet *exactly* where the money is on the Web, but we're all sure looking for it. And now, scads of large and small organizations want to help you in your own search. The hundreds and hundreds of response cards that readers sent me from the second edition of this book all asked for business information, so here's some more. I guess non-profits and social causes will have to wait until people feel a little more prosperous. Hey, it's the '90s.

This chapter contains an assortment of ten sites that I reviewed. For the most up-to-date names in this explosively growing area, try the index at Yahoo!. Just go to the Yahoo! home page, click Search, and use the keywords *Web* and *business*. Also, the actual Web addresses of many of these companies change in time, so rather than my listing URLs that are likely to go out of date in a few months, I recommend that you log onto Yahoo! and search on the actual company name.

AT&T WorldNet

`www.att.com/worldnet/`

If you're shopping around for a new Internet service provider, proceed to AT&T WorldNet and click everything in site. (I apologize in advance for the dreadful pun.)

MCI

`www.mci.com`

You can bet that MCI doesn't want AT&T to run away with all the Internet business. Check MCI for ferociously competitive offers.

GTE

`Superpages.gte.net`

The Web Yellow Pages lead you to GTE's own offers for hosting and publicizing your site. Face it, the Net is one of the ways in which "other" phone companies can attempt to expand.

Everyware

`www.everyware.com`

If you have the technical people to organize your own site software, check the Mac solutions at Everyware. From the Web database linker Tango for FileMaker to the Web site contact logger Bolero, this company has the right stuff to put a Mac-based business online.

4D

`www.acius.com`

4th Dimension is the leading big-time Mac database product, and the latest version has built-in Web server capability. Check out 4D to see an impressive demonstration.

Wilson Internet Services

www.wilsonweb.com

For a short course in the realities of Web-based business, it's hard to top the advice found at this site. This site has less hype and more facts than you'll find at most consulting operations.

GetSet! Communications

www.getset.com

GetSet! provides more hand-holding than most other Web consulting services. If you think you're missing out on a hot business opportunity but don't know much about the Web, this organization is a good first contact.

EarthLink

www.earthlink.net

EarthLink is a service provider with a nice cheap deal for small-business Web sites. They also do better Mac service than the other nationals.

BizProWeb

www.bizproweb.com

BizProWeb specializes in services for small and medium-sized businesses and maintains a great Web site packed with useful tips and news. They also maintain a great software archive.

Digital Sand

www.digitalsand.com

This exceptionally competent service is more Mac-friendly than most, possibly because its home is walking distance from Apple. Digital Sand has done tons of key sites in Silicon Valley, although its name is still mysterious.

Chapter 21

Ten (More or Less) Free Web Deals

*T*he cheapest way to distribute anything is via the Web, so you may expect that offers of free goods and services would abound — and you'd be right. The only small catch is that you're probably stuck looking at advertising while you download (hey, think of it as TV), but that's not too repellent. This list concentrates on Internet freebies, but for those people out there who are interested in actual objects, I also include a killer "stuff" link.

Permanent Address

Other than a tombstone, that is. The site at `http://netaddress.usa.net` gives you a single address that never changes. These guys are quite reliable — some aren't. I've had two lifetime addresses at companies that died.

Free Everything

This one's the stuff link. The diligent Web surfers at `www.thefreesite.com` have shored up a pile of links to every free deal they could find on the Web.

Free Web Page

If you have any curiosity at all, hop on down to `www.freetown.com` and check out the chat, the free user Web pages, and the bewildering variety of services.

FreeNets

It's a lot to type in, but a visit to `www.yahoo.com/Business_and_Economy/Companies/Computers/Networking/Online_Services/Free_Nets/` turns up a long list of local freenets, where you can get a free Internet access account if you're in one of the lucky communities.

Big Time

For the best-maintained Mac freeware and shareware archive, I've always turned to the University of Texas (`wwwhost.ots.utexas.edu:80/mac/pub-mac.html`). If you can't find it here, it's not legal.

Big and Free

The site at `www.primenet.com/~btn/free.software.html` is all free software only. You don't have to brood for weeks about ponying up your software registration fee like a good citizen.

Teacherware for the Web

You can tell from the name that it's an education site:
`www.rowan.k12.nc.us/Technology/M.Software.html`

However, it's the best-organized set of Mac Web freeware out there.

Linkage

After you have a site, how do you get it noticed? One way is to head out to
`http://dynamic.strides.com/`. Here, you can have links to your site
distributed to indexing services for free. Many comparable services exist,
but I've been lucky with this one.

Free Sound

The Free Radio Network (`www.frn.net/`) is totally cool. I'm listing it here
because more people read the free stuff list than any other part of the book.
Check it out!

Part VI

Appendixes

The 5th Wave   By Rich Tennant

"QUICK KIDS! YOUR MOTHER'S FLAMING SOMEONE ON THE INTERNET!"

In this part . . .

*L*ots of information about the Internet is contained in Net documents and lists of various sorts. This part gives you the essentials you need to find interesting topics on the Net, and a few other tips to help you become a fine upstanding Internet citizen.

Appendix A

Your Internet Phone Book

● ●

1 wish I could tell you that this was going to be easy. Well, I could tell you that, but you'd find out anyway and send me nasty e-mail.

Most e-mail programs offer a convenient way to add e-mail addresses to an address book built in your program. After you use the typical way to add an address (this process varies from program to program, so I won't try to describe it), you can probably give the address a more pronounceable or easier-to-remember name in your book. That is, a normal phone book doesn't give the number first in the listing in the mistaken belief that you'll know the person's name by the number, right? Same is true with the difference between "bwayne@wayneentinc.com" and "Bruce Wayne." So, be sure to add a name to the heading of each address so that you can find and add senders quickly to messages.

On the other hand, you can make a text file (using Word, for example) of Internet names and addresses and then just cut and paste the name(s) into the *To:* part of a message. This text file becomes your very own Internet phone book. After you get the correct entries, you won't make any typos (a truly dreaded Internet problem). This method always works, and you may find it simpler and more portable than the built-in address books in the mail functions of browsers. In real life, I never clear my e-mail Inbox, so I can pick entries for returning mail just by highlighting the entry and picking Reply. Disk space is abundant; your time is not.

That's the good news. The bad news is that after years of explosive growth, tracking down names and Internet addresses is very difficult. In this appendix, I tell you some resources to use, but you're on your own after that. Good luck!

Just Say What?

If you're talking to someone who you may want to reach someday by e-mail, ask that person for an Internet address on the spot. Maybe you won't need it for months, but months from now you probably won't be able to find it. Also, at least for the next few years, (until Internet numbers are assigned at birth) asking for an e-mail address makes you look cool.

I know that this plan sounds simple, but it's the most reliable.

Da Phone, Boss, Da Phone!

Most organizations provide lists of e-mail addresses; simply ask the receptionist at the other end of the phone. Take it from me, the boss's nephew who's answering the phone for the summer has more intelligence than the best search service. And if he doesn't know what you need to know, he can almost always find someone who does.

(In case you couldn't tell, I just delivered a searing indictment of the pitiful organization in modern online communications. Welcome to the information supersidewalk.)

Find Someone Using Four11

Many large e-mail systems are linked to the large directory at www.four11.com. If you know enough to guess parts of the address (is it a .com or .edu?), you can narrow down the resulting list — looking for Smiths is hard.

Now it happens that the home pages of big search services such as Excite and Yahoo! have a link to a PeopleFinder or some such name. These are almost always links to Four11, ultimately. So, you may as well just go there in the first place, and fill in your own little SimpleText directory.

The Special Case of AOL

AOL has its own internal directory for e-mail, and about a fourth of all Mac users are on this service, so it's a good place to start. There's the additional bonus, for the extra snoopy, that people put the most astonishing stuff in their member profiles. Just unbelievable.

AOL also has an address book for its e-mail that works pretty well (and doesn't have problems when you switch back and forth between Versions 3 and 4, either). So, you may consider making AOL your main e-mail center, even if you have another Internet account with another provider.

Appendix B
Netiquette, or Playing Nicely Together

● ●

*A*s the Internet expanded, it gradually shed its role as an online gentlemen's club whose members were university researchers. Old hands felt obliged, however, to post some of the informal rules of conduct that they had developed over the years.

Back when only a few million people were on the Net, these considerations were simply good manners, like not leaving chewing gum on a subway seat. Now that 100 million Net denizens exist, these rules take on new importance, like signs that make sure that you drive on the right side of the freeway.

Here are four simple rules. Please take them seriously as friendly advice.

Watch Your) and (

Probably 90 percent of the content of face-to-face messages lies in expression and tone (this is even more true in Japan, which is why Internet e-mail is not so popular there). When you send e-mail, all these little clues to meaning that we've developed over the centuries are absent.

My advice is if you're saying anything that may be taken two ways, throw in a smile (see the list of "emoticons" below). And look over your mail carefully before you send it.

The Keyboard Symbol	What It Says
:)	smile
;)	wink
: *	kiss
: (	things are not OK
: >	fiendish grin

Download FAQs First and Read Them Offline

Every newsgroup and Web site usually has a set of FAQs (Frequently Asked Questions). You'll be amazed (and I cast no aspersions on your originality) how often the things you want to know about rhododendrons or seismology are the *same things everyone else* wants to know. Reading these FAQs will prevent you from getting very nasty replies to any basic questions you have from users of the newsgroup that hate it when they're asked the same questions for the hundredth time.

In addition, read any newsgroup's guide to local customs at your leisure, a file usually called etiquette.txt.

Don't Send E-Mail to Thousands of People at Once

It's called *spamming*. After you use the Internet for a while, you figure out how to post e-mail to platoons of potential victims automatically. I didn't tell you how to do so, though. And for a good reason. I don't want you to. Neither does anyone else.

E-mail Privacy Is an Illusion

This is an etiquette issue, because etiquette means not hurting feelings.

If you use e-mail at work, I can guarantee you that if you characterize someone as a jerk in an e-mail, the jerk in question will at some point see that e-mail. I can't tell you how, and I can't tell you when, but it's a law of physics. Maybe your friend will pass along the note, maybe a system administrator will see it, or maybe it will get discovered by accident. I've been working for large organizations that have used e-mail since the 1970s, and I have hundreds of tales to tell on this count.

None of the tales concerns me, because I'm paranoid. I bad-mouth people in person, exclusively. If you take this one point seriously, this book will at some point save you your job, save a friend, or keep you from endless trouble.

Appendix C

alt.newsgroups

• •

*T*he alt newsgroups arose as a way to distinguish popular topics from the original core topics (physics, math, computer science, and other serious matters) in the Usenet universe. They loom large in the mythology of the Internet because they're still where much of the fun is, among other things.

This list is a severely edited version of a list posted regularly to a newsgroup called `news.lists`, which you can join from any Internet provider that offers Usenet newsgroups. The list is maintained by a volunteer named David C. Lawrence (Internet address `tale@uunet.uu.net`), who is the person to notify when groups are created or disappear. It's another example of the remarkable way the Internet operates — the list is a key piece of information about the Internet, and it's not under the control of an organization or business.

If you want the full version of the list, you should download it yourself. The complete list has topics and descriptions that are too X-rated for this little fun-for-the-whole-family book, and there's also an amazing amount of repetition — very similar topics often appear in three or four separate newsgroups. The groups identified as "moderated" here have someone who edits out the worst *flames* (messages that harshly and rudely criticize or sometimes question the parentage of another writer) or the most inappropriate postings. The rest are just the absolute, raw, unedited transcripts of all the messages contributed to the newsgroup.

Social Issues

This list is about one-fourth of the social-issue groups on Usenet. Different types of activist communities staked out their turf fairly early in Internet history.

`alt.abuse.recovery`	Helping victims of abuse to recover
`alt.activism`	Activities for activists
`alt.activism.d`	A place to discuss issues in `alt.activism`

(continued)

`alt.activism.death-penalty`	For people opposed to capital punishment
`alt.adoption`	For those involved with or contemplating adoption
`alt.child-support`	Raising children in a split family
`alt.censorship`	Discussion about restricting speech/press
`alt.current-events.clinton.whitewater`	The Clinton Whitewater scandal
`alt.current-events.russia`	Current happenings in Russia
`alt.current-events.usa`	What's new in the United States
`alt.dads-rights`	Rights of fathers (Moderated)
`alt.discrimination`	Quotas, affirmative action, bigotry, persecution
`alt.education.disabled`	Education for people with physical/mental disabilities
`alt.education.distance`	Learning from teachers who are far away
`alt.feminism`	Like `soc.feminism`, only different
`alt.fraternity.sorority`	Discussions of fraternity/sorority life and issues
`alt.individualism`	Philosophies where individual rights are paramount
`alt.missing-kids`	Locating missing children
`alt.parents-teens`	Parent-teenager relationships
`alt.politics.greens`	Green-party politics and activities worldwide
`alt.politics.usa.constitution`	U.S. Constitutional politics
`alt.recovery`	For people in recovery programs (for example, AA, ACA, GA)
`alt.recovery.codependency`	Mutually destructive relationships
`alt.sexual.abuse.recovery`	Helping others deal with traumatic experiences
`alt.support`	Dealing with emotional situations and experiences
`alt.support.cancer`	Emotional aid for people with cancer
`alt.support.depression`	Depression and mood disorders

`alt.support.divorce`	Discussion of marital breakups
`alt.support.step-parents`	Helping people with their stepparents
`alt.support.stuttering`	Support for people who stutter
`alt.war`	Not just collateral damage

At the Extremes

These groups contain plenty of interesting speculative material.

`alt.alien.visitors`	Space Aliens on Earth! Abduction! Government Cover-up!
`alt.conspiracy`	Be paranoid — they're out to get you.
`alt.conspiracy.lady-di`	Where's the white Fiat?
`alt.out-of-body`	Out-of-body experiences.
`alt.paranet.skeptic`	"I don't believe they turned you into a newt."
`alt.paranet.ufo`	Naming it "UFO" identifies it.
`alt.paranormal`	Phenomena that are not scientifically explicable.
`alt.sci.physics.new-theories`	Scientific theories you won't find in journals.

Computer Stuff

Please note that these are discussion groups, rather than sources of software. You can, however, get plenty of advice if you want it.

`alt.bbs.internet`	BBSs that are hooked up to the Internet.
`alt.best.of.internet`	It was a time of sorrow, it was a time of joy.
`alt.gopher`	Discussion of the gopher information service.
`alt.lang.basic`	The computer language that would not die.
`alt.online-service`	Large commercial online services and the Internet.

(continued)

`alt.online-service.america-online`	Discussions and questions about America Online.
`alt.online-service.compuserve`	Discussions and questions about CompuServe.
`alt.online-service.freenet`	Public FreeNet systems.
`alt.online-service.prodigy`	The Prodigy system.
`alt.sources.mac`	Source file newsgroup for the Apple Macintosh computers.

Creatures Great and Small

I expect that as more dog and cat owners get on the Internet, there will be postings of upcoming shows and the like. It's pretty hard to believe there's a skunks group and not at least one for Persian cat fanciers.

`alt.animals.badgers`	Badgers (meles meles and others)
`alt.animals.dolphins`	Flipper, Darwin, and all their friends
`alt.animals.foxes`	Everything you ever wanted to know about vulpines
`alt.aquaria`	The aquarium as a hobby
`alt.fan.lemurs`	Little critters with BIG eyes
`alt.pets.rabbits`	Coneys abound
`alt.skunks`	Enthusiasts of skunks and other mustelidae
`alt.wolves`	Discussing wolves and wolf-mix dogs

Games, Anyone

There are more groups actually playing games in newsgroups than discussing them.

`alt.anagrams`	Playing with words
`alt.games.mtrek`	Multi-Trek, a multiuser Star Trek-like game
`alt.games.netrek.paradise`	Discussion of the paradise version of netrek

`alt.games.video.classic`	Video games from before the mid-1980s
`alt.sega.genesis`	Another addiction
`alt.super.nes`	Like `rec.games.video.nintendo`, only different

Sports

I'm only listing a few of the groups for professional sports teams. Your favorite team is almost certainly listed, in the same format as these, as alt.sports.<sports>.<team-name>.

`alt.archery`	Robin Hood had the right idea.
`alt.caving`	Spelunking.
`alt.fishing`	Like `rec.outdoors.fishing`, only different.
`alt.skate-board`	Discussion of all aspects of skateboarding.
`alt.sport.bowling`	In the gutter again.
`alt.sport.darts`	Look what you've done to the wall!
`alt.sport.falconry`	The taking of live game by using a trained raptor.
`alt.sport.jet-ski`	Discussion of personal watercraft.
`alt.sport.officiating`	Problems related to officiating athletic contests.
`alt.sport.pool`	Knock your balls into your pockets for fun.
`alt.sport.racquetball`	All aspects of indoor racquetball and related sports.
`alt.sport.squash`	With the proper technique, vegetables can go very fast.
`alt.sports.baseball.`	My favorites! `chicago-cubs`.
`alt.sports.basketball.`	Los Angeles Lakers NBA basketball. `nba.la-lakers`.
`alt.sports.college.`	Ivy League athletics. `ivy-league`.
`alt.sports.football.`	Minnesota Vikings NFL football. `mn-vikings`.
`alt.sports.football.`	Green Bay Packers NFL football. `pro.gb-packers`.

(continued)

`alt.sports.hockey.nhl.`	Toronto Maple Leafs NHL hockey.
`tor-mapleleafs.`	
`alt.surfing`	Riding the ocean waves.

Fan Clubs

This listing represents roughly eight percent of the fan-club material on the lists. These were selected for no other reason than personal eccentricity.

`alt.books.anne-rice`	The vampire stuff.
`alt.elvis.king`	You've heard of this guy.
`alt.fan.blues-brothers`	Jake and Elwood ride to 2000!
`alt.fan.disney.afternoon`	Disney Afternoon characters and shows.
`alt.fan.hofstadter`	Douglas Hofstadter, Godel, Escher, Bach, and others.
`alt.fan.howard-stern`	Fans of the abrasive radio and TV personality.
`alt.fan.jimmy-buffett`	A white sports coat and a pink crustacean.
`alt.fan.laurie.anderson`	Will it be a music concert or a lecture this time?
`alt.fan.letterman`	One of the top ten reasons to get the alt groups.
`alt.fan.noam-chomsky`	Noam Chomsky's writings and opinions.
`alt.fan.penn-n-teller`	The magicians Penn and Teller.
`alt.fan.rush-limbaugh`	Just what it says.
`alt.fan.u2`	The Irish rock band U2.
`alt.fan.wodehouse`	Discussion of the works of humor author P.G. Wodehouse.
`alt.fan.woody-allen`	The diminutive director.
`alt.music.peter-gabriel`	Discussion of the music of Peter Gabriel.
`alt.tv.barney`	He's everywhere. Now appearing in several alt groups.

The Arts, More or Less

This list uses a fairly elastic definition of art.

alt.artcom	Artistic community, arts, and communication.
alt.arts.ballet	All aspects of ballet and modern dance as performing art.
alt.binaries.pictures.cartoons	Images from animated cartoons.
alt.binaries.pictures.fine-art.d	Discussion of the fine-art binaries. (Moderated)
alt.binaries.pictures.fine-art.digitized	Art from conventional media. (Moderated)
alt.binaries.pictures.fine-art.graphics	Art created on computers. (Moderated)
alt.books.reviews	"If you want to know how it turns out, read it!"
alt.folklore.urban	Urban legends, à la Jan Harold Brunvand.
alt.guitar	Strumming and picking.
alt.magic	For discussion about stage magic.
alt.music.a-cappella	Like rec.music.a-cappella, only different.
alt.music.alternative	For groups having two or less platinum-selling albums.
alt.music.blues-traveler	For "All fellow travelers."
alt.music.progressive	Yes, Marillion, Asia, King Crimson, and so on.
alt.music.synthpop	Depeche Mode, Erasure, Pet Shop Boys, and much more!
alt.music.techno	Bring on the bass!
alt.music.world	Discussion of music from around the world.
alt.prose	Postings of original writings, fictional and otherwise.
alt.zines	Small magazines, mostly noncommercial.

Religion

This area is full of many lively discussions. It's sometimes strange to think of comments on ancient manuscripts flying back and forth on high-speed, fiber-optic links.

alt.christnet	Gathering place for Christian ministers and users
alt.christnet.bible	Bible discussion and research
alt.christnet.philosophy	Philosophical implications of Christianity
alt.christnet.theology	The distinctives of God of Christian theology
alt.hindu	The Hindu religion. (Moderated)
alt.messianic	Messianic traditions
alt.philosophy.zen	Zen for everyone
alt.religion.christian	Unmoderated forum for discussing Christianity
alt.religion.gnostic	History and philosophies of the gnostic sects
alt.religion.islam	Discussion of Islamic faith and society

Funny Business

Humor is a giant newsgroup topic. If you're the only person in Nonesuch, Wyoming, who thinks Dave Barry is funny, you can find pals on the Net. In Usenet humor newsgroups like alt.humor.best-of-usenet, off-color jokes are typically encoded in a simple substitution cipher, so if you go to the trouble of decoding it, you don't have much business complaining about your sensibilities being assaulted.

alt.comedy.british	Discussion of British comedy in a variety of media
alt.comedy.firesgn-thtre	Firesign Theatre — in all its flaming glory
alt.comedy.standup	Discussion of stand-up comedy and comedians
alt.fan.dave_barry	Electronic fan club for humorist Dave Barry
alt.fan.monty-python	Electronic fan club for those wacky Brits
alt.humor.best-of-usenet	What the moderator thinks is funniest (Moderated)

Appendix D
Glossary

• •

*T*hese are terms that you're likely to encounter while roaming the Net or planning your next adventure.

address

A person's Internet *e-mail* address is the line with the @, as in `chseiter@aol.com`. From the Internet's point of view, an address is a set of four numbers, such as 132.34.115.31. The numbers correspond to a name that you can remember, such as `zapp.com` or `simple.net`. Check Appendix A for more on addresses.

alt

The newsgroups with the highest entertainment value are all in the unofficial alternative newsgroup hierarchy, and their names start with alt. Look in Appendix C for examples.

Anarchie

Anarchie is a Macintosh shareware program that performs Archie searches on FTP files. It's very good, and `www.shareware.com` has it in Mac software libraries.

anonymous FTP

Anonymous FTP (see Chapter 5) is a procedure for logging onto computers that maintain file archives that are accessible to anyone. You use *anonymous* as your username and your e-mail address as your password.

AppleTalk

Apple's own set of hardware and software for managing local-area networks. It's a slow protocol, best for smaller networks.

Archie

Archie is an older Internet system for finding FTP files. An Archie server is a computer that has lists of available archived files all over the Internet.

archive

An archive is a collection of files. At a site that maintains archives, someone is responsible for updating files and checking the archive for viruses.

ARPA

An acronym for Advanced Research Projects Agency, the government agency that funded ARPANET, a precursor to the Internet.

ARPANET

The ARPANET was the basis for networking research in the 1970s. The ARPANET has essentially disappeared into the Internet.

ASCII

An acronym for American Standard Code for Information Interchange, a definition that associates each character with a number from 0 to 255. An ASCII file is a text file of characters. Most computers base their character set on this standard, which is why a PC's message of "Hi, there!" doesn't look like "#$5!!dor!fd" when read on a Mac.

backbone

A high-speed set of network connections. On the Internet, this usually means the fiber-optic links between large computer sites.

BBS

An acronym for for bulletin board *system*. A BBS can be an old Mac II in a garage or a gigantic system with 10,000 users. Before the modern popularity and availability of the Internet and during the heyday of the old online services like Delphi, GEnie, and CompuServe, a local BBS was the best way for a computer user to access a free or inexpensive electronic community experience.

binary file

A file of 0s and 1s, which can represent pictures and sound as well as text.

BinHex

A common way to send programs and documents from one Mac to another on the Internet. Basically everything on the Internet is transmitted as pure text (ASCII), so a BinHex utility program converts programs and documents (also known as *binaries*) to ASCII so that people can mail you a binary file. At the receiving end, you or your e-mail program has to decode the file back to binary with a decoder such as StuffIt Expander.

biz

A newsgroup where you find discussions that have to do with (gasp!) money. Generally, you're not supposed to use other newsgroups for commercial purposes.

bounce

When you send a piece of e-mail and it comes back as undeliverable, it's said to have "bounced," much like an uncashable check.

bridge

A bridge is a set of hardware and software that lets two different networks appear to be a single larger network to people connecting from outside the system.

bug

A software programming or design problem. Unfortunately, bugs are plentiful in large, rapidly changing communications programs.

chat

If you send messages to an electronic mailbox, that's e-mail. If you're sending messages back and forth to someone in real time, that's chat.

ClarisWorks

ClarisWorks is an integrated software package (word processor, spreadsheet, database) for the Mac that also has some of the features of Claris Home Page for constructing Web pages.

com

This is the top-level Internet domain name that identifies businesses.

comp

The term *comp* in the middle of a newsgroup name means that the discussions will be computer-oriented. I'm sorry to report that the majority of these groups are oriented towards UNIX or PCs, not Macintoshes. But the few groups that cater to Macs are alive and well, thanks.

Computer Currents

A tabloid-format computer magazine that turns up on newspaper racks in big cities. A good source of local bulletin board numbers.

country code

A top-level domain name that identifies a site by country: `well.sf.ca.us`, for example, has the country code `us` because San Francisco is physically, if not emotionally, part of the United States. France is `.fr`, Singapore is `.sg`, and so forth.

cyberspace

This somewhat overworked term first appeared in the science fiction novel *Neuromancer,* by William Gibson. It refers to the digital world represented by all computers and their interaction.

dial-up

A dial-up connection is one that works only while you're connected by phone. The other type of connection is direct, where you're wired to a network and are connected all the time.

DIALOG

A huge information service, managed by Lockheed, with lots of technical databases.

DNS

An acronym for domain name system. DNS is used to convert Internet names to their corresponding Internet numbers.

domain

An Internet site address has two parts, the domain and the top-level domain name. For America Online — `aol.com` — aol is the domain name and com is the top-level part. The domain roughly corresponds to the name of a particular network.

DOS

The original operating system that Microsoft cooked up (actually, Microsoft bought it in a one-sided deal) for IBM PCs. Don't bother looking in DOS file collections.

dotted quad

Every now and then you'll hear an old-time Internet hipster refer to the four numbers of an Internet address (like 123.456.789.012) as a "dotted quad."

Electronic Frontier Foundation (EFF)

This organization is something like the conscience of the Internet, as opposed to its administration. Go look for the EFF area on your Internet service provider.

e-mail

Electronic mail. It's a message that you compose on your computer to be received on someone else's computer, although some services also deliver your message as a fax or (this sounds weird, but it's true) *an actual piece of paper!*

edu

Usually, this is the Internet address identifier for a university. The universities of the United States are the original reason the Internet is the vast wonderland it is today.

Ethernet

An Ethernet network is a very common, much faster alternative to Apple's original built-in networking stuff. Today's Macs all have Ethernet capability as part of the system.

Eudora

A Macintosh program for handling e-mail. The first versions were freeware, and Eudora Light still is, but now it's also available in commercial form (and with stronger features) from QUALCOMM software.

FAQ

Frequently asked question. Trust me, your questions will be just like anyone else's. When you sign up with an Internet service provider — and before you make any contributions to newsgroups — read the FAQ files that are prominently displayed in menus. This step saves you embarrassment and saves everyone else from your three-millionth-time newbie questions.

Fetch

A truly wonderful Macintosh FTP program from Dartmouth College, available from all Internet service providers.

file transfer protocol

See *FTP*.

firewall

You may wonder how other computers you can reach by telnet keep you out of private areas. Networks have electronic security programs and hardware called *firewalls* in different places to block access to unauthorized users.

flame

A flame is the sort of extreme opinion that the sender probably wouldn't have the nerve to deliver in person. Although some Internet old-timers seem to generate four flames a day, I think that as a matter of decorum you should never flame (it's a verb or a noun) anyone ever, no matter what.

FreePPP

FreePPP is Mac software for simplifying a dial-up connection to the Internet. As a result, it turns up in many ISP packages. If you're using Mac OS 8 or later, you can consider using Open Transport/PPP or Apple Remote Access 3.1 instead.

freeware

Freeware is software that's offered by its author for no charge. This is different from shareware (see *shareware*). You can find some amazingly good freeware on the Net.

FTP

FTP stands for file transfer protocol. On the Internet, it usually refers to a UNIX-system utility program that enables you to collect files from archives at other sites. Programs like Fetch enable you to download files by FTP to your Mac very reliably.

gateway

A gateway is hardware that enables you to send messages between two different kinds of networks. You need a gateway, for example, to communicate at network speeds between a Macintosh AppleTalk-based network and a UNIX-based network.

Gopher

A Gopher is an early file search-and-retrieval system. Web browsers can read the older Gopher files.

gov

Gov is the top-level domain name, or zone, for any type of government organization.

Graphics Interchange Format (GIF)

GIF stands for graphics interchange format — you see it as a file extension on picture files such as `flower.gif`. GIF files are very common on the Web and most sites offer shareware programs such as GIFwatcher to read them. Adobe Photoshop and other large image-handling programs also can work with GIF files.

host

Most kinds of Internet access using a modem require you to dial a host computer, which is a big computer with its own Internet address.

hqx

When you see this as a file extension, it means that the file is in BinHex (see BinHex) format. BinHex files contain programs or documents for Mac computers, typically. To use the contents of a BinHex file, you have to decode it using programs such as StuffIt Expander or BinHex 4.0.

HTML

An acronym for Hypertext Markup Language. HTML is the primary programming language for making Web pages (see Chapter 13).

HTTP

An acronym for Hypertext Transport Protocol. HTTP is the specification that underlies all Web files and tells computers how they are to be transmitted.

hyperlink

A hyperlink is underlined text in a Web document that enables you to click it to jump to another document.

hypertext

Hypertext is a set of text files in which individual words link one file to the next.

information superhighway

No one knows what this means, including me, so I thought I'd put it in the glossary. Internet fans think it means the Web, cable TV companies think it's what will happen when cable fibers carry data, and phone companies think it's what will happen when they can force you to buy computers from them. By 2005, it will simply be a nostalgic catch-phrase.

Internet protocol (IP)

A set of definitions that govern transmission of individual packets of information on the Internet.

Internet Society

A bunch of good people who discuss policies and make recommendations about Internet management.

InterNIC

An acronym for Internet Network Information Center. The word *InterNIC* turns up on the menus of many Internet service providers, because it's the place where people and companies request names (such as www.apple.com) for their Web sites.

IRC

IRC stands for Internet Relay Chat, an early type of chat format before chat got included as a function of Web browsers or America Online.

Java

Sun Microsystems developed this language, which has turned up all over the Web and works with the main browsers. Java, in theory, lets programmers write programs that can be used on any computer that understands Java, whether it's a Macintosh, Windows PC, or UNIX computer. It's the subject of a furious battle, because Microsoft is opposed to the idea of a language that doesn't depend directly on Windows.

JavaScript

A simple scripting language that works within HTML to provide all sorts of special functions, like menus in a Web page.

JPEG (or JPG)

A compressed file format for images. Stands for Joint Photographic Experts Group format. JPEG files are very small in size but can have good photographic quality.

LISTSERV

LISTSERV programs manage mailing lists by sending messages automatically to everyone on a given list. They're responsible for great information exchanges and also annoying spam (junk commercial ads or offers).

log in

Log in and *log on* are different terms for making contact with a remote computer. They're used interchangeably.

lurking

In Internet jargon, you're said to be lurking if you join a discussion group and just read other people's messages. Oh, well, better a lurker than a flamer.

MacBinary

A special format for storing Macintosh binary files on non-Mac computers. Mac files consist of two parts, one part with your data, the other with the item's icon and other Mac-like info. MacBinary files keep that information together; otherwise, the icon data would be lost if a Mac file were stored on other computers because no other computer cares about Mac icons.

MacTCP

An Apple program (a control panel, actually) that you need to use most Internet accounts. In Mac OS 7.6 and later, it's been replaced by the Open Transport network software and a control panel called TCP/IP (see Chapter 10).

mail server

A mail server is a program on a host computer that saves your mail for you until you make a dial-up connection and have a chance to download your mail and read it.

Matrix

Lots of early Net visionaries use the term Matrix to denote the total of all connected computers in the world. It used to be used as a cool name for the Internet plus everything else.

Metaverse

A fictional version, more or less, of the Web, but with a better plot. This electronic structure is the basis of Neal Stephenson's science fiction master-piece *Snow Crash*. Like the word *universe* — get it?

MicroTimes

A tabloid-format computer magazine that turns up on newspaper racks in big cities. A good source of local Internet service providers.

mil

The top-level domain name of military sites on the Internet. Just about all U.S. military sites are Internet sites.

MIME

This acronym stands for Multipurpose Internet Mail Extension, an Internet standard that enables you to add sound and images to e-mail.

mirror

A mirror site is an archive that keeps a copy of the files in another site.

misc

Newsgroups that don't fit under any other recognizable category get put into misc.

modem

The device that enables your computer to make telephone calls to other computers.

moderated

A moderated newsgroup has someone who filters out the really pointless or offensive material, leaving only moderately pointless or offensive messages.

Mosaic

Mosaic was the original freeware browser for access to the World Wide Web. It turned into Netscape Navigator, and most of its features also were copied by Microsoft into Internet Explorer.

NCSA

National Center for Supercomputing Applications, managed by the University of Illinois, was the home of Mosaic and of Netscape founder Marc Andreesen, along with lots of big computers.

Netcom

A large national Internet service provider, one of the first.

network

Any set of computers that can communicate directly with each other constitutes a network.

newsgroup

A collection of people and messages on a particular topic of interest.

node

The term *node* in Internet context means a central computer that's part of an Internet-connected network. Sometimes used interchangeably with *site* or *host*.

NSFNET

An acronym for the National Science Foundation Net. NSFNET was an original Internet traffic carrier.

packet

A block of information, complete with addresses for destination and source, traveling over the Internet.

page

The basic unit of the World Wide Web information service is the page. Pages are linked by hypertext references to other pages.

password

Okay, you know what a password is. Just think of a nonobvious password (usually, it shouldn't be a real word from a dictionary, much less your nickname) to save yourself potential grief.

ping

An Internet program that's used to determine whether a site is still active.

point of presence

A local phone number for high-speed access maintained by an Internet provider.

poker

Okay, you may be wondering why I keep putting definitions next to their acronyms. Years ago at Caltech, I asked a French postdoc in my research group if he wanted to join the lunchtime graduate student poker game. He looked puzzled (he was learning vernacular English, although he could write better than we could). I wrote the word "poker" on a blackboard, he looked at it, frowned, and looked it up in a bilingual dictionary, where the entry read (I'm not kidding)

poker (n.) *poker*

The light bulb went off, he said, "Ah, poker!" sat down, and cleaned us out.

POP

An acronym for Post Office Protocol, an e-mail protocol used for downloading mail from a mail server.

PPP

An acronym for Point to Point Protocol. PPP became the standard connection protocol after a brief competition with another protocol called SLIP for dial-up Internet access.

protocol

A protocol is a definition that controls communication on a network.

rec

Newsgroups for recreational purposes are signaled with rec. There's plenty of overlap between rec and alt, in practice.

RFC/RFD

Requests For Comment and Requests For Discussion are study-group documents with an important role in settling general Internet questions about design and use.

router

A router is a gateway (see gateway) between two networks that use Internet protocol.

sci

Serious research newsgroups in science and mathematics belong to this newsgroup hierarchy.

sea

This file extension stands for self-extracting archive. When you double-click a .sea file, it usually turns itself into a folder containing an application and some documentation files.

server

A computer that stores files as a central resource for other computers, called clients, and can connect to the server to get files for themselves.

shareware

Shareware is software that you can download free to test. If you like it and use it, you're obliged as a matter of honor to send the requested payment to the author.

sit

Files compressed with StuffIt from Aladdin Software show this file extension. You can expand them with UnStuffIt or StuffIt Expander, available from all the national online services and most bulletin boards, and included with Mac OS 8.

SMTP

An acronym for Simple Mail Transport Protocol. SMTP is the e-mail protocol standard for the Internet.

soc

The soc newsgroups on social issues overlap many of the alt social issue newsgroups.

tar

This file extension indicates files compressed with a special UNIX program. You can expand them with StuffIt Deluxe.

TCP/IP

The whole system, Transport Control Protocol and Internet Protocol, makes up a standard guideline for network hardware and Internet software design. To simplify things, Apple just made up a control panel of the same name.

telnet

The core of all Internet services is the UNIX utility telnet, a program that enables users who are connected to one host to dial up a different Internet host.

terminal

In the old days, a terminal could only receive and send characters to the real computer at the other end of the wires. A terminal program enables your sophisticated Macintosh to mimic this primitive arrangement.

thread

A series of connected messages in a newsgroup.

UNIX

The operating system that runs the biggest Internet services. Developed over many years, it's capable of meeting any networking challenge and is very thrifty with computing resources. The downside consequence of these virtues is that UNIX is hard for beginners to use.

Usenet

The network, linked at different points to the Internet, that supports all the newsgroups.

VT-100/102

These are two very common terminals and, hence, two very common terminal-software options. As a first guess, pick VT-100 as the terminal setting when you dial up almost any service using standard communications software.

WELL

A very popular Bay Area bulletin board with full Internet access. About half the computer journalists on earth seem to hang out on this service.

Windows

Windows 95 succeeded in wallpapering a Macintosh-like face over the ugly reality of DOS. Nonetheless, the Mac has been responsible for more Web site creation than Windows.

WWW

The World Wide Web, complete with audio, video, and Java, is now what most people think *is* the Internet.

z

Another type of UNIX-system compressed file extension, also expandable with UnStuffIt.

zip

The most common compressed-file format for PCs. Unless it's a text file, you probably won't be able to do anything with a .zip file on a Mac, even if you expand it, so don't bother unless you have a compelling reason to put yourself through the trouble.

ZTerm

A favorite early shareware communications package for many Mac users.

Index

• *O* •

• Y •

• Z •

Playing games is really fun...
The Dummies Way™!

Pressman®
©1998 Pressman Toy Corporation, New York, NY 10010

Crosswords For Dummies™ Game

You don't have to know how to spell to have a great time. Place a word strip on the board so that it overlaps another word or creates a new one. Special squares add to the fun. The first player to use up all their word strips wins!
For 2 to 4 players.

Trivia For Dummies™ Game

You're guaranteed to have an answer every time! Each player gets 10 cards that contain the answer to every question. Act quickly and be the first player to throw down the correct answer and move closer to the finish line!
For 3 or 4 players.

Charades For Dummies™ Game

Act out one-word charades: when other players guess them, they move ahead. The special cards keep the game full of surprises. The first player around the board wins.
For 3 or 4 players.

...For Dummies and The Dummies Way are trademarks or registered trademarks of IDG Books Worldwide, Inc.

IDG BOOKS WORLDWIDE BOOK REGISTRATION

Register This Book and Win!

We want to hear from you!

Visit **http://my2cents.dummies.com** to register this book and tell us how you liked it!

- ✔ Get entered in our monthly prize giveaway.

- ✔ Give us feedback about this book — tell us what you like best, what you like least, or maybe what you'd like to ask the author and us to change!

- ✔ Let us know any other *...For Dummies*® topics that interest you.

Your feedback helps us determine what books to publish, tells us what coverage to add as we revise our books, and lets us know whether we're meeting your needs as a *...For Dummies* reader. You're our most valuable resource, and what you have to say is important to us!

Not on the Web yet? It's easy to get started with *Dummies 101*®: *The Internet For Windows*® *98* or *The Internet For Dummies*®, 5th Edition, at local retailers everywhere.

Or let us know what you think by sending us a letter at the following address:

...For Dummies Book Registration
Dummies Press
7260 Shadeland Station, Suite 100
Indianapolis, IN 46256-3917
Fax 317-596-5498

...FOR DUMMIES™

BESTSELLING
BOOK SERIES